Prais MW00982405

'Remarkably researched so as to explain one of Australia's most extraordinary criminal cases. The intricacies of the police investigation are clearly set out and the mind of a famous criminal is revealed.'
Chester Porter QC

'Mark Tedeschi has given us a detailed and compelling account of events, unfolded with his customary forensic skill and interspersed with interpretation and analysis that informs and provokes. Greed will continue to motivate some people – not all like Stephen Leslie Bradley – to criminal offending; but not often (fortunately) does it have the deep personal consequences or arouse the public's interest, indignation and anger as the events in this case did. It was a case that also provided a quantum leap in crime investigation techniques, as Tedeschi explains.'
Nick Cowdery AM QC

'Few know the mind of the murderer like Mark Tedeschi. This is an utterly compelling account of the kidnap and murder of schoolboy Graeme Thorne from an author with unparalleled knowledge of the investigation and prosecution of crimes which have terrified Australians. From a distance of 55 years, Mark's analysis shows that the criminal justice system of the time was both efficient and effective.'
Margaret Cunneen SC, Deputy Senior Crown Prosecutor

'The kidnap, ransom and subsequent killing of schoolboy Graeme Thorne in 1960 was one of the most widely reported and closely followed crimes of twentieth century Australia. Mark Tedeschi's careful telling of the story is at once a study of kidnapper Bradley – suave continental chancer, bungler, family man and killer – and at the same time it presents a picture of an insular Australia encountering a strand of icy pragmatism direct from war-damaged Old Europe. Finally Tedeschi brings a senior jurist's insight to the complex police investigation and Bradley's trial for murder.'
Peter Doyle, writer, academic, and occasional curator at
Sydney's Justice & Police Museum

Also by Mark Tedeschi

Eugenia – A True Story of Adversity, Tragedy,
Crime and Courage

Mark Tedeschi AM QC

KIDNAPPED

The crime
that shocked
the nation

SIMON &
SCHUSTER

London · New York · Sydney · Toronto · New Delhi

A CBS COMPANY

KIDNAPPED
First published in Australia in 2015 by
Simon & Schuster (Australia) Pty Limited
Suite 19A, Level 1, 450 Miller Street, Cammeray, NSW 2062

10 9 8 7 6 5 4 3 2 1

A CBS Company
Sydney New York London Toronto New Delhi
Visit our website at www.simonandschuster.com.au

National Library of Australia Cataloguing-in-Publication entry
Author: Tedeschi, Mark, 1952– author.
Title: Kidnapped/Mark Tedeschi.
ISBN: 9781925310221 (paperback)
             9781925310238 (ebook)
Subjects: Thorne, Graeme – Kidnapping, 1960.
             Bradley, Stephen Leslie.
             Forensic sciences – Australia – History.
             Murder – Investigation – New South Wales – History.
             Kidnapping – New South Wales – History.
Dewey Number: 363.25

Cover design: Christabella Designs
Cover images: Courtesy of the Justice & Police Museum Collection,
Sydney Living Museums
Typeset by Midland Typesetters, Australia
Printed and bound in Australia by Griffin Press

The paper this book is printed on is certified
against the Forest Stewardship Council® Standards.
Griffin Press holds FSC chain of custody
certification SGS-COC-005088. FSC promotes
environmentally responsible, socially beneficial
and economically viable management of the
world's forests.

I dedicate this book to the three teachers in my family,
who have played such a large role in my life:
my late grandmother, Rosina Tedeschi (1893–1971),
my late mother, Ruth Tedeschi (1926–2003),
and my wife, Sharon.
Their talents and dedication as teachers
and their support of and confidence in me
have been the foundations upon which
I have built my professional career
as an advocate.

CONTENTS

Insatiability

(translated from Italian, which in turn has
been translated from the original Romanesque)

*God took mud from a swamp, modelled a puppet
and blowed on its face.
The puppet suddenly moved
and a man emerged at once
who opened his eyes and found himself in the world
like someone who awakes from a great sleep.*

*– What you see is yours – God told him –
and you can use it as you like:
I give you all the Earth and all the Sea,
except for the sky, because that's mine …
– What a pity! – said Adam – It's so beautiful …
Why don't you give me that too?*

Carlo Alberto Salustri (pen name: Trilussa)
Italian poet (1873–1950)

ACKNOWLEDGEMENTS

Alan Gold, literary mentor extraordinaire, who continually badgered me to write another true crime book.

Chief Justice the Honourable Tom Bathurst, who gave me permission to access the State records relating to the trial of Stephen Bradley.

State Records New South Wales, and in particular the ever-helpful and patient staff at the Kingswood Repository.

Nerida Campbell, Curator of the Justice and Police Museum, Sydney Living Museums (formerly the Historic Houses Trust of New South Wales), for giving me access to the holdings of the Museum on the Graeme Thorne kidnapping and the extradition and trial of Stephen Bradley.

Warwick Abadee and Robert Henderson, who provided much information on the movement of P&O ships between Australia and Britain.

Christine and Pauline Vizzard, nieces of the late Fred Vizzard QC, for a photograph of their uncle and information about his career.

Walter Glover, for his personal recollections of his neighbourhood friend, Graeme Thorne.

Robert Teicher, for an account of his mother's brief confrontation with Stephen Bradley.

Chester Porter QC, Nick Cowdery AM QC, Margaret Cunneen SC and Peter Doyle, for their generous pre-publication comments. Chester Porter also for permission to refer to his account of Fred Vizzard QC. Peter Doyle also gave me access to the papers of his late uncle, Detective Sergeant Brian Doyle.

Dr Michael Diamond, psychiatrist, for permission to quote from a forensic psychiatric report.

To the team at Simon & Schuster Australia, particularly: Larissa Edwards, for her encouragement and support; Anabel Pandiella, for her enthusiasm and joie de vivre; Claire de Medici Jones, for an excellent job of editing; and Roberta Ivers, for many helpful suggestions.

My wife, Sharon, for her patience, encouragement and wise advice.

Mark Tedeschi AM QC

PREFACE

Greed is the most ubiquitous of the seven deadly sins. We all know what it looks like. We have all seen it in others and harbour it in ourselves. Some say that it is the root evil from which all the other deadly sins emanate. It is the vice addressed by the tenth commandment: 'You shall not covet your neighbour's house, your neighbour's wife, his male servant, his female servant, his ox, his donkey, or anything that is your neighbour's.'

We all covet from time to time: possessions or accolades, recognition or acceptance, power or security, wealth or the fulfilment of our sexual urges. Most of us who are mentally healthy are able to keep our covetous desires in check and appreciate the differences between our needs and our wants. Deep down we understand intellectually that even if we were somehow able to fulfil our cravings, within a short time we would be no happier than before, and other equally powerful desires would emerge. We are able to appreciate the destructive potential of unrestrained greed and to prevent it from overwhelming our thoughts and deeds, consuming us, and ultimately destroying us.

There are a few among us, however, who are so totally consumed by greed that, although technically sane, they are unable to think rationally about their cravings and desires. They seek the fulfilment of them so voraciously that they destroy the boundaries between their own valid needs and the legitimate rights of others. Some – mercifully only very few – are so over-whelmingly driven by greed that, like the man I describe in this book, they are prepared to kill to acquire the objects of their desires. So overpowering and all-consuming is their sense of entitlement, and so irrepressible is the allure of the desired goal – generally wealth – that such people are unable to appre-ciate the terrible risks they run of destroying their own lives and the lives of others dear to them.

Over many years, I have prosecuted a number of such people for murder. The feature I have observed that they most commonly share is an ingrained, almost unshakeable, belief that they are owed something by the universe. The man I describe in this book was so gripped by his desires and so intent on achieving his ends that he lost the ability to see what most other sane people would have realised in an instant: that he was hell-bent on a path of inevitable self-destruction. His downfall was almost assured by the brazenness of his covetous pursuits and the risks inherent in his chosen methods.

Some people are of the view that any person who commits a serious crime, particularly murder, must necessarily be mentally ill. In my opinion – based upon many years' experi-ence as a prosecutor and defence barrister – murders are often committed by people who are perfectly sane but consumed by intense passions, such as greed, lust, jealousy, or the fear that comes from a loss of control or an overpowering sense of inadequacy. I believe that most of us, given the right circumstances, are susceptible to these powerful passions; that some of us are liable to be blinded by them; and that a few of us – thankfully small in number – are capable of being driven by them to commit murder.

This book is about Stephen Bradley, who perpetrated the 1960 kidnapping-for-ransom of eight-year-old Sydney schoolboy Graeme Thorne. The crime gripped the whole nation – turning a sleepy, prosperous and safe post-war Australia into a place with dark undercurrents, where children could be snatched off the streets. The author, who was the same age as Graeme, vividly remembers the anguish caused by the boy's disappearance.

The case is presented not only because it is such a stark example of a man so consumed by greed that he was driven to commit a terrible crime, or because it is the only example of the kidnapping of a child for ransom in Australia, but also because it marked the beginning in Australia of modern-day forensic science as a tool in the investigation of serious crime. Many of the techniques of scientific detection used to implicate Bradley, which have since become commonplace, had never before been used in a police investigation. To some degree this explains why the police took so long to focus their attention on him. This case therefore marked a watershed in the annals of modern criminal investigation.

At the time, there was much controversy over exactly how Bradley abducted Graeme Thorne and the circumstances that came to mark the end of his venture. As Bradley went to his death professing his innocence, that controversy has endured. The version of events that I present here, which in many respects is different to other commentators, is based on my own synthesis of information from a variety of sources. I have relied, in part, upon Bradley's oral and written confessions to the police some months after the kidnapping – confessions he later retracted. It must be remembered that these confessions were intended to portray himself in the best possible light, so his words should be viewed with considerable scepticism.

My version of what occurred relies heavily on the scientific evidence led at Bradley's trial, which is a much more reliable source of information about what actually happened than any later explanation by him. I have also given much credence to the hypotheses that were put to Bradley during cross-examination at his trial by Bill Knight QC, the Senior Crown Prosecutor who prosecuted him, because Knight had the benefit of hearing all the witnesses first-hand and had direct access to the investigating police. The version I have advanced also takes into account my own professional experience as a Crown Prosecutor over the past thirty-two years, including nearly 200 murder and attempted-murder cases, and also the six years that I practised at the defence Bar representing persons accused of serious crime.

This book depicts, among other things, the planning and commission of a kidnapping and its consequences from the point of view of the perpetrator, Stephen Bradley. I have obviously not had access to him. There has, of necessity, been a need to engage in creative reconstruction in order to present what I believe were the thought processes, emotions and motivations that lay behind this egregious offence. My understanding of Stephen Bradley, as well as his wife, Magda, is entirely my own subjective, personal view. I feel that my experience as a prosecutor has enabled me to get inside Bradley's mind and experience his thought processes. This is something which I seek to do in every case that I prosecute. I am convinced that if I can understand the motivations for a crime by getting into the mind of an accused person, I am able to present the case more thoroughly and convincingly to a jury. I have prosecuted many people who, like Bradley, were blinded by their unrestrained desires and innermost fears, and this is an important reason why I have striven to understand his motivations.

There was much debate at the time of Bradley's trial as to whether his wife, Magda, knew in advance of her husband's plan to commit the kidnapping – an allegation she strenuously denied. I have witnessed numerous cases in which close family members have refused to accept that their loved one could be capable of committing a heinous crime. I am confident that I have accurately assessed Magda Bradley's unrelenting hope – against all odds – that her husband was innocent of the terrible crime with which he was charged.

In this book I have also set out what I believe would have been the emotions and thoughts of the victims – primary and secondary – of Bradley's criminal actions, including members of Graeme Thorne's immediate family. Stephen Bradley's daughter and step-children were also secondary victims of his crime, albeit in a completely different way. I believe my contact over many decades with victims and their families has enabled me to intuit what they might have felt and thought at the time. My apologies in advance if I have misinterpreted any of them.

This reconstruction of the commission and investigation of a terrible crime that gripped the nation in 1960–1961 has necessitated my own creative input, based largely on my professional practice over many years. However, I have not allowed my subjective interpretations to detract from the accuracy of the factual details of the case, which were extensively documented at the time. Where there are direct, contemporaneous accounts of conversations, I have quoted them verbatim. Otherwise, I have interpolated my best assessment of what I believe would have been the substance of conversations, based upon the known facts.

I have used pseudonyms for only one set of names – in order to protect Bradley's step-children from further embarrassment. They were incidental, secondary victims who do not wish to have their identities disclosed. This has necessitated using the same pseudonym for their father's surname and for their mother's surname before she married Bradley.

I have used imperial units of length that were applicable at the time. If any Gen-Xers or Gen-Yers are unfamiliar with them, there are many websites that provide conversion details.

Mark Tedeschi AM QC
Sydney
2015

1

WINDFALL

Stephen Bradley stared with disdain at the photograph on the front page of the newspaper. It showed an elated thirty-seven-year-old Bazil Thorne holding his winning lottery ticket – Number 3932 – which had been drawn the previous day, 1 June 1960. It was the tenth draw of the Opera House Lottery, which the New South Wales Government had established to raise money to build what they promised would become the pre-eminent Sydney icon.

Stephen's disdain was tinged with envy for the lucky winner of the £100,000 prize.[1] What had Bazil Thorne done to warrant a windfall that would ensure his financial security and comfort for the rest of his life? Stephen was sure that this man, who stared with such provocative glee at him from the newspaper, had not had to go through the many traumas that had shaped

1

his own life. Bazil had not lived through the Nazi occupation of Hungary, or suffered Bradley's experiences of the political turmoil, disempowerment and poverty that accompanied post-war communism and Soviet domination in Stephen's native country. Bazil had not been through the trauma of a migration, as Stephen had endured in an attempt to find a better life. Bazil did not have the millstone of speaking English with a foreign accent like the one that constantly marked Stephen as an outsider. Bazil had not been compelled to change his name, unlike Stephen who, because of the constant mispronunciations of his dignified birth name, Istvan Baranyay, had chosen to metamorphose to the unmemorable anglicisation 'Stephen Bradley'.

Whereas boring Bazil was probably still married to his childhood sweetheart, the thirty-four-year-old Stephen was a man of the world who had had a multitude of relationships, and had been married three times – a rarity in those days. Stephen had undergone a divorce from his first wife in Europe, and had stoically borne the sudden, tragic death of his second wife in Australia. A man like Bazil Thorne had never had to confront the denigrating looks that Stephen and his third wife, Magda, frequently faced whenever they mentioned that they had previously been married and that their three children were products of their former marriages. Magda's eldest son, Paul Weinberg, was now thirteen, and her second boy, Ross, was just five, while Stephen's own daughter, Helen, was seven. Stephen doted on all three children – treating each of them equally, as though they were all his own flesh and blood – and they in turn responded with genuine love for him. The five of them wanted more than anything to spend time together enjoying the simple pleasures of life, such as romping around at the beach. Stephen had to bear the burden of his stepson Ross, who was totally deaf and largely unable to communicate with words, and who had to be picked up each week (in view of inquisitive neighbours) by a special bus to take him to a special school – St. Gabriel's School for Deaf Boys at Castle Hill – run by the Christian Brothers, who went to such effort to convey to the five-year-old boy the language, social interactions and cultural nuances that other children soaked up effortlessly. Because of the ordeal of caring for Ross, Stephen and Magda had chosen not to have any more children together.

The newspaper photo of Bazil Thorne, who worked as a commercial traveller in partnership with his elderly father, showed him in an old-fashioned, cheap overcoat and holding an utterly standard hat. His wife probably bought his clothes for him once a year at downmarket stores like Gowings or Lowes, whereas Stephen was always immaculately groomed and dressed in clothes from the most chic stores. Although he was not tall, many people had told Stephen that he was classically handsome, and his past successes with women were testament to that. Magda had been instantly and irrepressibly drawn to his sexual magnetism, despite the fact that she was married to someone else at the time. He was proud of his taut body and his physical strength, but it was his personality, his education and his class that gave him entrée into the upper echelons of Sydney society. He was able to project that personality to impress people well above his station in life. He was most attracted to – and envious of – people with vast amounts of money, as demonstrated by their impressive houses and cars. That was why it was so important to have a sizeable home of their own in a good suburb and a car that people would notice.

***

Unbeknown to Stephen Bradley, before their lottery win Bazil and Freda Thorne led lives that were in some respects less fortunate than his own. Freda was a country girl, born in Eugowra, New South Wales, to Sophia and Hilton Thorncraft. She was brought up in the township of Cowra. She met Bazil Thorne during the Second World War when he was stationed at the Japanese prisoner-of-war camp in Cowra. Freda was a keen pianist who used to play at local dances. After their marriage, Bazil and Freda settled in Sydney, and Bazil joined his father working as a commercial traveller, which involved him hawking clothing and other smallgoods to large country stores. This occupation required relentless travel and lugging of heavy samples. Whereas once upon a time a commercial traveller was financially well rewarded, by the 1950s the modern world had largely overtaken the role, so that Bazil's income was just barely enough to live a reasonable life. Bazil and Freda's firstborn child, Cheryl, suffered from a severe handicap which precluded her from living with her parents, so they were forced to take the grim decision to place her in an institution to the north of Sydney for severely handicapped children. Unlike other families in the same predicament, they always acknowledged the existence of their eldest child. Freda and Bazil had two more children: Graeme in 1951 and Belinda in 1957. The Thornes were a typical, conservative Australian family, who lived modest but honest lives that required them to struggle to make ends meet. In late 1959, they moved into a basic, ground-floor rental flat in Bondi, which was small but in reasonable condition. There was virtually no prospect of them ever owning their own home. That is – until the lottery win.

Bazil and Freda doted on their children: Graeme, who had an amiable, reserved disposition and was always courteous and well behaved, and Belinda, their gorgeous girl whose birth had allowed them to finally overcome the tragedy of their eldest, Cheryl. Like most Australian parents of the time, Bazil and Freda were strict with their children, but also loving and attentive. The move to Bondi in 1959 gave them the added bonus of living opposite Dickson Park – a large expanse of terraced grass with very little vegetation. After Graeme turned eight in December of that year, Freda finally let him go across the road on his own to the park where he would play with his Dinky toy cars together with some neighbouring children. Her protective nature caused her to frequently keep an eye on him. At least he was close by and not associating with the rough boys who hung out and frequently fought with each other in the thick bush at the Thomas Hogan Reserve in nearby Francis Street.

Bazil's work would often take him away from Sydney for days at a time, requiring Freda, a typical Australian housewife who had given up employment upon marriage, to care for her family alone. Their financially constrained circumstances allowed them few luxuries, so holidays and outings to restaurants were rare and much appreciated.

The lottery win initially caused Bazil and Freda to pause in their lives and gave them an opportunity to consider exactly what it was that they wanted for themselves, their children, and their elderly parents. They were determined that they would not allow the windfall to change them as people, or to alter their established friendships. They eventually decided to continue with their lives uninterrupted for a period, and then after some months, in an atmosphere of calm reflection, they would make decisions how best to use the money to enhance their lives and the lives of others. In the meantime, the lottery payout was sitting in a bank account accumulating interest at a rate which matched Bazil's earnings as a commercial traveller. The only step that they did take immediately was to make arrangements to have the telephone installed in their Bondi flat, so that Freda would not have to walk up to the nearby public telephone box, which was often occupied or out of order. It also meant that Bazil could give her advance warning of when he was due home from his trips to the country.

***

For days, at the family home the Bradleys owned in Clontarf – a swish, new, northern Sydney suburb with leafy views of Middle Harbour – Stephen was repeatedly drawn back to the photograph of Bazil Thorne. It was as if it taunted him every time he walked past the folded newspaper. The more he looked at it, the more it exemplified the marked contrast between Bazil Thorne's easy, simple, undeserved life and his own life of struggle and hardship.

Then, in a seemingly serendipitous coincidence, four days after Bazil had won his prize, in a magazine called *The Weekend* Bradley saw a two-page article headed 'The Vilest Crime of All', which described a number of kidnappings-for-ransom that had occurred in overseas countries. Most Australians who read the article felt secure in the knowledge that such shocking events did not occur in their own decent, law-abiding society, but Bradley soaked up every detail of it. One of the cases concerned the kidnapping in France earlier that year of four-year-old Eric Peugeot, grandson of Jean-Pierre Peugeot, the sixty-three-year-old head of the French automotive dynasty, who was then estimated to be worth $US40 million. Bradley read how the kidnappers had conducted intensive surveillance of the family before kidnapping the boy on 12 April 1960, leaving a ransom note near a sandpit from which they had taken the child. The child's father, Roland Peugeot, meticulously followed the kidnappers' instructions – including a firm warning not to involve the police – and three days later he readily paid the 50 million francs[2] ransom, which was followed by the safe return of his son. Bradley was shocked that the kidnappers had demanded such a paltry amount when clearly the Peugeot family had the capacity to pay far more. He felt that with his negotiating skills the amount would have been much larger. At the time of the article, the French police had failed to identify the kidnappers of Eric Peugeot.[3]

The article got Bradley thinking: why should Bazil Thorne be entitled to keep the whole of the £100,000 entirely for himself? Stephen was sure that such a simpleton would have no idea how to invest or spend such a substantial sum of money. He would be utterly susceptible to pathetic requests from family and friends – even from strangers – seeking his support for charitable or benevolent causes, or for fantastic and imagined projects, or to pay for desperately needed medical procedures or pharmaceuticals. He was sure that Bazil would dissipate the full amount in less than twelve months. Stephen, on the other hand, knew exactly how to invest such a sum, to make it grow into an even greater amount. Looked at logically, Stephen came to the view that he was just as entitled to such a windfall as anyone else – actually more so, because of what he had been forced to endure during his life so far. Just a small proportion of the money – say, £25,000 – would make his and Magda's lives a lot less stressful, so that they could focus more time on their children and he and Magda could finally live the life they imagined and deserved.

As disparate notions of inequity and entitlement coalesced in Stephen's mind, a plan began to emerge, seemingly from a source beyond his consciousness – a plan so simple and remarkably free from risk to anyone that he was surprised nobody had already thought of it.[4] The newspaper article about Bazil's lottery win was accompanied by a photograph of his wife, Freda, and mentioned that they had three children: Cheryl, aged eleven, Graeme, aged eight, and Belinda, aged three. The article even listed their address at 79 Edward Street in the middle-class, seaside suburb of Bondi. Stephen found that he was increasingly preoccupied with the idea of carrying out a kidnapping for ransom of one of the Thorne children, who were around the same age as his and Magda's. This gave Stephen the confidence that he could entice one of them to come with him, and that he could keep the child calm during the time it took to negotiate with Bazil and Freda Thorne. Stephen was so good with children that he could even make the incident trauma-free, so that the child would be unaware that anything untoward had occurred until being reunited with their parents. It would be almost like a game, with some real-life rewards for him at the end. Stephen was also sure that, as had happened in the Peugeot kidnapping, he could convince the parents not to involve the police while he had their child.

Surely his possession of their child would be sufficient to convince them to hand over a small part of their windfall in exchange for the child's safe return. He could drive the youngster around, keeping him or her occupied with playful imaginative games, while the Thornes collected the money, and within a few hours he would make another phone call to tell them where to leave it. They would undoubtedly follow his instructions to the letter, whereupon he would pick up the money, release the child in a safe place and notify the parents where to find him or her. The child would be oblivious to what had happened behind the scenes, and Stephen would be £25,000 richer. Although he was aware that the parents would be distressed, it would only be for a short time as they were gathering the ransom together, and it would immediately dissipate when they were joyously reunited with their child after the money was paid.

Within a few days, Stephen Bradley was resolute that he would carry out this venture, which would set him and Magda on a path to prosperity. He was convinced that he had all the characteristics necessary to accomplish it – attributes that most people lacked. He believed that he had the intelligence to carefully work through every detail of the plan, so that any risks could be anticipated and eliminated. Anyone else would probably do something stupid that would alert the child to danger, or give the parents a clue to their identity, or leave some evidence that the police would later be able to pursue. It was a magnificent idea and he was the ideal person to execute it. He delighted in the intellectual exercise of planning this unique venture, as it provided the kind of challenge and excitement that his mundane jobs had failed to offer him. For the first time in ages he felt that his true creative talents were being utilised. Whether at home or at work, his thoughts constantly drifted to the details of the plan. He would also spend countless hours imagining different ways to invest or spend the £25,000. Most of his musings involved the purchase of a grand new home and expensive cars, as well as trips overseas with Magda and possibly also the children. At a level deep within his psyche, he already had the money in his possession and it was his to spend as he wished. The thrill was like a drug of addiction.

It was simple to locate the Thorne family's modest downstairs flat in a two-storey duplex at 79 Edward Street, Bondi. The building was on the lower side of the street opposite a large park that stretched up a hill, making covert surveillance of their home an easy task. One morning, Stephen Bradley went to the park and settled down on the grass with a newspaper as disguise to observe the Thorne family's morning rituals. He watched as Bazil left for work. A little later Graeme came out in his school uniform and walked up the street to a corner store, where he was picked up in a car by a woman with two young boys, whom he presumed were her sons. Later still, Freda appeared with her younger daughter on their way to the shops. It was clear that they were a typical, ordinary Australian family.

Stephen's attention was initially directed at the youngest of the Thorne children, Belinda, because at the age of only three she would be unable to provide the police with any meaningful information about her abductor. However, he soon realised that it would be very difficult to abduct such a young child because she was almost always in the company of an adult. After conducting surveillance several times, Stephen's attention became focused on the Thornes' middle child – eight-year-old Graeme Frederick Hilton Thorne. At his age, the boy would not be able to provide the police with any meaningful description of him. At no time did Stephen sight their oldest child, Cheryl, aged eleven, who would, in any event, be able to put up more of a fight.

Before he could move ahead with his plan, however, Stephen needed to confirm the telephone number attached to the Thornes' flat – a necessary detail, because without this Stephen would not be able to make the call to demand the ransom. The Thornes had only made arrangements to have the telephone connected after they learned of their lottery win, and although the handset had been installed and they had been allocated a phone number, the connection was not yet functional.

Stephen looked up the telephone directory, but there was no entry for the Thornes' home. So he rang a special enquiry number at the telephone exchange to investigate. These were the days when there was no such concept as the right to privacy, and information such as phone numbers and addresses was readily available to the public, and Stephen was easily able to obtain the number from the exchange operator. However, when he called the number to check, the call was unsuccessful.

As the whole plan depended upon phone contact, Stephen realised that he had to find out why the number allocated to the Thornes' family home was not connected and, if the information he had been given by the exchange was wrong, he had to find out the correct number. It was possible that Bazil and Freda had applied for a 'silent number' – not published in the annual phone book – to deal with the volume of requests they were receiving from people wanting to share in the bounty from their lottery win. He thought long and hard about how to overcome this hurdle, and considered it a serious test for a man with his all-round abilities. In a way he enjoyed such a challenge, as it stretched his resolve to accomplish the plan, and it felt so good when his mind miraculously came up with a solution. After much consideration he decided to take a bold, necessary step: he would go to the Thornes' home and, using the clever ruse of posing as an investigator, would obtain their phone number.

The story he devised was to pretend to be a private enquiry agent engaged in a divorce investigation and seeking to know the whereabouts of a previous resident of their block of flats. He had once spoken to a real private detective who worked for a local agency, and he had told him that when they were making enquiries about 'new Australians' – as all immigrants were then called – they had been instructed by the principal of the agency to use the excuse of looking for a man by the fictitious name of Bognor. Bradley decided that this was as good a cover story as any, and if necessary he could provide the name of a real detective agency as a subterfuge. Although this deviation from his original plan would mean that the members of the Thorne family would see his face and hear his voice and accent, Stephen was confident that a time lapse of several weeks before the kidnapping would ensure that their memories of the man who had made the enquiry at their door would dissipate or even disappear. He thought it unlikely that they would connect his enquiry with the later abduction and, in any event, even if they did remember his visit, they had no way of identifying him, as his plan did not call for any further face-to-face contact.

On 14 June 1960 – twelve days after first seeing the newspaper article about Bazil Thorne – at about 7.30pm, when most families were cleaning up after dinner, Stephen Bradley arrived in Bondi and parked his car in an adjoining street. His heart was racing as he walked towards number 79 Edward Street. He hesitated as he got close enough to the block of flats to see that there were lights on and activity in both the downstairs and the upstairs flats. For a moment, he contemplated abandoning this preliminary step, and perhaps even the whole venture, but as soon as the thought had registered he dismissed it as a trick of the mind, and purposely rekindled his determination to press on. This stage of the plan was as much a test of his resolve as it was an exercise in information-gathering. While it did not commit him to pursuing the central part of the plot, and involved nothing illegal in itself – since he was merely using a pretence to obtain information – it was a means of assessing whether he would be able to carry through with the real plan when the time came. Mustering the strength of purpose that he knew he possessed, he walked down the steps to the Thornes' front door and knocked loudly.

Freda answered the door, and Stephen could see Bazil, seated in a chair, looking his way from a room deep inside the flat. They were both surprised by the unexpected intrusion into their family space at a time when most suburban families were cleaning up after dinner. Nobody they knew would unexpectedly come to their home at that time unless it was an emergency. Freda's face told him that she thought he was a hawker trying to sell them something. Stephen gave her his most engaging smile and, in line with his plan, told her that he was looking for a Mr Bognor. She looked enquiringly at him and replied that the previous tenant had been a Mr Bailey and she had no knowledge of a Mr Bognor. Stephen looked down at his notebook and said, 'Is the phone number at this flat 30-7113?' Freda was surprised and immediately asked, 'How did you get that number?' He replied, 'I have my ways and means of getting information. I'm a private enquiry agent and this is a husband-and-wife affair.' Freda, having no knowledge of divorce disputes, looked even more quizzically at him, not knowing what 'a husband-and-wife affair' meant, and said, 'That happens to be my telephone number and it has not even been connected yet.' She then suggested that he go upstairs to consult with the tenant there, Mrs Dorothy Lord, who had been living in the building much longer than they had.

Although Stephen had obtained the information he required, he felt the need to maintain his cover, in case Freda was still observing him, so he went upstairs and spoke to Mrs Lord. However, instead of saying that he was looking for a Mr Bognor, he decided to utilise the information he had garnered from Freda and told the woman upstairs that he was looking for a Mr Bailey. Mrs Lord told him that Mr Bailey had lived downstairs, but that she had no idea where he was living now.

Having achieved his objective by finding out that the number provided by the exchange was correct, and that he just needed to wait for it to be connected, Stephen left the block of flats and returned to his car, proud of himself for having taken this first, important step in the plan that was going to change his and Magda's fortunes forever. He thought to himself how easy it had been to induce Freda to give him the information he required. It never ceased to amaze him how readily people accepted the lies he delivered to them in a confident and easygoing manner. He was pleased that he had been able to overcome his initial jitters, and carry out this step with confidence and aplomb. Then again, not many people had his ability to deliver lines without a trace of doubt or hesitation.

Stephen knew that he now needed to wait a sufficient time to allow the memory of his visit to fade in Freda and Bazil's minds, and also for the telephone installed at Edward Street to be connected. It would be easy to determine when the latter occurred by simply dialling the number every few days. If someone answered, there was no need for him to speak, and he would know that the lines of communication were open.

***

Freda Thorne felt uneasy about the strange request for information from the man with a distinctly European accent who had knocked at their door at an odd hour of the night. How did he know their new telephone number when it had not yet been connected? And why had he come to their home looking for a man with such a peculiar name? What did he mean by 'a husband-and-wife affair'? She was sure that he was up to no good – possibly he was gathering information for a person or organisation that wanted to sell them something or solicit money from them. She made a mental note to look out for him in case he ever came back to their door. She would surely recognise his accent if ever he contacted them by phone.

The next day, Freda spoke to Mrs Lord and learnt of the discrepancy between the enquiry that had been made of her and the one made of Mrs Lord. This made her even more uneasy, and she became convinced that his enquiry was not a genuine one, but a ruse of some sort. Freda expressed her concerns to Bazil, but he seemed unperturbed. Mrs Lord, however, was of a similar view to Freda that the man was on some sort of suspicious mission. They both commented on how unusual it was for a man with such a distinctive foreign accent to be knocking on doors in their area at that time of night. Mrs Lord mentioned the matter to her husband, who was the desk sergeant at the Bondi police station.

***

A week after his visit to the Thornes' home, Stephen Bradley felt that enough time had passed for him to undertake the next stage of his grand plan. This required him to engage in more intensive surveillance of the Thornes – and Graeme in particular. In order to have the time to do this properly, on 21 June Stephen resigned from his position as an electroplater for poker-machine manufacturer Nutt & Muddle at Darlinghurst, telling them that he needed treatment for a slipped disc in his neck. He was not perturbed at losing his income, as he had tired of the job, and he did not plan to work after the massive injection of funds he was expecting, which would dwarf his salary as an electroplater. He did not tell Magda that he had left his job, and she asked no questions.

Over the course of the next fortnight, Stephen often awoke at around 6am and left his home at Clontarf to conduct surveillance on the Thorne family, either from the park opposite their home or the streets nearby. Stephen observed that at about 8.30 each weekday morning, Graeme – dressed in his private-school uniform and carrying his school case – would invariably leave his home on foot, turn left into Wellington Street and walk two blocks down a hill to the corner of O'Brien Street, where he would go into a corner store and buy a packet of chips. He would then sit on his school case outside the store, eat his snack and wait to be picked up – generally about ten minutes later – by a woman in a station wagon with two young boys of about the same age and in the same uniform. On one occasion, Stephen followed the station wagon and learnt that the boys were students at the Scots College in Bellevue Hill.

Another day he discovered that the woman who picked up Graeme and drove him to school lived in Cox Avenue, Bondi. Stephen thought that if he could find out the woman's name, it might prove useful in enticing Graeme to come with him. He knew a family by the name of Teicher, who also lived in Cox Avenue, so Stephen approached Mrs Teicher and asked her if she knew the name of the woman. Mrs Teicher was suspicious of the enquiry, thinking that Bradley might have designs on the woman, and so denied any knowledge of her.

Stephen observed that Bazil's work as a commercial traveller sometimes had him leaving the house very early, but that on other days he remained at home until late in the morning. His surveillance also revealed that Freda, like most wives of working men of her day, would spend much of her day at home when she was not shopping or doing other errands or visiting friends.

Stephen realised early in his planning that it would entail too great a risk to forcibly drag the boy into his car from a public street, and that he would instead need a ruse to entice the eight-year-old to voluntarily enter the vehicle – an easy task for a father of three children. That way, Bradley could delay the forcible part of the venture until he had driven the boy to a secluded location. After observing Graeme over many weekdays during that fortnight, Stephen initially thought that the most opportune time to approach the boy was when he was outside the corner store waiting to be picked up. However, on further reflection, he considered that this approach would necessitate speaking to him right outside the shop, where there would be an unacceptable risk of being observed or overheard by the shopkeeper or customers. He therefore decided that the safest approach was to intercept

Graeme at the intersection of Wellington and Francis Streets, one block back from the store. He would park his car close to the intersection so that it would impede Graeme's path and the boy would have to deviate around it. This would place Graeme so close to the car that Stephen could speak to him in a quiet voice that was unlikely to be overheard by anyone who happened to be nearby.

After much thought, Stephen decided that an eight-year-old was most likely to accept a story that involved only a slight change to his regular routine; he would tell Graeme that the woman who normally picked him up was sick and that he, Bradley, had been sent instead to take Graeme to school. Even if the boy had initial reservations about getting in the car, Stephen would be able to impress upon him that he had no other way of getting to school, and that his parents would be very upset with him if he didn't arrive at school on time. He would convince Graeme of his authenticity by demonstrating his knowledge of the names of his parents, and even his sisters, and, if need be, their ages as well. He could also mention the boy's school and where it was located. Surely all this would satisfy Graeme that Stephen could be trusted to take him to school. Once inside the car, he could then tell Graeme that they were also picking up another boy, giving Stephen time before Graeme would became alarmed that they were not driving towards his school.

By the late stages of planning, Stephen had realised that he would not be able to keep an eight-year-old boy entertained for the time required for Bazil and Freda to get the ransom money together and deliver it in accordance with his instructions. His earlier idea that the child would suffer no trauma had been replaced by the reality that a child of eight would inevitably realise at some stage that something was seriously amiss. The challenge was to delay this as long as possible. How would he keep Graeme under his control and still be able to make the phone calls? What would he do when the boy suddenly panicked upon realising that he was not being driven to school? It slowly dawned on Stephen that the plan would inevitably require some physical force and some degree of restraint. He was still determined that he would limit the trauma to the child as much as possible but, eventually, he came to the conclusion that the most merciful way to execute his plan was to quickly render the child unconscious – and to keep him in that state for the duration of his abduction, secured out of sight in the garage of his Clontarf home – so that by the time he regained consciousness the ordeal would be over and he would wake up safely in his parents' arms. This plan would leave him with little or no memory of the events of the day – somewhat akin to a long, daytime sleep.

The only car in the Bradley family at that time was a cream Goggomobil sports roadster[5] on which he still owed a substantial amount of money. It was small, open-roofed, stylish and rare, which meant that it constantly attracted attention. It was clearly unsuitable for inconspicuously taking a child off the street and keeping him secure until the ransom could be paid. Stephen discarded the idea of stealing a car to use in the venture, because the risk of detection of the theft was greater than the risks associated with the kidnapping.

Instead, he decided to buy a new car which would be more suited to his plan. In early July 1960, he bought on hire purchase[6] an iridescent blue, 1955 Ford Customline sedan, which was much larger than the Goggomobil and was the kind of vehicle that attracted no particular attention. At a cost of around £900, the five-year-old Customline was well beyond his means, but Stephen didn't care, because he knew that within a few weeks he would be flush with funds.

Once he had settled on the details of the kidnapping plan and called the Thornes' home to confirm that their telephone had been connected, Stephen was overcome with a desire to urgently carry it out while he still maintained his resolve and before Bazil could spend or give away his winnings. At the same time, Stephen was seized by yet another of his frequent impulses – this time to sell his home in Clontarf, in anticipation of soon having the finances to purchase a far grander one. In order to secure Graeme during the ransom negotiations, however, Stephen needed unrestricted access to the house without Magda and the children being present. The fusion of these ideas propelled Bradley to put their Clontarf home on the market, start looking for a new one and make arrangements for the house to be vacant on the day of the kidnapping. This all took a considerable amount of time – which was facilitated by the fact that he had surrendered his position at Nutt & Muddle.

Stephen informed Magda that it would be best for them to sell their Clontarf home and move into rental accommodation for a time, so that they could find another, even better home to buy – and possibly take a holiday after vacating their home. When Magda heard this, she was alarmed at his bizarre, grandiose ideas that seemed well beyond their means. However, she knew that to defy him would threaten their harmonious marriage, so she went along with this seemingly unattainable proposal. They prepared to pack up and store all their worldly possessions, and the Clontarf property was put on the market.

It was not difficult to sell the house at Moore Street; it was in a desirable suburb, had distant water views, and a buyer was quickly found. A Mr Douglas Palmer, a company director, and his wife, Paula, agreed to buy the property for £8,800 – a profit of £800 for Stephen and Magda over the price that they had paid less than twelve month before. Stephen considered that he had done well on the transaction, although he still had substantial loans to pay off. It was less than five weeks since he had first read the newspaper article detailing the Thornes' lottery win, and Stephen was proud that he had been able to set everything up so quickly. He believed that few others would have had the organisational skills and the determination to achieve so much in such a short time.

In the meantime, Stephen took Magda to inspect a number of impressive homes priced between £12,000 and £13,000 – amounts well beyond their means, even with a few rubbery figures to enhance a substantial loan. One such house was at 16 Grandview Grove, Seaforth – a suburb with superb views just a mile or two from their existing home in Clontarf. Stephen told one agent that he had a deal coming through very soon and that when it did he would be in a position to buy the property outright – and to pay cash. Magda could not understand why Stephen was taking her to view houses so far outside their range, because, as far as she knew, they had little equity in their existing home; but as usual she knew better than to question, let alone challenge, her husband.

Mr Palmer was anxious to finalise the purchase. Arrangements were made for the sale of the Clontarf home to be completed and possession to be handed over a week later on Saturday 9 July. Although this date placed Stephen under intense time pressure if he was going to use their Clontarf home as a staging post for the kidnapping, he readily agreed to this hurried completion of the sale, believing that it was yet another challenge to his ingenuity and resolve. It also meant that Bazil Thorne had less time to spend or otherwise dissipate his winnings. There were now two reasons for Stephen to have his house cleared and his family out of the way before the following weekend.

Stephen had no qualms about his family having nowhere to go after vacating their home, because he relished the idea of sending Magda and the children on a holiday away from Sydney, thus giving him access to the property on the day of the kidnapping. He planned to join them several days later and joyfully announce that they were all going on a grand overseas holiday. He would tell Magda that he had done a business deal – too complex to explain – that had netted him an unexpected windfall. On their return, he and Magda would purchase a magnificent new home befitting their enhanced financial status. Stephen arranged for a firm of removalists to arrive at their home between 10 and 11am on Thursday 7 July to collect the family's possessions. He planned to convince Magda and the children to depart on their holiday that same day. This would leave the following day – Friday the 8th – clear to accomplish the kidnapping. However, Stephen and Magda still faced the prospect of packing up their worldly possessions, so that removalists could pick them up and store them.

Stephen arranged for the removalists to store the larger items of furniture until he could find alternative accommodation, while some valuable paintings were given for safekeeping to their neighbours, the Telfords. Magda was concerned about where they would live, as it was obvious that there would be a gap between leaving their Clontarf home and buying a new one.

Stephen had seemingly taken no steps to find rented accommodation in the meantime, but she was delighted when he told her that on vacating their home they would drive to a holiday resort at Surfers Paradise on the Gold Coast of Queensland, six hundred miles north of a cold Sydney winter. She was sure that when they returned Stephen would find suitable rental accommodation until they found another house to buy. But first, there was the enormous task of packing up all of their household goods.

As the day for the removal approached, it suddenly occurred to Stephen that he had unnecessarily limited the execution of his kidnapping plan to a single day – the following Friday. He contemplated that if, for some reason, Graeme did not go to school that day, or did not follow his usual route to the shop in Wellington Street, or if there was someone in Wellington Street near Graeme who knew him, the whole plan would have to be indefinitely postponed and completely reformulated. He decided to increase the odds by giving himself two chances to carry out his plan – the first on Thursday, thereby leaving Friday in reserve. However, this change required Stephen to convince Magda to leave the house with the children late on Wednesday, or at the latest early on Thursday morning. Stephen had already invested a great deal of time and thought into his plan, and there was now no possibility of abandoning it. In his mind, the money was almost within his grasp, and no one was going to stand in his way of getting it – not even Magda.

As Magda feverishly packed up their household goods in the days before their move – a tedious task that she had dutifully performed on too many occasions – what sustained her mood was the knowledge that she and her family would soon leave on a driving holiday to Surfers Paradise. The plan was that they would drive north in the Ford Customline, taking their cat and dog with them. However, late on the evening before the removalists were due, when Stephen and Magda had completed much of their packing and were desperately tired, without any warning or discussion, Stephen announced that Magda and the children would fly to Queensland the following morning without him, and that he would join them in the Customline a day or two later, after supervising the removalists on his own.

Magda was livid – not just at the sudden and unilateral nature of the decision, but also that these new arrangements would mean that she would be absent when the removalists came to collect their possessions. She immediately objected to this change of plans, arguing that the flights would cost them money they could ill afford. Magda was also angry that the new plan meant that she would be on her own with the children in Queensland for the first few days of their holiday. This was not what she had had in mind. More than anything, Magda had been looking forward to the leisurely drive to Queensland, and she was resentful that Stephen wanted to deprive her of this chance to relax after the ordeal of packing up their property.

As a result, the two of them had a furious row. Stephen, however, remained adamant that she and the children would leave by plane as early as possible the following morning. He phoned the airline and booked tickets on the first available flight to Coolangatta, which was due to depart at 11.35 the following morning – Thursday 7 July. He then rang their favourite hotel in Surfers Paradise, the Seabreeze Private Hotel, and made a booking for one room for Magda and the children. Magda was mystified that during this call he made no mention of the fact that he would be arriving a few days later, in which case they would require two rooms. Still smarting from their argument, Magda finally went to sleep at about 2am, knowing that the following morning she and the children would leave their Clontarf home forever.

***

On the night of 6 July, Stephen and Magda's neighbours heard the sounds of a furious argument coming from within the Bradleys' home. Although they could not make out the words that were being shouted, the neighbours realised that something was seriously amiss in the Bradley household.

***

On the morning of 7 July, Magda awoke still feeling resentful from the argument the previous night. Stephen was nowhere to be seen, having already left, so Magda got up and prepared to depart in time to catch their flight. Realising that she could not rely on Stephen to take them to the airport, Magda called for a taxi, which arrived between 9.30am and 9.45am. Their neighbours, the Telfords, who had been told that the Bradleys were going for a holiday to Queensland, saw Magda and the children get into the taxi, and were surprised that there was no sign of Stephen. That was because earlier that morning Stephen Bradley had left his home in his Ford Customline to kidnap a child for ransom – a crime so heinous that it had never before been committed in the 172 years of European settlement in Australia.

2

FROM ISTVAN TO STEPHEN

Very little can be verified about Stephen Bradley's life before his arrival in Australia on 20 March 1950. Many of his assertions are highly unlikely to be true, because of his penchant for telling tall, self-aggrandising stories. He had a constant, desperate need to impress, and the personality, persuasiveness and high IQ to do it convincingly and unflinchingly. He was suave and could quickly sway others with his warmth and enthusiasm. He was particularly attracted to people who had money, status and influence, and he craved acceptance by them as an equal. He had the ability to charm people into doing things for him and, in particular, giving him jobs or money. If anyone challenged his claims, he would remain eminently composed and quietly explain to them why their scepticism was unwarranted. He had an overwhelming need to be seen as a man of status, affluence and class, and he firmly believed that respect came from having an abundance of wealth. He had a penchant for ostentatiously portraying himself as a man of money – particularly through owning an expensive home and car. When he went to restaurants or hotels, he would tip generously and assume the air of a man flush with money. While he was short and, for a man in his mid-thirties, rather pudgy, he was invariably well dressed and his dark hair was always well groomed. Most people considered him quite handsome.

What *is* a proven fact is that Stephen Bradley came from Budapest in Hungary, where he was born Istvan Baranyay on 15 March 1926, the son of József Baranyay, an architect, and Klara Baranyay née Kramer. Stephen claimed that his father was Christian and his mother Jewish, with the result that during the Nazi occupation of Hungary he was required to wear a white armband to show that he was a 'half-breed'. He maintained that in 1944 he was a prisoner of the Gestapo for five months, during which time he was lined up beside a river to be shot with other people of Jewish descent, but that when the shooting started a bullet grazed his right eye, so he dropped into the water and managed to escape.

After the war, at the age of nineteen, he migrated from Hungary to Italy, with the intention of salvaging a semblance of an education of which he had been deprived in his homeland as a result of the war. He later told people that he had studied in Rome to be a doctor and then an engineer. Istvan's first marriage took place in Europe. Very little is known about it, except that it resulted in divorce in 1948. At some stage, he realised that Europe had little to offer him – professionally or socially – and so he chose to uproot himself and spend his precious remaining monetary resources to come to a new land full of opportunity – Australia. However, the 'land of milk and honey' failed to live up to many of his expectations.

When he arrived in Melbourne aboard the SS *Skaugum* on 28 March 1950, Istvan Baranyay claimed to be a qualified male nurse. His foreign education was not recognised, and so he was reduced to working in mundane occupations where his real talents were rarely utilised. He took on a number of trade or sales jobs, at which he quickly became adept. However, he found that his bosses were generally stupid and insular, and they failed to recognise what he regarded as his superior intelligence, education and insights. Any advice he gave them was resented or ignored. As a result, he would soon tire of these jobs and restlessly move to a new one – often in a completely different industry – where he hoped to be given the recognition and opportunities he deserved.

Istvan readily adapted to the culture of his adopted country, because of his ability to mould his personality to meet whatever circumstances confronted him. His capacity to understand people's motivations and desires allowed him to manipulate them as he wished. He could be anyone he wanted to be, in order to ingratiate himself to whomever he needed to impress. His ability to charm was a particularly valuable asset to overcome the pervasive prejudice against migrants that Istvan encountered in his new country. His olive complexion, his Hungarian accent, and even his European education frequently provoked initial discrimination, denigration and distrust by ordinary Anglo-Australians, which he was able to overcome with his engaging personality.

FROM ISTVAN TO STEPHEN

On 1 March 1952, Istvan married his second wife, Eva Laidlaw, also a Hungarian migrant, who had changed her surname from Laszlo. They were married at the Presbyterian Church in Gardiner, a suburb of Melbourne, and lived in that city, where he worked as a motor mechanic. It was from this marriage that Istvan's only natural child, Helen Jennifer, was born in June 1953. Upon their marriage, Eva's father, Dr Franz (Frank) Laszlo, a lecturer in engineering at Melbourne University since his arrival in Australia in 1939, transferred a valuable house into his daughter's name, in which the couple lived. After several years of marriage, the house was sold and a new one was purchased in their joint names.

Several months later, on 26 February 1955, Eva was tragically killed at Heidelberg when the brakes of the car she was driving mysteriously failed. Their baby daughter, Helen, who was also in the car, sustained an injury to her thigh that left her with a slight but permanent impairment. Istvan inherited Eva's entire estate. The accident was investigated by the police, but no unequivocal evidence could be found to prove foul play. Dr Frank Laszlo, who had never liked his son-in-law, pressed the police to continue their investigations, but they assured him that everything that could be done had been. Dr Laszlo and his wife, Ilse, realised that if they were to maintain contact with their granddaughter, Helen, it was imperative to have as good a relationship as possible with their son-in-law, so they made the decision to sublimate their true feelings and suspicions about him. Stephen, of course, was well aware of his parents-in-law's hostility, but he allowed them contact with Helen, because it suited him to have somewhere to leave her.

Not long after this tragedy, in October 1955, Istvan met another Hungarian migrant – Magda Weinberg[1] née Klein. Magda was attractive, vivacious and possessed an inherent sensuality that drew men to her. As opposed to Bradley's dubious wartime background, Magda's experiences during the Nazi period were probably genuine. Together with both her Jewish parents, she had been a prisoner in Auschwitz concentration camp, and she still bore the prisoner number A-11-663 tattooed on her left arm. Both her parents had been killed in the gas chambers. Magda had survived, but an injury in the camp had deprived her of sight in one eye.

Magda married her first husband, Gregor Weinberg, in Hungary, where their first son, Paul, was born in 1947. They migrated to Melbourne in April 1949, where their second son, Ross, was born in 1955. Ross was born with a severe, permanent hearing impediment that caused him to be functionally mute. In October 1955, with her marriage floundering, Magda went to a penny poker card night at a friend's home where she met the charismatic widower, who, at that time, was still named Istvan Baranyay. She was instantly attracted to him and within a short time they began an affair. On learning of their relationship, Gregor Weinberg initiated divorce proceedings against Magda on the grounds of her adultery.

In August 1956, Istvan Baranyay changed his name by deed poll to Stephen Leslie Bradley in the hope that the anglicisation of his name would go some way to alleviating the prejudice he confronted daily from most Anglo-Australians. Around the same time, Magda and Stephen set up home together with their three children – Paul, Helen and Ross – initially in Melbourne. Magda readily became Helen Bradley's principal cater and treated the now three-year-old as if she were her own natural daughter. In 1957 they moved to Sydney, largely because Magda's ex-husband, Gregor, had taken his elder son, Paul, to live there with him, leaving Ross with his mother and Stephen. On arriving in Sydney, Magda quickly reclaimed Paul, and all five of them moved into a flat at Waverley. The move to Sydney meant that Frank and Ilse Laszlo lost most of their contact with their granddaughter, Helen. They disliked Magda and their feelings about Stephen had only worsened since the death of their daughter.

It was a constant struggle for Stephen Bradley to provide financially for himself and his family in a manner befitting his education and class. He was a master wheeler-dealer, who was able to supplement his meagre salary from semi-skilled jobs by using his superior financial expertise. He could see opportunities where others saw only folly. Where others were risk-averse, he was adventurous and bold. His financial credo was that riches went to those who were open to new opportunities, and he believed that he had the perspicacity to see them when most others did not. He would regularly buy and sell the houses in which he, Magda and the children lived – largely on borrowed money – generally making small profits each time, which enabled him to buy a bigger and better house the next. He was not averse to fudging the details of a loan application so that a bank or finance company would advance a greater amount than their rules permitted, or making a secret profit on the side, or converting a piece of property that belonged to an employer to his own use. If his infractions were ever detected, he had the capacity to lie his way out of trouble, and in any event he would rarely stay anywhere long-term, so even if his lies were exposed, he would often have already moved on. To Stephen Bradley, the world was full of opportunities waiting to be exploited.

Armed with his new identity in Sydney, Stephen Bradley arranged for a business card to be printed on which he described himself as 'Dr Stephen L Bradley. Psychotherapist, DOM (Italy)'. Presumably DOM stood for doctor of medicine. Despite these supposed qualifications, or perhaps because of them, in May 1957 he obtained a job as a psychiatric nurse at Broughton Hall Psychiatric Clinic, which later became part of the Rozelle Hospital. Five months later, for reasons unknown, he precipitately lost his position at the clinic. He told his wife and friends that he had been forced to leave after he was knocked over by a patient, causing a back injury that aggravated a wound sustained during the war when he had worked with the Hungarian underground against the Nazis. However, so strong was Bradley's desire to remain within the walls of the clinic that he immediately applied for admission as a patient, claiming to suffer from extreme anxiety – a request that was refused. In the same year, Bradley was charged with false pretences after he sold a motor vehicle that was still financially encumbered to a lender, however the charge was never pursued, due to insufficient evidence.

At the end of 1957, Magda and Stephen took over the management of the Wunulla Club – part of the prestigious Royal Motor Yacht Club in Rose Bay. Stephen was able to talk his way into this venture despite having no qualifications or previous experience. He relished the opportunity of contact with the wealthy, eastern suburbs boat owners who were members of the club. He and Magda lasted barely three months before the club terminated the contract, but the experience gave them a taste for the hospitality industry, and they believed that in that direction lay their future financial destiny.

In June 1958, Magda and Stephen purchased the Carinya Guesthouse in the Blue Mountains village of Katoomba, largely from money that Magda had received in her divorce settlement from Gregor Weinberg. They threw themselves into creating a holiday venue at which guests could enjoy the best of European food and hospitality, surrounded by the stunning natural beauty of the Blue Mountains just 70 miles west of Sydney. By this time, Magda's ex-husband Gregor was running another guesthouse in the adjoining village of Leura, and relations between the former spouses had become quite cordial. Paul Weinberg regularly went between his parents in the Blue Mountains, but because of Ross's severe hearing handicap, the younger boy had little contact with his father. Magda relished fulfilling the role of mother to Stephen's daughter, Helen, who, being only three years old when Magda came into her life, had no memory of her deceased natural mother. Helen immediately latched on to Magda as her primary care-giver. It was while they were at Katoomba that Stephen brought home a present for Magda and the children – a female Pekinese dog they named Cherie.

Magda became Stephen Bradley's third wife on 8 December 1958 at the Registry Office in Sydney. She brought to their marriage not only her substantial contribution to the guesthouse at Katoomba, but also £3500 in savings. Stephen brought to their union his charisma and panache. After marrying Stephen, Magda gave vent to an aspiration she had harboured for many years – to write and sell music and song scores – but she met with virtually no artistic recognition or financial success.

Magda and Stephen's venture running the Carinya Guesthouse lasted only one summer-holiday season. By mid-1959 the business was floundering and the proprietors had realised just how much effort was entailed in running a guesthouse with accommodation for fifty-five people, as well as a restaurant. The newly married couple were only saved from financial oblivion when, in the early hours of the morning of 8 June 1959, the guesthouse mysteriously caught fire and burnt down, enabling the Bradleys to collect the insurance money and sell the land. After payment of all debts, they were left with only £42. The cause of the fire was never determined.

Once again in Sydney, Stephen Bradley tried his hand working as a life insurance salesman for the T&G Insurance Company. Ross was placed in a school that specialised in the education of children with hearing impairments – St. Gabriel's School for deaf children at Castle Hill – which was residential during the week but allowed the boy to return home at weekends. In December 1959, Stephen and Magda purchased an elegant house at 28 Moore Street, Clontarf, which had a good, if distant, view of the water at Middle Harbour, but was well beyond their means. The £8000 purchase price was covered by a loan from the T&G Insurance Company for £5000 and a second mortgage for £3300, which also allowed a margin for additional expenses. Shortly afterwards, there was a 'misunderstanding due to carelessness' concerning £136 Stephen had collected in client premiums that had not found its way to T&G, and Stephen was obliged to leave his employment. He then secured a job at a lower salary as an electroplater with

Nutt & Muddle, a firm of poker machine manufacturers at Darlinghurst. This position was the latest in a long line of jobs in varied industries in which he quickly perfected his role.

Stephen's income from Nutt & Muddle was a mere £20 per week, which meant that he and Magda had grossly overextended themselves in purchasing the house at Clontarf, leaving them in a precarious financial position. The mortgage repayments were £11 per week, leaving the family only £9 for living expenses. With outgoings far exceeding their income, clearly the Bradley family was living on capital and, without a massive injection of funds, faced financial ruin. Stephen knew that if he was to maintain his family's status and their standard of living, he had to pull a mythical rabbit out of a magical hat. Desperate situations called for definitive solutions.

Magda and Stephen Bradley had a good marriage – she ensured that it was so. She was determined that this marriage would be successful after the failure of her previous one to Gregor Weinberg. Magda constantly told Stephen what a wonderful husband and father he was. She was full of praise for his looks, his intelligence and his enterprising business acumen. She would often compare him favourably to men of vastly greater means and assets, so as to appease his jealousy for their affluent lifestyles. She understood why they had to live up to the appearance of wealth and why it was important for them to associate with people above their true station in society. Magda also knew when to stay quiet, even if something about her husband troubled her. She rarely expressed her concerns for his wild and unpredictable financial ventures, and so his failures generally passed without discussion. Magda put up with Stephen's fantastic schemes as the family seemed to veer from one financial disaster to another. She offered no resistance when he wanted to use her divorce settlement monies to jointly purchase the guesthouse in the Blue Mountains, or when he placed her savings in both their names. She got used to the frequent moves when he bought and sold their homes in an attempt to shift up-market, and she accepted the often sudden changes in his work placements and his constant complaints about the stupidity of his bosses. She humoured his grand plans of how they were going to become prosperous and be accepted by Sydney's high society – the upper-class, wealthy people that Stephen craved to emulate. Stephen still exerted a magnetic effect on her, and their sexual attraction to each other was still as strong as the heady days when they had first consummated their unbridled and dangerous lust for each other.

Stephen Bradley doted on his wife and their three children. He did not distinguish between his own flesh and blood – Helen – and Magda's two boys from her marriage to Gregor Weinberg. The family loved nothing better than to spend time together at the beach or a picnic ground. Stephen was loving and attentive to Ross, and never lost his patience when the boy had difficulty understanding him or making his needs known. He was tolerant of Magda's continuing friendship with her ex-husband, and indeed was not averse to using Gregor to their advantage. He was supportive of Magda's dream of becoming a successful songwriter, and would always come up with utterly believable excuses whenever she complained of her lack of progress.

An objective observer would have concluded that theirs was a well-functioning, upwardly mobile family with goodwill on all sides and every chance of leading happy and productive lives. But beneath the surface, Stephen harboured an undercurrent of intense envy and greed, fuelled by a desperate need for social acceptance, a readiness to undertake appalling risks, an unrealistic sense of his own perspicacity, and a perverse thrill in the face of great danger.

3

TESTING METTLE

On the morning of Thursday, 7 July 1960, Stephen Bradley arose early while his wife and children were still asleep. He was comforted to think that by the time he returned home, they would be on their way to Queensland, leaving the house vacant and available to him. He took a family picnic blanket from the boot of his Ford Customline and opened it neatly on the back seat. Then he drove from Clontarf to Bondi, arriving at about 8.15am. This was a routine he had followed many times before when conducting surveillance of the Thorne family in preparation for today. He was quite sure that his observations of the Thorne home had not aroused any suspicions, and he was confident that he had allowed a sufficient time after his visit to their door for their memories to fade. This time, of course, was different – a fact reinforced by his racing heartbeat.

His emotions reminded him of the times many years earlier in Hungary when he had walked through the streets of Budapest, past Gestapo officers, feigning a lack of concern for his safety. Today was also very much a test – of his mettle, his meticulous preparations, and his ability to anticipate and allow for every eventuality that could arise during such a potentially perilous undertaking. It was as though everything he had done in his life so far had been in preparation for the events of today. He felt hyper-aware and his nerve endings were suddenly super-sensitive, as though he could detect the slightest change in the wind or the air temperature, but at the same time he felt a calm resolve, as if his destiny had finally arrived.

Bradley parked his car in Francis Street, right at the inter-section of Wellington Street, where he had observed Graeme walk every day. Any person crossing on that side of the street would have to walk right past his car. He then settled back in the driver's seat to await the arrival of his intended victim. Bradley was unperturbed by the fact that he was using his own car or that he was undisguised. His Customline was one of thousands in Sydney alone. On this cold winter's day, he was wearing an unremarkable grey gabardine overcoat and had a plain felt hat to cover his head. He was quite convinced that if everything went according to plan and the boy got into his car, it would be an event so unremarkable that no one would pay it the slightest attention. He hadn't removed or covered the number plate on his car, because he felt that doing so would be more likely to attract attention. He had, however, taken the precaution of wearing driving gloves to avoid the possibility of leaving fingerprints on Graeme or his possessions.

Bradley sat in his car waiting for the familiar figure of the boy to appear. Based on his previous observations, he expected Graeme to walk past at around 8.25am.

***

That day began very early in the Thorne household. Bazil left before 6am to catch a plane from the airport at Mascot to the North Coast town of Kempsey on one of his frequent business trips as a commercial traveller. After he had gone, Freda made up Graeme's school lunch, making sure that his sandwiches were neatly cut in half and his apple was peeled, with the skin carefully placed back around the fruit, so it would not turn brown before he ate it. Then began the busiest part of the morning when Freda got her two children up and ready for the day. This entailed helping three-year-old Belinda to get dressed, while Graeme got ready for school. Both children then sat together to eat the breakfast that Freda had cooked for them. Graeme was unusually late that morning, and his mother bustled him out of the house at 8.30 with a peremptory goodbye, worried that he might hold up her friend, Phyllis Smith, who routinely picked him up to take him and her own two sons to school at Scots College in Victoria Road at Bellevue Hill.

It was a financial struggle for Bazil and Freda to send their son to Scots, but it was a sacrifice they willingly made to ensure he received a good education in the Scottish Presbyterian tradition, which they admired, despite the fact that both their families were of English origin. In addition, it was close to their home. Like most parents, they hoped that their son would have better opportunities than they had had – having lived their formative years during the Great Depression and the Second World War.

Graeme walked down Wellington Street towards the corner store where, as usual, he planned to buy a packet of chips before being picked up by his mother's friend, Mrs Smith. The trip in her car normally took around ten or fifteen minutes, depending on the peak hour traffic. Graeme was dressed in his grey school uniform with a cap and was carrying his school case, which contained his lunch, school books and a few odds and ends. As he walked down Wellington Street, one of his friends, twelve-year-old Peter Sneddon, who was being driven to school, waved to him.

***

As soon as Bradley saw Graeme approaching, he opened his driver's-side door to step outside and position himself where he could interact with the boy. As he did so, a car approaching the corner from behind him on the same side was forced to deviate slightly to pass the stationary Customline with its open door. This did not concern Bradley, as events like this were commonplace, and he deliberately chose not to look at the passing car or whoever was inside it, so as not to draw any additional attention to himself.

***

As Graeme crossed Francis Street and came within a yard or two of a parked car, a man who was standing by the open front passenger door said to him: 'You must be Graeme.' Graeme nodded, and the man continued: 'I've been sent to pick you up to take you to Scots, because the lady who normally picks you up is sick. Her two boys are already at school, and I've been asked to pick up you and another boy. Your mother, Freda, has been told, so you'd better get into the car, then we'll pick up the other boy and I'll drop you off at school.' Graeme looked at the man, who was smiling kindly at him, and thought to himself that he looked like someone's father. The fact that the man knew his mother's name and his school gave him an air of authority and authenticity that disarmed Graeme sufficiently to dismiss any concerns. Not for a moment did he think back to the many times his parents had told him that he should never, ever, go with a stranger. This was no stranger. This was a friend of his mother's friend.

Without any hesitation or apprehension, Graeme walked the few steps to the front passenger door of this slick-looking car, which was being invitingly held open by the man who had spoken to him. Graeme slid onto the front bench seat and placed his school case on his lap. As he did so, the man slowly but firmly closed the door of the car, calmly walked around the front, opened the driver's-side door and slid in beside him. As the man turned the car key and started the engine, he looked across at Graeme with a wry smile that Graeme didn't quite understand. It was not a smile of warmth or friendship, nor of reassurance, nor an invitation to converse. It was a smile that Graeme had seen on taxi drivers when his father had given them a particularly generous tip.

***

Stephen Bradley knew that if he drove past Bellevue Hill where the Scots College was located, even an eight-year-old would become alarmed that he was not being taken to his school by the usual route.[1] Graeme readily accepted the explanation that they were diverting from the usual journey to Scots College to pick up another boy to take them both to school, but Bradley anticipated that this explanation would allay the boy's concerns only for a while, and that at some point he would become worried and then alarmed. If this occurred while they were driving in a public street in the eastern suburbs of Sydney during peak hour, the boy might attempt to leave the car or raise the attention of a passer-by – an unacceptable risk. Therefore, while the boy still believed he was on his way to school and his suspicions had not yet been aroused, Bradley decided he would stop the car on a pretext at a suitably private place and convert the voluntary lift into a forcible abduction. This, undoubtedly, would be the critical moment on which the success of this whole venture rested. If it was done successfully, the boy would be completely under his control and secured out of sight, without anyone having seen the momentary scene of pandemonium. If it was unsuccessful, someone who saw the incident might come running to the car to assist the boy, or the police might be informed and given a description of Bradley and his car, including the registration number. It was therefore essential to carefully select a suitable location for this conversion of a lift into an abduction. He was convinced that his superior physical strength and the element of surprise would ensure everything went according to plan at this decisive moment.

During his weeks of surveillance of the Thorne family, Bradley had scoured many possible venues in the suburbs between Bondi and Bellevue Hill, and had settled on Centennial Park, an expansive, sparsely wooded area of parkland situated about a ten-minute drive from Bondi – sufficiently short that it would not be likely to raise Graeme's concerns. The park contained a circular driveway and several crossroads. On a Thursday morning at around 8.45, the park would be almost deserted.[2] He had concluded that, once in the park, the safest place to overcome the boy without being observed was within the confines of his car. In visits to the area, he located a spot about 400 yards from one of the gates where he could park his car in a position that could not be seen from any surrounding houses. From here he would be able to scan the vicinity to make sure that nobody was walking, cycling, or driving nearby at the critical time.

***

As he drove from Bondi through the nearby town centre of Bondi Junction and on towards Woollahra where Centennial Park was located, the driver chatted amiably with Graeme, asking him questions about the sports he liked to play and the subjects he was taught at Scots. Graeme readily answered the questions and after a while was quite entranced by this man who was unusually interested in the minor details of his personal life. The minutes passed without any lull in the conversation, until the man slowly eased the car through the stone gates of Centennial Park. As he did so, Graeme became slightly anxious, as he had never before been into Centennial Park on a school day. His parents had taken him there on numerous picnics on weekends and during his holidays, but it seemed strange to be picking up a boy from the park to take him to school. Graeme began nervously fidgeting in the passenger seat and looking around in an attempt to assess where they were going and why they were in such a strange location. His main concern was that if this took longer than expected, he might be late for school.

As he drove into the park, the man said to Graeme, 'We're picking the other boy up here. He lives just on the other side of the park and his mother is bringing him. This is the quickest way to go.' Graeme didn't reply. The man stopped the car on the side of the road, saying to Graeme, 'He should be here in just a minute.' For the next thirty seconds or so, the driver looked around in every direction, which Graeme found strange. Surely, if he was picking up another boy, the driver should know from what direction the other boy was coming. He felt uneasy – there were no houses nearby, so where was the boy coming from? What occupied his mind the most, however, was the thought that being late for school would earn him a detention. His parents would not be pleased.

The driver then said, 'I need to look up his name,' where-upon he reached over the back of the bench seat to the back and pulled over a small travel bag, which he placed on his lap. For another half-minute or so, the man rummaged around in the bag with both hands, and then placed it on the floor under his legs. He then turned to face Graeme. At the same moment, Graeme turned to face this man and was alarmed to see a com-pletely different look on his face – one he had not seen before.

Suddenly, both of the man's hands darted at him across the seat and grabbed him firmly around the neck, pulling his head swiftly down onto the man's lap, jamming him between his abdomen and the steering wheel. Graeme's school cap went flying to the floor and his school case tipped loudly onto its side, but Graeme didn't even have a chance to whimper. As Graeme struggled to breathe, the man kept a firm grip with one hand around his neck, and with the other he reached down into his bag and brought up a piece of rag soaked in a pungent-smelling liquid, which he placed firmly over Graeme's mouth and nose. This made breathing even more difficult, and also prevented him from calling out. Gasping for air, his arms vainly flailed around, one of them occasionally hitting the man lightly on the chest and head, the other pushing the man's legs in an attempt to sit up. Graeme's mind was entirely focused on the primal urge to draw breath, so there was no space for any thoughts of why the man was doing this. His overarching sensation was the vile smell of the rag over his mouth and nose. Within thirty seconds or so, everything went blank.

***

Stephen Bradley held the rag over the boy's mouth for a further minute to ensure he would not wake up too soon. He then laid his limp body down on the front bench seat and placed the rag into the bag at his feet. He then reached over with his left arm to the picnic rug which was neatly laid out on the back seat, pulled it over to the front and covered the boy's now motion-less body with it.

Bradley caught his breath, intensely aware of the significance of the moment, furtively looked around, and was gratified to see that there was still no one in sight. The whole episode had taken less than a few minutes, and he was elated that it had all gone according to plan. He opened the driver's-side door and stepped out, gently laying the boy's head on the driver's seat, and carefully adjusting the rug to make sure that no part of the boy's body was visible. He went around to the large boot of the Ford Customline and opened it, then, still very aware of his surroundings, opened the passenger's-side door. He carefully scooped up the boy and carried him, still wrapped in the rug, to the back of the car, where he gently laid him down inside the boot.

Bradley was confident that he had done no real harm to his precious cargo by rendering him unconscious in this way. He had been to the local library and read textbooks on the medical uses of chloroform³ as an anaesthetic, and he was sure that the time he had held the rag over the boy's mouth was less than anything that would place his life in any danger. He fully expected that Graeme would awaken in an hour or so, with little, if any, memory of what had happened.

Bradley had come fully prepared for the next stage of the venture. He had a roll of strong twine and an old silk scarf that he hadn't worn for years ready in the boot. In preparation for the boy waking from his induced state of unconsciousness, Bradley unwrapped the rug from around him and bound his hands together behind his back, then tied his feet together, and lastly tied the silk scarf tightly around his mouth as a gag, so that when the boy awoke he would not be able to create enough noise to attract the attention of any passer-by.

Bradley took Graeme's school case and cap and his own travel bag from the floor inside the car and placed them next to the boy in the boot. He looked down at his immobilised little captive with triumph, firmly shut the boot and returned to the driver's seat. Bradley allowed himself a deep sigh of relief and a smug smile as he contemplated for a few delicious seconds how easy this most testing and treacherous part of the venture had been, and how everything had gone exactly according to plan. His extensive preparations had paid off handsomely and he had found this whole episode much easier than he had contemplated. Not at any time did he have to look at the boy's face as he desperately struggled for air. Once the boy was unconscious, the rug was both a device to secrete what he had done from outsiders and also a means to psychologically distance himself from his victim. The hardest part of the plan had been accomplished with a minimum of risk, and the boy was now safely under his control. Bradley restarted the engine and drove slowly out of the park, careful to a fault not to do anything that might attract attention to himself or his car.

It was in this comatose condition that Stephen Bradley conveyed Graeme Thorne in the boot of his car across the Sydney Harbour Bridge towards the Spit Bridge on the northern side of the harbour. As he momentarily stopped the car to pay the toll collector on the Harbour Bridge, he was confident that nothing would be audible from the boot of his car – like a boy's screams or inexplicable kicks from inside. As Bradley approached Middle Harbour and the Spit Bridge, at the corner of Spit Road and Medusa Street[4] he parked his car near a public phone box where he planned to make the first call to the Thorne household. He got out, and before walking away from his car he put his ear down to the lid of the boot, but he heard no sound from within and was confident that Graeme was still asleep.

As he strode to the phone box, Bradley had nothing but disdain for the conservative, suburban couple whose lives he was about to disrupt forever.

4

FEEDING SHARKS

At 8.40am on Thursday, 7 July 1960, Phyllis Smith edged her station wagon next to the kerb in front of the general store in Wellington Street, Bondi, and was surprised that she couldn't see Graeme Thorne sitting on his school case outside the shop, where he invariably waited for her. Thinking that he must still be inside the shop, she lightly touched the car horn to urge him to come out, and when he didn't emerge she sent her younger son, who was the same age as Graeme, into the shop to get him. Within a few seconds her son came out, telling her that Graeme was nowhere to be seen. Mrs Smith waited a few more minutes, thinking that Graeme must be running late, but still there was no sign of him.

Thinking that Graeme might be running late or might not be going to school that day, Mrs Smith drove the short distance to the block of flats where the Thornes lived. Leaving her two sons in the car, she walked briskly to the front door and knocked. Freda answered and was surprised to see Phyllis Smith. Her initial thought was that Graeme must have forgotten something that he needed for school. When Phyllis explained that Graeme had not been waiting at the usual place, Freda immediately became alarmed. She was sorry that Bazil was not at home, because he always knew what to do. Phyllis assured Freda that Graeme must have gone to school with someone else, and stated firmly that she would go straight there with her two boys and make sure that Graeme had arrived safely. Phyllis felt that Freda's concerns were unwarranted. Having two young boys herself, she knew that they were capable of doing the oddest things without any concern for their parents' anxieties.

Phyllis drove to the Scots College, dropped off her two boys and then went into the administration block where she requested one of the secretaries to enquire whether Graeme had arrived at school. With a throng of students milling around in the playground and masters bustling furiously to get ready for the bell that marked the beginning of classes, it took a good ten minutes before Phyllis was informed that Graeme had not been seen at school. With regret and some alarm, she drove back to Freda in Bondi and gave her the bad news.

By this stage Freda was beset with panic and dread. She already had an overwhelming instinct that something dire had happened to her son and no amount of reassurance from Phyllis could comfort her. Freda insisted on calling the Bondi police station to report her son missing, telling the officer, 'We only recently won a lot of money and I feel something has happened.' Her alarm was so patent that the station sergeant agreed to send someone to her home immediately. 'Immediately' meant about twenty minutes.

At about 9.30am, Sergeant Lawrence O'Shea of the Bondi police station arrived at the Thornes' home. On entering the house, he saw immediately that Freda was frightfully upset, so he asked her to sit down and, as calmly as she could, give him a description of her son which he would write down. She explained that her husband was away on one of his frequent business trips to the North Coast. As she began to describe Graeme's appearance, and before she had had any opportunity to explain why she held grave concerns for her son, the telephone rang. The ringing caused Freda to suddenly leap out of her chair and grab the phone, hoping that it was the school letting her know that Graeme had arrived.

'Yes, hello?' she said in a hopeful, enquiring tone.

On the other end was a man with a smooth voice and a distinctly European accent. 'Is that you, Mrs Thorne?'

'Yes,' she replied.

'Is your husband there?' asked the man.

'What do you want him for?'

Then the man said the fateful words: 'I have your son.'

Freda Thorne reeled from the phone as if she had been struck by a bolt of lightning emanating from the handset. Sergeant O'Shea thought she might faint as she held the phone out to him and said, 'Take this.'

The sergeant took the phone from her and said: 'What can I do for you?'

The male with the foreign accent said, 'Is that you, Mr Thorne?'

Thinking quickly, O'Shea thought that it would be best if he pretended to be the boy's father. 'Yes,' he said.

In a very deliberate manner, with a seemingly calm voice and without the slightest hesitation, the man said, 'I have got your boy. I want twenty-five thousand pounds before five o'clock this afternoon.'

Unfortunately, Sergeant O'Shea was one of the few people in Sydney who did not recognise the Thornes' name, and Freda had not had a chance to tell him about the £100,000 lottery win. The police officer's next response on the phone would be the cause of much regret in the days and weeks to follow.

'How am I going to get money like that?'

The caller replied, 'You have plenty of time before five o'clock. I'm not fooling. If I don't get the money, I'll feed him to the sharks.'

It should be remembered that during the 1950s shark attacks in and around Sydney were much more prevalent than they are today. The man's threat caused Sergeant O'Shea to shudder.

'How am I going to contact you?' he said.

'I'll contact you later,' the man replied, and the telephone went dead.

Sergeant O'Shea's face was deathly pale as he put down the handset, turned to Freda and said, 'I think your boy's been kidnapped.'

∗∗∗

When Stephen Bradley made the telephone call to the Thorne household at about 9.40am on that fateful day in July 1960, it never occurred to him that the police might already have become involved in the disappearance of Graeme Thorne. In fact, his timing of the call – an hour after he had enticed Graeme into his car – had been carefully calculated to allow an opportunity for the parents to be informed that their boy had not been picked up from the usual spot in Wellington Street, but also to be sufficiently soon after his disappearance so that they would not yet have contacted the police. He anticipated that the parents would be worried about where their son had gone, but would presume that he had gone walkabout or was truanting from school. Bradley himself had done just that on numerous occasions in Budapest when he was the same age. It never crossed his mind that the police would be involved within an hour of the boy being whisked away.

When Freda Thorne answered the phone, Bradley noticed the anticipation in her voice and the deflation when he asked for her husband. Bradley had never heard Bazil's voice, so when Freda handed over the phone, he assumed he was now speaking to her husband. When the man queried how he was going to get an amount like £25,000, it confirmed just how unsophisticated and unimaginative Bazil was to think that anyone who had the skill and determination to abduct his son would be put off by such a pathetic response. In a fit of pique, he delivered the threat of feeding the boy to the sharks to impress upon this simpleton just how determined he was to get the ransom.

Having made the call, Stephen Bradley was confident that by five o'clock that afternoon the Thornes would be able to withdraw the money from their bank account in which it was languishing. He was so confident that in their panic they would not contact the police that he forgot to tell them that they must not notify the authorities. When he realised this after completing the call, he was not troubled, because he believed that in their fear they would not do anything to prejudice the safe return of their son.

When Bradley returned to his Ford, there was still not the slightest sound from the boot. He drove across the Spit Bridge and up the hill towards Seaforth and Clontarf. He knew that by now Magda and the children would have left in a taxi for the airport, and that he would have a little time before the removalists arrived – enough to check his human cargo, and if necessary administer some more chloroform. As he drove along, he felt a sense of smug satisfaction that everything was going exactly according to plan. He was in no way concerned at the distress he had caused to Graeme's parents, as they were masters of their own destiny for having unjustifiably enriched themselves through no effort or attributes of their own. Neither did he have any concern for the prisoner in his boot, as he was certain that within a few hours the boy would be released unharmed to resume life in the midst of his family.

***

As soon as he hung up the phone, Sergeant O'Shea realised that he had made a feeble attempt at dealing with what was clearly a dire situation. He vainly attempted to comfort Mrs Thorne, who was now in a shocking state. Between sobs, erratic breathing and periods of light-headedness, she told him about the £100,000 lottery win. The sergeant immediately contacted the Criminal Investigation Bureau (CIB) at the Central police station in the city, to inform them that a young boy from Bondi had been kidnapped for ransom. A team of police from the CIB immediately swung into action. Within a short time they had ensured that any further calls to the Thornes' home were monitored, and alerted points of departure from Australia to keep an eye out for the boy. Because a child had never before been kidnapped for ransom in Australia, the police had no experience in investigating a crime of this kind. The only vaguely similar event in living memory had involved an adult victim who had been abducted in 1932 – coincidentally in Bondi – and forced to write a £10,000 money order, which the kidnappers had been unable to cash. The victim had been released unharmed and the two kidnappers had been apprehended and gaoled. It was with some dismay that the police discovered that because of the rarity of this crime, there was in fact no offence of kidnapping for ransom on the statute books of New South Wales.

It was not until about 1pm that day, four-and-a-half hours after Graeme's disappearance, that Bazil Thorne learnt of his son's kidnapping. As he stepped off a plane at Sydney's Kingsford Smith Airport on his way home from Kempsey, his name was called over the airport public address system. As he approached the enquiry desk, thinking that there would be a message about his work, he was approached by a police officer, Detective Sergeant S. Workman, who explained to him that his son was missing. Realising how distressed Freda would be, Bazil immediately went home to comfort her. By the time he arrived, Freda was so overwrought that she required medical sedation, which gave her the appearance of being drunk, but did nothing to anaesthetise her fears or allay her anguish. Sergeant O'Shea informed Bazil about the phone call. Bazil was terribly distressed that he had not been at home when the kidnapper rang, as he was convinced that he could have negotiated Graeme's swift release. Three-year-old Belinda, who was still at home, knew that something was amiss. Bazil told her frankly that Graeme was missing, but that he was hopeful that her brother would be found and brought home before nightfall. Belinda wanted to know what 'missing' meant, and Bazil told her that her brother was 'lost'.

Bazil and Freda assured the police that they would pay any amount, even the full £100,000, if it meant getting their son back safely. They were able to tell the police about the suspicious visit to their home three weeks earlier by the man who claimed to be looking for a Mr Bognor, and Freda was confident that his voice and accent were the same. They remembered him as being thickset, in his thirties or forties, with dark brown hair that was longish at the back, having a sallow complexion, bushy black eyebrows and with a distinctly European accent. Both of them, particularly Freda, felt that they could identify the man if the police could locate him. The upstairs neighbour, Mrs Dorothy Lord, was able to confirm that the man with the accent had also come to her door. The discrepancy in the man's story – telling the Thornes he was looking for Mr Bognor but Mrs Lord that he was looking for Mr Bailey – immediately raised grave suspicions that this had been the kidnapper conducting surveillance on his intended victim's home. Surely it was more than mere coincidence that a man with a strong European accent had made a clumsy and suspicious enquiry three weeks earlier and that a man with a European accent had made the vicious and determined demand for ransom over the phone.

The police decided not to release to the media or the public any details of the man's earlier visit to the Thornes' home, but unfortunately news of Graeme's kidnapping and the ransom demand spread like wildfire around the Central police station. The information was broadcast on the police radio, which had the unintended and undesirable consequence that police roundsmen from the newspapers heard about these extraordinary events within minutes of the CIB becoming involved.

Reporters for the afternoon papers were placed under extreme pressure from their editors to get the basic details of this alarming offence in sufficient time to publish them that very day. Otherwise, if the news was delayed, the morning papers the following day would get the advantage of first run of the story. Commercial pressures therefore ensured that on the afternoon and evening of the day of Graeme Thorne's disappearance, the newspapers and the evening television and radio broadcasts carried the story. The *Sun* had a short note on page three about the disappearance of an unnamed eight-year-old schoolboy from Bondi and the police search for him. The *Daily Mirror* carried a front-page story headed 'Kidnapped! Son of £100,000 winner' in which Graeme Thorne was named and details about the location of his disappearance were given. The news immediately attracted the attention of the nation to the fate of this little boy and the suffering of his unfortunate parents, whose lives had so markedly changed in the course of a single day.

In the meantime, police commenced to extensively canvass the area around Graeme's home and Wellington Street in an effort to find witnesses who might have seen anything untoward at the time of his disappearance. Even young children living in the surrounding streets were interviewed by investigators. It seemed extraordinary that nobody had witnessed a young boy being abducted in broad daylight on a public street in suburban Sydney. Arrangements were made for a police officer to be on hand at the Thornes' home twenty-four hours a day. Detective Constable Lloyd Noonan effectively took up residence at their home, to be relieved at weekends by Sergeant Dave Paul. Bazil and Freda gave these two officers strict instructions that Belinda was to be protected from a full appreciation of what was happening. She obviously could not be prevented from knowing that her brother was missing, but the real story was to be kept from the three-year-old.

That afternoon a distraught Bazil Thorne waited by his phone for the pre-arranged 5pm call from the kidnapper, but it never came. He continued his vigil for several hours after the appointed time, desperately praying that the kidnapper would make contact. By this stage of the night, Bazil and Freda were in a frightful state. Freda kept mentioning her regret that she had not properly said goodbye to Graeme that morning. Bazil kept mumbling: 'If only I had been home this morning'.

At 9.47pm the phone suddenly rang. It was answered by Detective Sergeant David Valentine, who had replaced Sergeant O'Shea at the house. When Valentine answered the phone, a man with a European accent said, 'Is that you, Mr Thorne?'

When Valentine said that it was, the man asked, 'Have you got the money?'

Valentine answered in the affirmative.

The man continued. 'Put it in two paper bags ...'

Before he could continue the instructions, Sergeant Valentine interrupted, saying, 'Wait a minute. I want to take your instructions down. I don't want to make a mistake.'

The caller was obviously baulked by this response, because he mumbled something in an agitated fashion which the policeman was unable to understand, and then abruptly hung up. Sergeant Valentine was bitterly disappointed that he had failed to keep the caller on the line, and Bazil Thorne, who was nearby, was intensely distraught that contact had been broken off, feeling that the police officer had mismanaged the call and that he himself could have handled it far better. While it was generally agreed in police circles that this call had come from the kidnapper, because Sergeant Valentine had not heard the earlier call he was unable to verify that the voice and accent were the same.

Following the phone call, Bazil and Freda went to the Bondi police station, where Bazil made an emotional television appearance in which he said:

If the person who has my son is a father, and has children of his own, all I can say is, for God's sake, send him back to me in one piece.

He then broke down and, just before the transmission was terminated, Freda could be faintly heard in the background calling out 'Keep your chin up, darling'. The transmission then transferred to Police Headquarters in the city, where the New South Wales Commissioner of Police, Mr CJ Delaney, made a personal request to the kidnapper to release Graeme unharmed, and called on the community to assist the police with any information that might progress the investigation. The whole of Australia was hoping that this little boy would be safely returned to his loving family and that their frightful ordeal would come to an end.

5

REMOVALS

Just before 10am, about ten minutes after making the ransom call from the public phone box at the Spit Bridge, Stephen Bradley arrived at his Clontarf home at 28 Moore Street with Graeme Thorne still in the car boot. He parked his car inside the internal garage of the house which was situated in the sub-floor space of the house's foundations, closed the large doors and contemplated with glee the massive ransom that he was confident of receiving later that day. He realised that time was tight. Magda and the children had left the house, but the removalists were due to arrive between 10 and 11am to pick up the family's furniture to place it into storage. He needed the boy to remain in his enforced slumber while the removalists did their work.

Bradley gingerly opened the boot of the car and, as the light streamed into this coffin-like prison, the boy began to squirm and groan. It was quite apparent that he was semi-conscious and might fully awaken at any moment. The gag was still in place over Graeme's mouth and his feet were still securely tied, but Bradley noticed that the twine he had wrapped around the boy's wrists had become slack. Without checking on the boy's condition, Bradley was concerned that if his young prisoner became fully conscious and managed to get the gag off his mouth, he might call out and be heard by the removalists or neighbours. Without any further thought, Bradley opened the travel bag which was still in the boot and again held the liquid-soaked rag over the boy's mouth and nose until he ceased squirming. His object was to ensure that he would remain in that state for several more hours, which would allow Bradley to interact with the removalists without being distracted by concerns that the boy might wake up. He then re-closed the boot, believing that his captive was sufficiently secured for several more hours.

***

Shortly afterwards, at about 10.15am, Magda phoned Stephen from Kingsford Smith Airport at Mascot as she and the children waited to board their plane to Coolangatta. Although Magda had woken that morning still smarting from the argument the night before, by the time she got to the airport she had calmed down. During the phone call, Stephen told her that he was still waiting for the removalists.

As Magda stepped onto the plane bound for Queensland, did she have some inkling that her husband was in the course of executing something far more serious than any of his previous, crazy financial escapades? Was she getting as far away as she could from what she knew or suspected would be an unfolding tragedy or was she merely a pawn in her husband's hands who was reluctantly complying with his insistent instructions to go on an interstate holiday so that he would have the house to himself?

**

About fifteen minutes after Magda's call, the removalists arrived. After backing their large van onto the driveway, they immediately began loading. Bradley strictly supervised their work, and indeed helped them by carrying some of the smaller items from the house to their vehicle. He refused them entry to the garage, saying that he would bring them the items they needed to load from there. As they did their work, the removalists constantly walked through the front garden in close proximity to the locked garage doors, which made Bradley distinctly nervous. At one point, as he was walking past the garage doors, he thought he heard a noise coming from within that could only be his young prisoner. Deeply surprised, he looked around to see if any of the removalists had heard anything, but thankfully they happened to be inside the house at that time. In a flash, he unlocked and opened the garage door, entered and closed it behind him. As he tentatively opened the boot lid, he saw his bound and gagged captive stirring. At the same moment, he heard one of the removalists just outside the closed, but now unlocked, garage doors calling out: 'Mr Bradley. Do you want this to go on the truck?' In a blind panic, without even checking to see if Graeme was in fact awake, Bradley impulsively reached over and grabbed one of the metal tools from the nearby work bench, and struck the boy's head with sufficient force to again render him fully unconscious.[1]

***

Four-and-a-half hours later, at about 3pm, when Bradley still had two hours before he was due to make the second ransom call to Bazil and Freda, the removalists finished loading and left the house. As soon as they departed, a relieved Bradley returned to his car and opened the boot to find, to his alarm, that Graeme had not moved since he had last seen him. Bradley pulled the gag down from the boy's mouth so that it hung loosely around his neck and realised with horror that he was not breathing. As he began lifting his body, he felt that it was cold to touch and stiffer than it should have been, and he immediately knew that the boy was dead. Recoiling with revulsion, he let the inert body drop back onto the floor of the boot and slammed the lid down, so as not to have to look at the corpse.

Bradley was devastated – not because he had killed an innocent child, but because his plans had gone completely awry. He understood immediately that it would be much more difficult now to convince the Thornes to pay the ransom without being able to provide evidence that Graeme was still alive. He was utterly deflated at the thought that all of his painstaking plans and preparations, including surveillance of the Thorne family over the preceding weeks, might come to nothing and that he might be deprived of the financial reward he had so eagerly been awaiting.

Having failed to anticipate these events, Bradley had no plan of how to dispose of Graeme's body. He needed time to think about how he was going to achieve this without drawing attention to himself or leaving clues that could implicate him. He was determined to get Graeme's body out of his house under cover of darkness before he retired that night, so that early the next morning he could set off for the long drive to Queensland.

Pacing agitatedly back and forth in his garage, Bradley decided on a plan. He re-opened the boot, wrapped the family's picnic rug, which was still in the boot, around the body and secured it with string. Bradley then took the corpse out of the boot and placed it on the floor of the garage, which was littered with dust, dirt and loose vegetation blown in from the garden. From the garage, there was an opening in the foundations of the house that provided access to the other sub-floor spaces. The first space was a dark, bare-earth alcove where nobody would accidentally stumble upon the body and Bradley would not have to view the wrapped bundle if he needed to access the garage or use the car.

Picking up Graeme's tightly wrapped body, he carried it into the dim cavern of this sub-floor space and laid it down on the damp, bare ground that was mixed with flecks of mortar from the brickwork of the foundations. He then returned upstairs and thought for a long time about how he might yet convince Graeme's parents to pay the ransom money. He still had some of Graeme's possessions – like his school case and its contents – with which he could prove that he had taken the boy, but what was he to do if they insisted on proof their son was still alive before paying the ransom?

Later that day, Bradley drove the Goggomobil to a news-agency at nearby Balgowlah, where he purchased both afternoon papers. He was horrified to see that they contained articles on the kidnapping. The *Daily Mirror* particularly had a lot of detail about the abducted child, including his name and his parents' lottery win. It completely baffled him why the Thornes would have involved the police, and why they would have allowed the incident to be disseminated so publicly when Graeme was still missing. Surely they would know that this would unnerve the kidnapper and thereby threaten the safety of the boy. He was irate with Bazil and Freda for acting in such an unpredictable and counterproductive way. Did they really think that the publicity would make it more likely they would get their son back? For Stephen Bradley, this foolishness in allowing all this publicity – so contrary to common sense – had disentitled Bazil and Freda to expect their son to be returned alive. He felt a sense of vindication in that the Thornes' actions had retrospectively contributed to what was now the inevitable, tragic ending. In his mind, they were, in part, the authors of their own misfortune – even if they were not yet aware of the extent of it. About one thing he was relieved – there was nothing in the newspapers that pointed in his direction. He felt that if the police had any substantial leads about the man or the car, they would surely have been included in the news reports. He returned home to contemplate his next move.

At about 9pm, Stephen Bradley placed his driving gloves back on his hands and laid Graeme's body – still wrapped in the family picnic rug and tied with string, with Stephen's scarf still loosely looped around his neck – back into the boot of the

Customline, together with the boy's cap, the school case and its contents. At a time when most people were inside their homes and traffic was light, he drove just ten minutes away to a bushy section of the Wakehurst Parkway, a little east of Bantry Bay. During the day, Wakehurst Parkway is a busy, major thoroughfare through a state forest in the midst of Sydney's Northern Beaches suburbs. Midway through the Parkway is the leafy suburb of Frenchs Forest, while at the southern end is the affluent suburb of Seaforth, overlooking Middle Harbour, an inlet of Sydney Harbour. Late at night, Wakehurst Parkway is a lonely and isolated road with long sections of rugged bush without any houses. Bradley stopped his car in a deserted, thickly wooded section of the Parkway where there was a flat, dirt area on the side of the road surrounding a stone memorial. From here, he had clear visibility for several hundred yards in both directions. Still wearing his driving gloves to avoid leaving fingerprints, after making sure that no one was lurking in the vicinity and no cars were approaching, he threw the boy's school case into the dense bush. He made no attempt to remove any identifying features that linked it to Graeme, because he felt secure that it could never be linked to himself. He then drove about a mile further along the Wakehurst Parkway, where he stopped to throw Graeme's cap, lunchbox and an exercise book into the bush on the other side of the road.

Bradley then drove back along the Wakehurst Parkway to Seaforth, about two miles from where he had discarded Graeme's school case, and just over one-and-a-half miles from his own home at Clontarf. Seaforth contained pockets of bushland suitable for disposing of a body. In fact, Stephen Bradley knew of one such area from a real-estate inspection of a house at 16 Grandview Grove some weeks earlier in anticipation of purchasing a larger home for his family. He drove into Grandview Grove and parked his car at a vacant allotment next to the house at number 16. After making sure that no one was about, he picked up Graeme's inert body, still wrapped in the picnic rug with the scarf now loosely looped around the neck, and carried it into the bush, where he placed it in a crevice under a large sandstone rock. The fact that the body may be found by local residents, or that this location was close to his home, was of no concern to Bradley, because he was utterly convinced that there was nothing to identify him as the perpetrator.

Having discarded Graeme's body and possessions, Bradley decided on his way home to make one – and only one – attempt to convince Bazil Thorne to hand over the ransom money without proof that Graeme was still alive. By this time he was thoroughly unsettled by the effect that this unforeseen death of his victim would have on negotiations with the Thornes.

He made the call to the Thornes at 9.47pm from a public telephone box at the corner of Seaview Street and Upper Beach Street, Balgowlah, only a mile away from his home. In fact, it was the closest public telephone box to Moore Street. He suspected that if a phone call went for long enough the police could trace its source and, mindful of the fact that he was so close to his home, Bradley was determined not to give them that opportunity. He was also concerned that a canny police officer might have the ability to discern that his accent was Hungarian, which would provide an important clue to his identity. When the phone call was answered, he immediately realised that it was not the same man who had spoken to him that morning.

Although the man assured him he was Bazil Thorne, Bradley thought that in all probability he was a police officer. When the man asked him to wait a minute to write down his instructions, Bradley knew that it was a trap. He impulsively uttered an expletive under his breath – in Hungarian – and then slammed down the phone in anger and frustration.

His chances of negotiating the payment of a ransom had evaporated. He could not risk any further calls that might provide the police with an opportunity to identify him. As he walked away from the phone box, he was utterly gutted. All his planning had come to nothing. All the dreams of how he and Magda would live in luxury had been dashed. In two days they would have no home, and once again he would face the prospect of finding a new one with meagre financial resources. This time, he had no job to go back to. What galled him the most was that he would have to explain to Magda why they had inspected a number of magnificent, expensive houses over the past few weeks when they now were unable to afford any of them. In fact, they would do well if they managed to find a home as good as the one they had just sold. How was he to explain their change in fortune? What he feared most was not Magda's disappointment, but her thinking less of him as a provider, a businessman and an investor. Why had life treated them both so harshly?

Bradley returned home angry and dejected that his grand plan for he and Magda to lead the lives they deserved had come to nothing. He doubted that they would ever get another opportunity like this one. All his plans to buy an impressive house and a new car, and to take a grand trip overseas with the children, had been dashed. He gave not a moment's thought to the fact that he had cut short the life of a perfectly innocent little boy, nor to the agony that Graeme's parents were going through, nor to the devastation that would inevitably hit them when they found out that their son was dead. He genuinely felt that it was not his fault that Graeme had died and he was mystified as to how it had occurred. How could he have anticipated that the boy would die from being locked in the boot or from the hit to his head – whichever it was that had caused his death? Bradley was purely focused on his own loss of the reward money and how he was going to explain to Magda that his ambitious plans for their new home had come to nothing. In his mind he railed against fate that had so unfairly plucked such a unique opportunity from him, just when it seemed so close.

6

CONTROLLING THE AVALANCHE

On 8 July 1960, the day following Graeme Thorne's disappearance, every newspaper carried a front-page article on the sensational kidnapping of the son of the recent winners of the Opera House Lottery. Comparisons were made to the kidnapping of the Lindbergh baby in the United States almost three decades earlier.[1] The threat by the kidnapper to 'feed him to the sharks' struck a raw nerve in the Australian psyche. There was mention that the ransom demand had been made by a man with a foreign accent, stirring prejudices that were often barely below the surface of what was still a predominantly Anglo society. The reports of the kidnapping prompted an Australia-wide outpouring of sympathy for Graeme's parents, a desperate hope that the boy would be safely returned, and extreme anger at the monster who

71

had carried out such a callous crime. People felt a sense of personal involvement that they had never before felt for victims of crime. In streets, shops, clubs, hotels, workplaces, on trains and buses, and in homes throughout the land people spoke at length about the kidnapping of this young boy. Many had their own theories about what kind of person would commit such a crime, and speculation was rife about possible outcomes. Australians have a long history of poor cooperation with police investigations – perhaps deriving from our convict past – but in this instance the reaction of the community was overwhelmingly supportive.

Within days, the New South Wales Government offered a £5,000 reward for information leading to an arrest, and John Fairfax Ltd, publishers of the *Sydney Morning Herald*, offered £10,000. Within a week, a further £5,000 reward was advanced by the publishers of the *Daily Telegraph*. This brought the total reward monies to £20,000 – almost as much as the ransom demand. The *Daily Mirror* reported that in an unprecedented act of cooperation, underworld figures had offered to help the police find the boy, saying that there were a dozen men – each bad by police standards – who would tear the kidnapper to pieces if they found him. By the weekend, there was barely a family in the nation that had not heard of Graeme Thorne. The whole of Australia was anxious to return this eight-year-old boy to the safety of his home and to relieve the agony of his inconsolable parents.

When the authorities realised that there was in fact no crime on the statute books to meet these circumstances, there was great consternation among the public and in police circles, and a community-wide clamour to amend the law. The State

Premier, Mr Robert J. Heffron, publicly asserted his opinion that, 'In my mind, and I am sure in the public's mind, the crime of kidnapping should rank with murder.' The government assured the community that this shortcoming would be remedied at the earliest opportunity. There were even calls for the reintroduction of the death penalty, which had been abolished in New South Wales only five years earlier. However, Premier Heffron and Mr Robin Askin, the leader of the opposition, stated that both personally and on behalf of their party they were against the reintroduction of capital punishment.

The police were only too aware that publicity would do little to assist Graeme's safe return from the clutches of his kidnapper or kidnappers, however it was impossible to control the avalanche of information, conjecture and rumour that swilled around the nation's newsrooms. As a result of the extensive reportage, the police were flooded with information from numerous well-meaning members of the public. The Commissioner of Police encouraged this deluge by publicly stating that 'the smallest snippet of information could be a vital clue'.

Never before in the history of Australian policing had there been such intense communal participation as seen in the attempts to locate this missing child and apprehend his abductor. People from all over the country rang the CIB and Bondi police station to report the most extraordinary observations and the most bizarre suspicions. There were countless false leads that had to be investigated by the police, tying up their valuable resources. The response from the public was in fact quite distracting to the substantial police team that had been quickly established. A group of more than forty police officers sifted through every piece of information that came in, and investigated those aspects that warranted further enquiry.

The information included sightings of a man who, for several days before the kidnapping, had been sitting on a seat in the park opposite the Thornes' home, but the descriptions of the man were vague and varied enormously. Additionally, on the morning of the kidnapping a number of people had observed a car parked at the corner of Wellington and Francis Streets, just where Graeme would have walked past. The descriptions of the vehicle, however, varied from a blue Ford to a green Holden to a black Dodge. A police artist consulted with Bazil and Freda and drew an artist's impression of the 'private investigator' who had come to their home, and this drawing was published in the newspapers as a person to whom the police wished to speak.

The snatching of a young boy from a suburban Sydney street while on his way to school not only excited abject horror at the cold-heartedness of the crime and overwhelming sympathy for Graeme's family, but also caused parents Australia-wide to be seized with panic and alarm at what dangers lurked in public for their own children. If this could happen to Bazil and Freda Thorne, it could happen to almost anyone who had a financial windfall. People who previously had allowed their children to walk to and from school would now accompany them. Children who had been permitted to play in the street for years were now told to restrict their games to backyards within view of nearby adults. Two mothers, who won second prize in the Opera House Lottery a day after the kidnapping, expressed concerns about the safety of their families. In sympathy, the newspapers published their names but not their addresses. Men with foreign accents were

subjected to especially critical scrutiny and even more prejudice than usual. Unfortunately, the publicity about Graeme's
kidnapping resulted in many callous, unscrupulous people
contacting the Thornes or the police, claiming to be the kidnapper and to have Graeme in their possession in an attempt
to cash in on the ransom money. These ghoulish individuals
caused untold anguish to the Thornes.

During the very early stages of the police investigation, a
decision was made by senior officers that certain pieces of information would be withheld from the public. These included
the fact that a man with a foreign accent had come to the
Thornes' block of flats about three weeks before the kidnapping
asking for a Mr Bognor. However, within a few days, even this
detail had been leaked to the newspapers.

***

On the afternoon of Friday 8 July, less than twenty-four
hours after dumping Graeme Thorne's lifeless body, Stephen
Bradley again went to a local newsagency and purchased the
morning and afternoon newspapers. He was amused to read
that although the kidnapper was described as having 'a slight
foreign accent', experienced detectives had stated their view that
'it could have been and possibly was assumed [i.e. fake], in view
of the "correct" English used in phrasing the demand'. He had
worried needlessly about someone with an acute ear picking
the origin of his accent when he made the second call. He was
chuffed to read in the *Sydney Morning Herald* that police had
conducted a swoop of known criminal underworld haunts in
search of the kidnapper. Let them waste their time in useless

enquiries! None would lead to him, because he had covered his tracks so thoroughly. The report in the *Daily Mirror* informed readers that:

> *Police have been told that a mystery man was seen about the flats in which the Thornes live, making enquiries about a fort-night ago. Occupants of the flats who saw the man are studying police photographs and it is felt that this angle of the enquiry could bring developments.*

Let them look at every single photograph in the police archives – nothing there could provide a link to him! One man, described as a tough and callous member of the Sydney underworld, told the *Daily Mirror*: 'I'll bet a thousand quid to a peanut it's not an Australian knockabout man responsible for this.' Bradley laughed out loud when he read that Mrs Kate Ryan (formerly Mrs Leigh), an infamous member of Sydney's underworld, had said:

> *I've got one of the biggest butcher's knives in Sydney and it would give me the greatest pleasure to use it on the mongrels. I hope I can hear something that will put me on their trail. By the time I finish with them they will make a good meal for the dogs' home.*

With some pride, Bradley read the opinion of the Police Commissioner:

> *The person or persons who abducted Graeme worked so silently that the kidnapping had obviously been planned with great thought and split-second timing.*

At least the authorities could recognise a clever and well-organised operator, even if they lacked the capacity to expose him.

That evening, Stephen phoned Magda in Queensland to tell her that the removalists had successfully taken all their possessions and that he would drive up to join them, bringing with him Cherie, the Pekinese dog, and the family cat.

***

In Surfers Paradise, Magda Bradley saw a television news broadcast about the kidnapping of eight-year-old Graeme Thorne in Sydney. Did she know, or guess, that her husband was responsible for this dastardly plot? While he might be capable of financial irregularities and mismanagement, or even the odd insurance fraud, did she consider that he was vicious enough to abduct a young boy who was around the same age as his own daughter and to put the poor parents through the agony of not knowing whether they would ever see him alive again?

That night, as Magda lay in bed at the Seabreeze Private Hotel worrying about her absent husband, did a terrible thought come to her that previously might have bubbled away beneath the surface of her consciousness, that was kept firmly at bay unless they had an argument: How was it that Stephen's second wife had tragically died in a car accident when her brakes suddenly and inexplicably failed, leaving Stephen as the sole owner of their joint property? He had once told her in an unguarded moment that before her death his previous wife had refused to cooperate with him in a plan he had devised to invest some of her money. Did Magda for one dreadful moment wonder whether she, and even her children, might be at risk from Stephen if she refused to go along with one of his crazy plans? Was that why she had never stood in his way when he wanted to recklessly invest the money she had received from Gregor Weinberg on some wild, new venture that she couldn't understand? As she drifted towards sleep, did her worries evaporate as she dismissed these negative thoughts as just petty insecurities derived from the tiredness of looking after the children on her own?

On Stephen's arrival at Surfers Paradise during the night of 9–10 July, all their previous tensions dissipated. Although Stephen was very tired – which Magda presumed was from packing up their possessions, supervising the removal and then driving the 600 miles to Queensland – he played beautifully with the children and he was particularly kind and attentive to her. How could she possibly have thought that he was capable of such an evil deed?

***

It was not until late on Friday 8 July, about thirty-three hours after Graeme had been abducted, that the police got their first major lead in the investigation. That evening, at about 6pm, a seventy-five-year-old man, Joseph Bell of Collaroy, called the police to report that he had found a school case with Graeme's name in it lying in thick bushland in Frenchs Forest, about 10 yards off the Wakehurst Parkway near the Lord Wakehurst Memorial, east of Bantry Bay. He told police he had been fossicking in the bush for discarded empty soft-drink bottles (for which there was a 3p refund for each bottle) when he came upon the case. Realising that it was likely Graeme Thorne's, he hid it in a hollow and went home. Inexplicably, he waited six hours to notify the police. Police immediately converged on the area around the Lord Wakehurst Memorial, and the school case was taken to police headquarters where it was closely examined. Unfortunately, there were no fingerprints on it.

Later that night, Commissioner Delaney made a further appeal to the kidnapper in this public statement:

Although every avenue open to my department has been thoroughly investigated, no information has been obtained to establish the identity of the kidnapper. We are gravely concerned for the safety of Graeme Thorne. His life means more than money or the observance of conventional criminal investigation procedure. We cannot and will not compromise with a criminal, but we have a great and grave responsibility to do all in our power to have the child returned unharmed. This is a desperate situation and it demands drastic measures. Therefore, as Commissioner of Police, I say this to the kidnapper of Graeme Thorne: make contact urgently with the boy's parents. Satisfy them that he is alive and well and that if payment is made he will be returned. We want, above all, to know that the boy is alive and well and that no harm has befallen him. I therefore urge you to make contact with his parents.

The Commissioner followed this up with instructions to all police that nothing should be done to frustrate the handing over of the ransom or anything else that could endanger the boy's life.

The following day, Saturday 9 July, as Stephen Bradley was driving his Customline to Queensland to join his family, a huge search was conducted in the bushland on both sides of the Wakehurst Parkway, extending on one side through the bush down to Bantry Bay. It involved 250 police, 230 soldiers, more than 200 members of the Warringah Shire Civil Defence Organisation, sniffer dogs, helicopters, divers and others. A reporter for the *Sun* stated that the scene resembled preparations for a wartime manoeuvre.

The search continued for a number of days, and it was not until Monday 11 July that Graeme's school cap, raincoat, mathematics textbook and lunchbox were found in bush beside the Wakehurst Parkway about a mile away from the school case and on the opposite side of the road. Ominously, the lunchbox contained the untouched food that Freda had prepared for Graeme on the morning of his abduction, including the apple she had lovingly peeled before carefully rewrapping the skin around it. Things were not looking good for Graeme.

7

IMPOSTORS AND INFORMANTS

The finding of the school case and its contents was considered by police to be a disturbing sign for Graeme Thorne's fate. However, the investigating team – indeed the whole nation – refused to give up hope that he might still be found alive.

Bazil and Freda Thorne were informed about the school case on the Friday night that it was found, and about the other items when they were located three days later. The police brought each item to them for identification purposes, and every time it was like a stab to the heart for them to sight the objects they knew so well. While logic told them that this was not a good omen for Graeme, they desperately hoped that the kidnapper had discarded these items because he didn't need them to get the ransom. They felt helpless that they could do nothing to assist their son in his time of need and, as each day passed, their fears increased. They could not understand why the kidnapper was being so elusive. Was he trying to torture them, so that they would more readily pay the ransom? Surely, with all the publicity about their willingness to pay, this was unnecessary. Each time the phone or the doorbell rang, their hearts would race with anticipation and dread in equal measure, only to be dashed when it was not news about Graeme. They both suffered extreme agitation which drained every ounce of energy from their bodies, and yet Bazil would restlessly pace around the house – particularly at night – trying to resist the ridiculous urge to go outside and look for Graeme. They constantly wished that they could turn back the clock by returning the money they had won – if only they could have their son back. The money now seemed dirty – as though they had done something wrong to obtain it – and they couldn't imagine ever enjoying the fruits of it in the future. How could they have been so stupid as to allow the papers to take Bazil's photo with his lottery ticket? Hadn't they been taught as children not to gloat! Freda was beset with thoughts that Graeme might be suffering from extreme cold, as the overnight temperatures often dropped to between 40 and 50 degrees Fahrenheit[1]. She would lie in bed for hours at night, clutching the blankets fiercely up to her neck, with tears silently oozing from her eyes. Day after day, Bazil and Freda tried to reassure Belinda that her brother would still be found and brought home. The youngster would ask repeatedly why Graeme was 'lost', and eventually asked the questions she really wanted answered: 'Will anyone else be lost?' and 'Will I be lost?' As each day went by, however, Bazil and Freda's assurances to their daughter sounded more formulaic and less convincing.

Following the finding of the school case and its contents, an impassioned message from Bazil Thorne was broadcast on the television and relayed through the newspapers in a variety of European languages:

To whoever is holding my son: I am ready to pay you the money you are demanding for his safe return. I will pay you in cash at any place and at any time you specify. You may contact me at my home. You will not be betrayed. Bazil Thorne.

Unfortunately, there was no response to Bazil's plea – other than from impostors. According to the *Sydney Morning Herald*:

Already tortured by the uncertainty about the fate of their son, [Bazil and Freda Thorne] were pestered by telephone calls from cranks, sadists and irresponsibles. Repeatedly, the Thornes answered the phone late at night, only to hear the heavy breathing of a caller who remained silent. But the telephone could not be left off the hook or disconnected for fear of missing a genuine contact by the kidnapper. Police were posted to the Thornes' flat to protect them and divert unwanted callers. Mr Thorne had personal assurance of [Police Commissioner] Mr Delaney that the police would make no move to frustrate a ransom meeting.[2]

On Sunday 10 July, by special arrangement, Bazil Thorne withdrew £25,000 in cash from the Bank of New South Wales. At first he kept the money at his flat, so that if the kidnapper suddenly made contact out of normal banking hours Bazil would be able to act swiftly to bring the money to him. At that stage, Detective Constable Lloyd Noonan or Sergeant Dave Paul were living in the flat day and night. These two officers had become an extension of the Thorne family and were a source of great strength and support to Bazil, Freda and Belinda. However, by now Bazil was determined to personally handle any further contact with the kidnapper, so he kept to himself and Freda many communications he received from would-be kidnappers. Several days later, Bazil took out another £25,000 because a person claiming to be the kidnapper had demanded an increase in the ransom. Bazil put the £50,000 in a bag and went on his own to the nominated meeting place, but nobody appeared and he returned home with the money in a state of utter dejection.

Over the next fortnight, Bazil and Freda were subjected to the most agonising torture of repeated extortion attempts by bogus callers pretending to have Graeme in their custody. Police on guard at their flat kept a close eye on Bazil, fearing that, because of his distraught state of mind, he would offer the £50,000 indiscriminately to anyone who said he could produce Graeme, or that he might be waylaid and robbed of the money on his way to a sham meeting. Eventually, on 25 July, because of police anxieties for his safety, Bazil returned the £50,000 to the bank, but special arrangements were made for it to be available on very short notice, even if the bank was closed.

On 11 July, four days after the kidnapping, a man with a foreign accent rang a phone number that was similar to the Thornes', but differed in the prefix (the first two numbers that varied by suburb), and demanded that the ransom be delivered to Matraville Post Office within half an hour or the boy would die. The police were informed and rushed to the post office, but nobody was there.

The Thornes' local minister at St Mark's Church of England in Darling Point, Reverend Clive Goodwin, offered to act as an intermediary and made his own public appeal to the kidnappers to use his services to facilitate the payment of the ransom and the return of the child, promising to keep the identity of the kidnappers confidential. He offered that they could approach him either at his church or home and gave an assurance that the police would not be involved. He indicated that his church would be left unlocked with a light on twenty-four hours a day, in the hope that the kidnappers might leave Graeme there, or at least a note to commence negotiations. This appeal did not result in the real kidnapper making any further approach, but it did produce a very convincing bogus ransom demand.

A woman rang Reverend Goodwin at the church to say that she was a go-between for the kidnappers and that he should have the money wrapped in two separate parcels and await a call from her at 5pm. After discussion with the police, both Bazil and the reverend went to the church, and at the appointed time Bazil took the phone and spoke to her. He demanded to speak to Graeme. The woman then put on the line another person with a thin, faint voice that didn't sound at all like Graeme. Bazil wanted to make absolutely sure that it was not his son, so he asked him, 'What's the name of your mate, Giddy, at school?'

The voice replied, 'I'm not allowed to answer that one.'

Bazil retorted, 'Then what's the name of our former landlady?'

'I'm not allowed to answer that one, either,' replied the voice.

By this stage, Bazil was convinced that it was not Graeme speaking and said as much to the person at the other end. The woman then came back on the line and said, 'I'm sorry, I can't put Graeme on the phone because he's been photographed too much and is too hot.' She then gave instructions on how the ransom money should be taken to a location in Merrylands.

Despite this woman's pathetic attempt at convincing Bazil that she had Graeme in her possession, Bazil was still determined not to let any possibility pass to be reunited with his son. He was reluctant to tell the police the instructions the woman had given him for the payment of the ransom, but he eventually did. The police advised him not to go to the location at Merrylands, however Bazil insisted. Reverend Goodwin agreed to go with him, but they wisely decided not to take the £25,000. When they went to the appointed place, no one was there.

On returning home, Bazil was so deflated that he broke down and wept. If only he had been home on the morning of Graeme's kidnapping when the first contact was made by the real kidnapper. If only he had ignored police instructions and insisted on taking the call when the real kidnapper rang back on the night of the abduction, then surely by the following day, at the latest, Graeme would have been safely home!

Eventually, Reverend Goodwin withdrew as an intermediary because of the continual harassment from people making bogus demands for the ransom money. He was immediately replaced by the Lord Mayor of Sydney, Alderman Harry Jensen, who was also plagued by frequent hoaxers and limelighters. One man, who said he was Italian, rang him nearly a dozen times. Although Jensen had his doubts about the authenticity of this man, he was not prepared to take the risk of abandoning contact with him. In one telephone conversation, which lasted ninety minutes, the man told Jensen that all the kidnappers were migrants, that he was involved in only a minor way, and that the others were divided about what should be done with Graeme. Jensen tried to bargain with him, telling him that if he had played only a minor part and gave himself up it was possible that he would be treated differently to the others. The caller said that he would do nothing to harm Graeme, but that the child was at risk from the other kidnappers. Finally, he named some Italians living on the south coast as being involved. Jensen gave this information to the police, but investigations proved that the man was either a hoaxer or insane.

One of the most infamous attempts to collect the ransom money was instigated by a woman who wrote a letter to Freda, inviting her to a rendezvous in Brisbane to arrange for payment of the ransom and Graeme's return. A Brisbane policewoman, who strongly resembled Freda, kept the appointment. The first meeting was to have been at Lennon's Hotel in Brisbane. The policewoman answered a telephone call at the hotel for Mrs Thorne from a woman who spoke with a foreign accent, and who told her to leave £25,000 in a ferry shed at Norman Park. The policewoman left a package as directed, but nobody picked it up. Several days later, Freda received a second letter from this woman in which she accused Freda of having foolishly allowed the police to be near the ferry shed. The woman wrote:

I told you, if you want your boy you must play it my way. If you didn't go to the police they must be keeping in close touch. I have told your son he will be home soon. He will not eat very much and has lost weight and is very happy about going back home. You have a few days to think it over. If you don't succeed this time you can blame yourself for your son's death. These instructions must be kept confidential. Do not tell your husband. Book a plane to Melbourne next Tuesday, but don't take it. Then book a seat on the plane to Brisbane under the name of Higgins. Make sure no one is following you. Lose them. Then go to Exhibition [Ground], enter the gates near the Museum [Brisbane's annual show was on at the time]. Make sure you are not followed. Go through the crowd around the ferris wheel and wait at the ticket box. I will send someone to collect the parcel containing £25,000 in notes in exchange for a letter telling where your son will be on Friday next.

In reply, an anguished and broken-hearted Freda Thorne wrote back to the post office address supplied by the woman:

I received your letter today and please God you are telling us the truth. Unfortunately I cannot carry out all your instructions as I had to show the letter to my husband and get the money. I did go to Brisbane as directed in your last letter. But my husband will not give the money until he has proof of your having the boy. Please, I beg of you as the boy's mother, give me some proof so that the money can be paid and my son given back. Please, if you have the boy, let him write a short note, or if he can't write, ask him these questions and send me the boy's answers. Ask him what is Giddy's Christian name? What is the name of Pam's dog? What did Father Christmas bring him last Christmas? What is the name of his barber? Please God, as the mother of Graeme, if you have my boy give me some proof so that I can get him back. There will be no hesitation on our part to pay the £25,000 when we are sure, but so many people have written saying that they have my son that I don't know what to believe.

Freda signed the letter 'Mrs Higgins'. The request for information that only Graeme would know produced no response. Despite this, the female police officer, again pretending to be Freda, went to the Exhibition Ground on the appointed day and waited at the nominated ticket box. A thirteen-year-old boy approached her and said that a woman had told him to ask a Mrs Higgins for a parcel. The boy agreed to take the police officer to the woman, but when they got to the spot where the boy had last seen her, she was nowhere to be found. Clearly, the two letters were part of a crude attempt by an impostor to get the money.

After numerous false hopes from attempts by impostors to enrich themselves, Bazil and Freda Thorne eventually adopted a standard method of testing the genuineness of contact from would-be kidnappers. Whether an approach was by letter or by phone, they would respond with this:

I received your letter/call relating to my son, Graeme, who is missing. I am not sending money as you asked simply because I am not satisfied that you are a genuine person and that you have Graeme. If you or anyone else has Graeme with them, and if they get in touch with me and let Graeme speak to me or write to me, I will pay the XXX demanded.

It should be noted, however, that the Thornes also received an enormous amount of cooperation and support from friends and strangers alike. The groundswell of community anguish for their plight was palpable throughout the nation. Church leaders of every denomination prayed with their congregations for the safe return of the boy. The police printed 5,000 posters carrying photographs and a description of Graeme, which were distributed to police stations, food and milk companies, suburban town halls, and places where people regularly gathered. The police were greatly moved when a blind man travelled by public transport from the city to the Thornes' home to offer his services as an intermediary, pointing out that it would be obvious to the kidnappers that a blind man could never identify them. The *Sun* newspaper reported that the Director of the FBI, J Edgar Hoover, was taking a personal interest in the case, and had asked to be notified immediately should there be a major breakthrough. Mr Hoover expressed his deep sympathy to the Thorne family, while a spokesman for the FBI stated that the organisation would be only too ready to supply 'the utmost help to Sydney police'.

***

For weeks, Bazil and Freda vainly hoped that the genuine kidnapper would again make contact, however each time they thought that a call might be the real thing, their hopes were dashed, causing them repeated intense anguish and despair. This rollercoaster drove them to the point of near-complete emotional collapse. Eventually, the calls died down, but so did Bazil and Freda's hopes for the safe return of their son. After several weeks of telling their daughter that Graeme would still be coming home, Bazil and Freda finally agreed that they should acknowledge to her that her brother might not be coming home after all. For three-year-old Belinda, the news was greeted with silence for a long time and then a series of questions: 'Has he gone to be with Jesus? Didn't he want to live with us? Can he come back one day? Is he sad? Are you sad? Am I sad?'

***

The police engaged in a huge amount of tedious investigative work, basing their enquiries at a central command post at the Bondi police station. For the first time, police utilised a 'running sheet' system that recorded in a central documentary archive every piece of information received and every enquiry made – all of which had to be cross-referenced. There were obvious advantages to this methodical approach, considering the size of the investigative team, but there were also pitfalls that had yet to be exposed.[3] The main risk was that once a line of enquiry had been recorded in the running sheet, it would disappear in a mass of paper without necessarily being fully considered or disseminated to the whole team.

The police were inundated by numerous people who claimed to have seen Graeme in a wide variety of unlikely places all over New South Wales. The reports went like this: 'I saw a man leaving a city theatre with the boy.' 'I saw the boy in a car at Kings Cross. He was crying.' 'I saw some men with binoculars watching the area of Graeme's home.' 'I saw this boy crying and calling out, "Is my mummy here?" There were two men with him.' A North Shore resident reported seeing a boy in a Scots College uniform carrying a case on the Pacific Highway thumbing a lift north of Sydney. Twelve hours after Graeme disappeared, a woman who lived near his home reported to the police that she could hear a whimpering noise in a nearby building. Police rushed to the scene, but found a colony of squealing cats. The police took every call seriously. All sightings, however unlikely, were logged and investigated, but they all proved groundless.

Numerous people contacted the police to report suspicious activity they thought might be connected with the kidnapping, and again each had to be investigated and discounted. A taxi driver reported a policeman as a possible suspect, claiming that the officer had hired his cab to go to the city from the eastern suburbs, but after travelling only a short distance he had abruptly and suspiciously ended the hire, whereupon he had been joined by some friends who arrived in a private car. A North Shore doctor reported that all the children's comics from his waiting room had been stolen and he believed that this might have some connection with the kidnapping. A woman reported seeing two men and a boy acting suspiciously in bush at Brooklyn on the Hawkesbury River, however they turned out to be on a fishing trip. One of the strangest limelighters to provide information was a man who drove up to a Sydney Harbour Bridge toll collector on the evening of 11 July, four days after Graeme's disappearance. The man appeared agitated, handed over £1, which was far more than the toll, and said, 'I have information; they might find the boy at Bundeena; keep the change.' He then sped off towards York Street. The toll collector was unable to read the registration number on the car because it was covered in mud. Numerous enquiries were conducted at Bundeena, but police failed to find any connection with the kidnapping.

Police were also besieged by numerous theories advanced by well-meaning people intent on assisting in the search for Graeme. A member of Sydney's underworld suggested that police should contact all estate agents dealing with holiday-home lettings, because it was likely the kidnappers had rented a house at some lonely spot in which to hold the child. He also suggested that proprietors of caravan-rental companies should be contacted, because Graeme could have been secured in a hired caravan that might have pulled in at one of the many caravan parks along the coast without exciting suspicion. Police Commissioner Delaney informed the public that it was thought unlikely that the child was being held in a heavily populated inner-city area, but rather in a secluded near-city location. He appealed to people with holiday cottages or weekenders in and around Sydney to inspect them as quickly as possible, stating that police believed that Graeme might be 'in a weekender or a secluded home in areas like Cronulla, Palm Beach, and even as far away as Katoomba'. Various theories advanced by members of the public, and even by the police, fed on racial and ethnic prejudices that were prevalent at the time. The Commissioner informed the public that his men had 'questioned roving gypsy bands seen in various parts of the Sydney area in the past few days … and questioned European market gardeners in outer Sydney suburbs'.

Police kept dozens of rendezvous with people who claimed to have confidential information about the kidnapper. Invariably the information was innocuous or malicious, but the possibility of a lead could never be overlooked. Every clue had to be followed up; every suspects had to be interviewed. Tedious hours were spent tracking the sources of anonymous reports, many of which were based on partially overheard snatches of conversation or even domestic squabbles. Some used the investigation as an opportunity to vent personal animosities by nominating as suspects people who had failed to pay them money or simply offended them in some way. Others reported men with foreign accents they knew or had met who had been acting suspiciously and should therefore be investigated. None of these reports proved fruitful and only tied up valuable police resources.

***

After a wonderful, but frustratingly short holiday, Stephen Bradley and the children returned by car to Sydney on 12 July and Magda flew down two days later. As soon as he could, Stephen approached a real estate agent and found rental accommodation for the family at 49 Osborne Road, Manly, in an old building divided into three flats. On 19 July, he went to his former employers at Nutt & Muddle and convinced them to give him back his old job.

It was not until his return to Sydney on Tuesday 12 July that Stephen Bradley saw the *Sun Herald* that had been published the previous Sunday. With some alarm, he read an article on page 2 headed 'Mystery man at flat', which disclosed that three weeks before the kidnapping a man had called at the Thornes' home describing himself as a private enquiry agent asking for people named Bognor or Bailey. The man was described as aged between thirty-five and forty, thickset, with black or dark brown slightly wavy hair, and thick, dark eyebrows. He was, according to the article, well-spoken and had a foreign appearance, and was wearing a grey coat over an open-necked shirt. The report stated that police would like to interview that man or receive information that could lead them to him.

Bradley immediately disposed of his grey overcoat, cut his hair short and trimmed his eyebrows. Although he was surprised that the residents at 79 Edward Street, Bondi, had remembered his visit weeks earlier – and even more amazed that they recalled the fake name he had used – he was still supremely confident that none of the information they had given to police could be linked to him.

***

By the week after Graeme Thorne's abduction, when the nation was still desperately hoping and praying that he would be found alive, there were essentially only two important lines of enquiry that the police felt were significant and worth pursuing. The first was to enquire of all private enquiry agencies to see if the man who had come to the Thornes' home three weeks before the kidnapping purporting to be a private investigator could be identified. During this aspect of the investigation, the police became excited when they located a real private enquiry agency that trained its agents to use the false name 'Mr Bognor', but questioning of the agency's employees failed to reveal the identity of the man who had used that unusual name at the Thornes' home.

The other major line of enquiry, which was kept from the media and the public, concerned reports of a car – described by the preponderance of witnesses as a blue Ford – that had been parked in Wellington Street at around the time of

Graeme's disappearance. The day after his abduction, a young man by the name of Cecil Denmeade and his fiancée, Dorothea Warren, came forward to say that they had seen a man standing next to a car parked at the corner of Francis Street and Wellington Street in Bondi at 8.32am the previous day. By now, the police were convinced that this was the location from which the kidnapper had abducted Graeme. Denmeade described the car as an iridescent blue 1955 Ford Customline, and he felt sure that he could identify the man again if the police found him. Being a car enthusiast, he was adamant that his description of the vehicle was accurate. The police were understandably sceptical about this claim, so Detective Sergeant Brian Doyle from the investigative team showed him a book of photographs depicting every model of Ford car for every year of manufacture and in every colour. Denmeade quickly established that he was capable of correctly identifying each model, year and colour. Doyle then took him outside and conducted a similar exercise with real cars, and again Denmeade passed with flying colours. After this exhaustive series of tests, the police were satisfied that Mr Denmeade was a reliable witness and that the kidnapper had used an iridescent blue 1955 Ford Customline vehicle.

Confident that they now had an accurate description of the vehicle used in the kidnapping, police set themselves the daunting task of conducting an exhaustive search of the records of the Department of Motor Transport to see how many 1955 Ford Customlines were registered in New South Wales. This exercise alone required a team of twenty-five police searching full-time for some weeks through more than 270,000 index cards of Ford motor vehicles. The initial conclusion from this search was that there were approximately 4,000 1955 Ford Customlines (in any colour) registered in the State. The officers-in-charge of the investigation made a decision that the search for a Ford Customline would remain confidential and not be disclosed to the public. There was no mention of it in the newspapers or on the radio or television, despite the fact that some journalists had got wind of it.

Armed with the information about the number of 1955 Ford Customlines, the New South Wales police embarked on a line of enquiry so vast and ambitious that nothing like it had been attempted before in the history of Australian policing. They decided to locate and interview every single one of the approximately 4,000 owners of 1955 Ford Customlines throughout New South Wales in an attempt to find the one that had been used in the kidnapping. However, the manner in which the police went about this task was, in retrospect, seriously flawed.[4] They came to the conclusion that the kidnapper would not have used his own car to carry out such a brazen child-snatching in broad daylight in a public street, and therefore what they were looking for was a 1955 Ford Customline that had been stolen or borrowed from the owner. Police also felt that there was a possibility that the kidnapper might have modified the car by repainting it. So, rather than focusing on owners of blue 1955 Ford Customlines, they decided to question the owners of all such vehicles, no matter what the colour. This massive exercise involved questioning every owner throughout the State as to where their vehicle had been situated on the morning of 7 July and who had had access to it. Each owner of a Ford Customline was asked three questions:

1. Has the car been lent to anybody?
2. Was it in the garage on 7 July?
3. Does your wife drive the car?

It was hoped that if owners answered these questions honestly and accurately, this would flush out the vehicle that had been borrowed or stolen from the owner by the kidnapper.

The exercise to exclude up to 4,000 Ford Customlines was laborious, painstaking and protracted, but the police were determined to accomplish the task. It involved police throughout the State locating owners of these vehicles, questioning them, filling in a standard form and remitting the information back to the nerve centre at Bondi. As several weeks went by without any positive results, police continued to question private enquiry agents and middle-aged men with foreign accents, and to pursue every lead provided by members of the public – no matter how bizarre or unlikely. In the meantime, Bazil and Freda Thorne maintained their vigil by their phone and continued to be harassed by well-meaning do-gooders and perverted, heartless extortionists.

8

SKELETON AT THE FORT

The children of Grandview Grove in Seaforth often played in the local streets and on nearby bush blocks. Seven-year-old Andrew McCue and his four-year-old brother, Peter, had for some weeks enjoyed romping on the bush-covered vacant block next to number 16 – mainly because lying under the large rock they called 'the fort' was a 'skeleton' wrapped in a blanket, which added to their imaginary games. Like most children their age, they had been mesmerised and horrified by the stories they had been told about the eight-year-old Sydney boy who had been taken from his parents and not heard of again. In fact, Andrew McCue often carried around with him a newspaper clipping with a photograph of the boy, so that he would recognise him if he saw him.[1]

On 16 August 1960, five weeks and five days after Graeme

Thorne's disappearance, Andrew McCue told some of his local playmates, including eight-year-olds Philip Wall and Eric Coughlin, about the skeleton, and they all went to examine it at the fort. The extra year of maturity of the eight-year-olds gave them greater insight, so that when they inspected it Philip proudly informed his friends that it wasn't a skeleton at all, but a body wrapped in a blanket.

When both eight-year-olds mentioned to their mothers about the blanket in the bush with 'something like a head in it', and four-year-old Peter McCue told his mother that 'Philip says there's a body there.' That night, when the fathers arrived home from work, Mr Wall and Mr Coughlin went to investigate. They found a brightly coloured picnic rug wrapped around an object and tied with string. On untying the string, they immediately saw two human arms, causing them to recoil in horror. They wisely did not touch the body any further and immediately returned home to notify the local police.

Within minutes, officers arrived at the scene, where they discovered the corpse of a young boy fully dressed in a Scots College uniform, and they immediately realised that it was the body of Graeme Thorne. His ankles were tightly tied together with twine and a silk scarf was loosely knotted around his neck – the size of the loop indicating that it had been used as a gag. Government Medical Officer Dr Clarence Percy examined Graeme's body where it lay under the rock, after which it was taken to the city morgue in George Street in The Rocks. The picnic rug, the scarf, the twine from the ankles and the string that had been wrapped around the body were all transported to the CIB laboratory in the city.

***

Detective Sergeant Ken Baret was given the odious task of informing Bazil and Freda Thorne that their son's body had been found. By this time, Bazil, Freda and Belinda had been relocated by the police to another eastern suburbs address. Baret arranged for Reverend Goodwin to come with him to break the news, but moments before they arrived, Bazil and Freda learned of the discovery of their son's body from a television broadcast.

Freda and Bazil received the news with outward stoicism and inner despair. It had been five weeks since their son had been taken, and nothing that could reliably be ascribed as contact from the kidnapper had occurred since the night of his abduction, so their expectations for his survival were not high. Their greatest fear, apart from constant worry that he was being ill-treated and in a state of intense anguish, had been that Graeme would be killed and his body disposed of in a place where it would never be found, forcing them to live the rest of their lives never knowing whether he was alive or dead. The discovery of his body at least saved them from that fate. They had suffered so much over the intervening five weeks and sunk so low after each contact had proven to be bogus, that when they were finally given the news that his body had been found it added an additional layer to an already crushing sense of grief and loss. Their fear of his death had been so great and so prolonged that when news of it finally came, it was something that they had already imagined and suffered many times over.

Graeme's younger sister, Belinda, had long since ceased to enquire if her brother would be coming home. When Bazil and

Freda informed their daughter that Graeme was definitely not coming home because he had 'gone to be with God', Belinda besieged them with questions: 'Why has he gone there?' 'Will he be happy there?' 'Will he go to school there?' 'Will he have a mummy and daddy there?' Extended family members and close friends rallied around the Thornes to lend support at this time of unimaginable pain.

***

News of the discovery of the body spread like wildfire around the country and caused an intense outpouring of grief from the whole nation. There also arose a terrible anger towards a person who could murder an eight-year-old boy when his parents had been so willing to pay the ransom money. Out of the grief and anger came a communal insistence that justice be done. In response, New South Wales Premier Heffron stated that the resources of the State would be applied to 'run the guilty parties to earth'.

The New South Wales Police approached their investigative tasks with renewed energy, resolute that they would find the person responsible for a crime so heinous that it had never before been committed in Australia. While there was a lot of pressure on the politicians to pass immediate legislation to remedy the gap in the law by creating a new offence of kidnapping-for-ransom, the Attorney-General advised the Premier that 'it would be improper at this juncture to introduce into Parliament legislation to strengthen the law relating to kidnapping, and in the interests of justice any such action should await the determination of proceedings'.[2] The government wisely decided to delay implementing any changes until after the matter had been finalised. In any event, any legislative amendment could never be retrospective and would have no influence on the outcome of this murder investigation.

The picnic rug, scarf, twine and string from Graeme's body were closely examined at the CIB laboratory. No fingerprints were found; indeed none of the items contained surfaces suitable for capturing them. A description of the rug, along with black-and-white photographs, was published in all the major daily newspapers, while weekly and monthly magazines carried full-colour images. Meanwhile, the unrelenting police search for the 1955 Ford Customline continued unabated.

On 19 August, three days after Graeme's body had been located, Mr William Telford and his wife Kathleen, who lived at 26 Moore Street, Clontarf, contacted the police to tell them of their suspicions about their former next-door neighbour, Stephen Bradley, at number 28. They had noticed that for about ten days prior to the kidnapping, Bradley – who had a strong European accent – had left home at about 6am in a Goggomobil Sports roadster. They informed police that Bradley also owned a blue Ford,[3] which he had purchased only about a week before the kidnapping. They were struck by the coincidence that he and his family had moved out of their home on the very day Graeme Thorne disappeared, after living there for about six months. They reported that on the morning of the kidnapping, Mrs Bradley and the children had left their home in a taxi to go on a holiday to Queensland, but that Stephen Bradley had not come out of the house to see them off. Around the middle of the day, the Telfords had heard Bradley moving inside his home and various other strange noises that sounded like a baby whimpering and a man mumbling unintelligibly. During the day, removalists had arrived and taken the Bradleys' furniture away, and later that day Bradley had called into the Telfords' home to ask if he could leave some valuable paintings with them. By the time Bradley called back at the Telfords' home ten days later to pick up his paintings, he had trimmed his eyebrows, which had previously been bushy, and his hair had been cut short. On a pretext, Mrs Telford had gone out and looked into Bradley's car – the blue Ford – but she saw nothing unusual. Mr and Mrs Telford informed the police that they were utterly convinced that this man was the kidnapper. Despite the Telfords' suspicions, they had inexplicably waited until 19 August, three days after Graeme's body had been found, to approach the police. A report of their observations was filed in the police running sheets, arousing no special interest or attention and failing to prompt any further investigation – perhaps because of their delay in relaying the information to the police.

On Wednesday 24 August, five days after the Telfords had provided their information to the police, Detective Sergeants Brian Doyle and Don Fergusson went to Nutt & Muddle Pty Ltd in Kings Cross to interview Stephen Bradley, who worked there as an electroplater. Their visit was not prompted by the Telfords' information, but rather by Bradley being one of the numerous owners of a 1955 Ford Customline. Indeed, Doyle and Fergusson had no knowledge of the information provided by the Telfords. The large investigative group was constantly receiving vast amounts of information, and even with the benefits of a police running sheet it was impossible for every member of the team to keep abreast of every piece of information. The running sheet with the Telfords' material was merely one of many thousands of reports that had been filed away and categorised as having no particular significance.

Despite the fact that these two officers had given Bradley no warning of their arrival at his workplace, he appeared to be completely unfazed by their visit. He seemed relaxed, he was quite personable and he readily answered all their questions with great assurance. He gave them a history of his arrival in Australia and his marriage to Magda, mentioning that they had three children. He explained that he and his family had formerly lived in their own home at Clontarf, but that they had recently moved to rented accommodation in Manly. He readily agreed to his ownership of two cars: a 1955 iridescent blue Ford Customline and a Goggomobil. When Doyle asked him where he had been on 7 July, Bradley casually replied in his mid-European accent, 'What day was that?' Doyle told him it had been a Thursday, to which Bradley replied, 'I remember it well. It was the day my wife and children went away for a holiday.' Bradley told the police that he had had a couple of days off work at that time so that he could move house while the rest of the family was away. He told them:

> I got up at about 8am and had breakfast. My wife and children left by taxi at about 10am and the furniture removalists arrived at 10.45am or 11am. I was with them until they left at about 2pm.

Bradley insisted that the Customline had never been out of the garage that day and that the only time he had left the house was to go in the Goggomobil to a hardware store in Balgowlah to buy some tie wire for packing cases. He had come straight home from the hardware store and seen his wife and children off soon after. Just to be absolutely clear, Sergeant Fergusson asked him, 'Were your wife and children with you up till the time they left the house?' Bradley responded, 'Yes, I saw them off and put them into a taxi at about ten o'clock. They were with me until then. Then I was on my own until the furniture men arrived.' He convincingly assured the police that he had not been in Wellington Street, Bondi, that day and had never gone to the Thornes' home posing as an enquiry agent. Sergeants Doyle and Fergusson left Nutt & Muddle without the slightest suspicions about the man they had just interviewed.

Later, the two sergeants checked the information Bradley had given them and confirmed that he had indeed taken leave from his work, that his wife and children had flown to Queensland for a holiday on the morning of the kidnapping, and that he had indeed moved to a rented flat in Manly. From the point of view of the investigating police, this was another Ford Customline owner whom they could tick off the list, because he could give an account of the whereabouts of his car on the day of the kidnapping.

⋆

The visit by the two sergeants to Nutt & Muddle on 24 August did not, in fact, come as a complete surprise to Stephen Bradley. The previous Sunday, 21 August, as he was driving along Pittwater Road between Manly and Collaroy in his Ford Customline, the notorious Detective Sergeant Ray Kelly[4] happened to be driving along the same road, but in the opposite direction. Kelly had an awesome reputation as an exceptional investigator with a remarkable instinct for sniffing out suspects and an uncanny eye for detail, as well as an unrivalled list of informants. He had been decorated many times for bravery while under fire in the course of capturing armed criminals and escaped prisoners. Knowing that police in the Graeme Thorne kidnapping team were looking for a 1955 blue Customline, when Kelly saw that model being driven along Pittwater Road, he immediately decided to do a U-turn and pull it over. Was it a whim or was it his instinct at work? Bradley initially assumed he was being stopped for a traffic violation, but after taking down his personal details, Detective Sergeant Kelly informed him that a Sergeant Doyle would visit him in the next few days to interview him about his vehicle as part of the investigation of the Graeme Thorne kidnapping. Bradley was taken aback at this information, however his concerns were partly allayed when Kelly told him that the visit by Sergeant Doyle was part of a routine enquiry into the owners of all 1955 Ford Customline vehicles. Trying to act as nonchalantly as possible, Bradley assured the detective that Sergeant Doyle was welcome to contact him at any time, and he provided his work address so that the interview could occur during office hours and away from his home.

In reality, Bradley was deeply shaken and astonished to learn that the police had narrowed their search to focus on 1955 Ford Customlines, because early in the investigation the newspapers had reported that they were looking at a number of different vehicles – none of which was that model. He realised that someone must have seen his car in Wellington Street, and as he cast his mind back to the events on the morning of the kidnapping, he suddenly recalled that a vehicle had edged past him as he was getting out of his car just as Graeme was approaching. While this revelation was a setback, when he thought about it carefully Bradley rationalised that the Ford Customline was a common car in Sydney and that if the police had any solid evidence pointing to him, they would hardly have given him warning of the interview. He felt confident that the police had no evidence to link him to the kidnapping, and he quickly recovered his composure. He had the advantage of several days in which to thoroughly clean the Customline to remove any possibility of Graeme's fingerprints being found, and also to carefully think about how he should respond to the police when they questioned him. While he felt perturbed at the prospect of a police interrogation, he was confident that he could withstand any questioning and convey the impression of being a typical, concerned member of the community. All he had to do was to act normally, not get flustered, and confidently assert that the vehicle had not left his garage that day. The police would then have no evidence to link him to the kidnapping.

At the end of the interview with Sergeants Doyle and Fergusson, Bradley felt a sense of superiority that he possessed information that they desperately wanted, and that these plodders lacked the ability to extract it from him. In a real sense, he held the upper hand, rather than the police, and he was quite proud of the adept manner with which he had feigned cooperation with them. He thought to himself that a professional actor could not have done a more convincing job.

However, while Bradley was sure that the two sergeants had accepted his story and discounted him as a suspect, he was realistic enough to appreciate that further investigations by the police might lead them in his direction. In particular, he was concerned that, as a man with a foreign accent who owned the same model vehicle suspected to have been used by the kidnapper, he might one day be asked to participate in an identification parade in front of Freda and Bazil Thorne or the woman who lived above them. If they identified him as the man who had come to their flats three weeks before the kidnapping, he had no viable explanation for his actions. Alternatively, he might be asked to provide a voice sample on one of the new electronic tape contraptions used to record sounds, which could then be played to whomever had answered his two telephone calls on the day of the kidnapping. The more he thought about it, the more Bradley became convinced that it would only be a matter of time before the police settled on him as a suspect. He concluded that the only solution was for him, Magda and the children to leave Australia at the earliest opportunity. They had often discussed travelling overseas to seek their fortune in another country, like Canada, but such ideas had always been shelved because Magda could not bring herself to take Paul away from his natural father. More recently – when he had expected the financial windfall of the ransom money – Stephen had suggested to Magda that they go on a world tour. But now there was a more pressing reason to leave: to place himself out of reach of the police. How was he to convince Magda that they should take such a major and unexpected turn in their lives?

***

Although Stephen Bradley had both a European accent and a 1955 blue Ford Customline, and he lived barely two miles from where Graeme Thorne's body had been located, the combination of these qualities was not sufficient to excite any particular suspicions or prompt any additional enquiries about him. At this time, the police viewed Stephen Bradley as just another one of the numerous Customline owners whose car had neither been lent nor stolen. The police were blinded by the criteria they had set themselves in their search for the kidnapper.[5] Having decided that no rational kidnapper would use his own car, they were immune to the suspicious circumstances pointing to Bradley as a potential suspect who *had* used his own car. All it would have taken would have been to show his photograph to Freda and Bazil Thorne or to Cecil Denmeade and the hunt for the kidnapper would have been over. Instead, the investigation still had a long way to go.

***

The funeral service for Graeme Thorne at St Mark's Anglican Church in Darling Point on 28 August 1960 was a most sombre affair. A large contingent of older boys from Scots College and a police escort accompanied the hearse carrying the coffin to the church, where a huge crowd, including family, friends and numerous members of the public, had congregated. The whole nation grieved with Bazil, Freda and Belinda for the loss of their beautiful, young son and brother. While Bazil and Freda were grateful for the support of the public, at this time they craved their privacy and some emotional space to grieve for their son and give attention to their daughter. It was, indeed, impossible for either of them to venture outside without being waylaid by well-meaning people wanting to express their condolences. In their despair, Bazil and Freda had reluctantly become national celebrities.

9

FLIGHT AND RUSES

On Thursday 25 August, the day after police spoke to Stephen Bradley at Nutt & Muddle, Magda Bradley went to the Union Steamship Company offices in the city to book and pay the deposit on a one-way passage to England for herself and her eldest son Paul on the P&O-Orient liner SS *Himalaya*, leaving Sydney a month later on 26 September. Four days after Magda's purchase, on 29 August, Stephen Bradley went to the same travel office to book and pay deposits for one-way berths on the same liner for himself and the other two children. The Bradleys could not afford airline flights for all five of them, and the SS *Himalaya* was the first liner available, considering the preparations they still had to make prior to travelling overseas for an indefinite period. Stephen then began the process of disposing of much of their personal property in anticipation of the family departing Australia on 26 September. They informed nobody of their plans to leave the country – not family, not friends, not neighbours, not the estate agent managing their flat, not Stephen's employer, not even Paul and Ross's father, Gregor Weinberg.

∗∗∗

While Stephen and Magda's preparations for departing Australia are well documented, the process of arriving at the decision to leave, which was tantamount to another migration for them both, is largely a matter of conjecture. Magda Bradley much later provided her own explanation in an unpublished manuscript.[1] She wrote the manuscript many months after their departure at a time when she was at a particularly low ebb and when she had every reason to justify their actions. She described the circumstances in which she came to fall in love with Stephen. She devoted much of the manuscript to describing how wonderful Stephen was as a husband and father. She gave an account of the many financial calamities and misadventures that had beset them, and how they had valiantly struggled to overcome their string of 'bad luck'. She attempted to justify their decision to leave Australia with a detailed and lengthy explanation that went back as far as the fire in Katoomba. Her account went like this: After the destruction of their guesthouse at Katoomba in June 1959, Magda and Stephen considered going overseas for a period, and Stephen had suggested Canada. However, when they discussed the idea with Gregor Weinberg, he was vehemently against the plan, because it would mean losing contact with his son, Paul. When Ross secured a place at St. Gabriel's School for deaf children, their decision not to go overseas was sealed. When it came to the crunch, Magda was also not keen on another migration, because she really loved Australia. When Stephen got the job at Nutt & Muddle, he was happier at work than he had been for a long time, and it paid him a good salary, but he still had an innate restlessness. In Magda's words:

> *He still had the feeling that things were against us, and was sure that if we went away for a couple of years to another country, we might be able to break the spell of bad luck which had been following us for so long. But still we didn't come to a definite decision. I wasn't altogether against the idea of leaving Australia for a while … I thought that it would take some time to sell the properties, especially the house in Clontarf, so I felt that there was still plenty of time to make a final decision as to whether we were going to stay in Australia and try to make a go of another business, or to go abroad for a year or two. It was such a hard decision to make, and I tried to stall for time – or perhaps I was waiting for Steve to make up his mind for us – but I don't really know. All I know is that it was very difficult to decide and a great responsibility.*[2]

After returning from their holiday in Queensland and moving into the flat at Manly, Stephen and Magda began looking for some land on which they could build a house. They found a lovely block at Narrabeen, and paid a deposit on it, but the owner then changed his mind about selling. Magda was terribly upset:

Everything was pointing to the fact that we were not very lucky, and I got to the stage where I was sick and tired of everything. I lost interest in life, and became very depressed in that flat in Manly. What with all those old things and the rather odd smell that hung about the place it was not very encouraging at all. I wish that I had never agreed to sell our home in the first place. Steve got worried about me and wanted me to go and finish my holiday for at least another fortnight, and then when I had had a proper rest I would be able to make up my mind what we really wanted to do. I must say that I didn't especially want to go, particularly without Steve and the children, but I realised that I was badly in need of a rest.[3]

Magda then spent fourteen days on her own at Hayman Island. Although she missed Stephen and the children dreadfully, she came back refreshed. It was while she was on the island that, according to her version, she decided to go to London:

During my stay on the island I had done a great deal of thinking, and I had decided to go to London to find my uncle and try to publish some of my songs. But when I arrived home I couldn't tell Steve straight away. I wasn't at all sure that I liked the idea of being parted from him, even only for six months. Especially when I saw him and the children again, my plans to go to London with Paul did not seem so good after all ... I told Steve what I had been thinking during my holiday. I told him that I would like to go to England for a few months, and if I saw that we had a better chance to progress there and I could find a market for my writing and songs, I would ask him to join me and we could stay for a couple of years. As usual, Steve agreed with me. He thought it would be a good idea if he kept his job, then if I didn't find what I wanted I could come back and regard my stay in England as a holiday. I intended to take Paul with me as it would be such a chance for a boy of his age to see another country. Also I wouldn't be so lonely.[4]

With this plan in mind, Magda made the booking on the *Himalaya* for herself and Paul. The reality that Magda and Stephen would be parted from each other for a long time then struck them both:

I made our bookings and at that very moment, Steve and I began to say goodbye to each other. Every hour that passed I felt worse and worse about the thought of having to part from my husband. Perhaps that sounds ridiculous but even though I had wanted to go in the first place, I was realising how difficult it would be to live without Steve even for a few months. Steve became sad too, and after a few days we admitted to each other that we could not go through with it. I asked him to come with us. We would all go together. But there was the question of booking their passages on the same ship as well as organising everything in such a short time, should we be able to get extra bookings ... We eventually agreed that if we were able to get extra tickets for the same ship we would all go together. If not, I would go with Paul as originally decided.[5]

After work the very next day, Stephen went to the shipping company's office and found that he was able to get tickets on the same ship. They were all overjoyed:

That night we were very happy, because that was really what we had wanted. I was already hoping that I might be able to find some new solution or method for curing little Ross's deafness in England. I was hearing every day about new possibilities for deaf people and new surgery too. Also Helen still had a slightly deformed thigh from the car accident, and I was planning to ask my uncle, who is an orthopaedic specialist, what we could do for her. Steve was excited like a little boy going to an unexpected party. I felt that God must have wanted us all to go together, and perhaps a journey like that would change the bad luck which had been following us around for years.[6]

***

Was Magda's peculiar step of booking tickets for only herself and Paul, followed by Stephen's separate reservation for the remainder of the family, a ruse so as not to attract the attention of the police to the family's plans to depart Australia? Did this rather lame manoeuvre mean that Magda knew why they urgently had to go and that they needed to adopt furtive tactics to hide that fact? Did she know or suspect that Stephen had committed a crime so heinous that it warranted leaving the land she dearly loved that had so readily accepted her after the Holocaust? Or was this a fabulous adventure for the whole family in order to seek their fortune elsewhere, as she and Stephen had often discussed?

Magda's tortuous explanation is convenient, self-serving and gives the impression of being contrived. It weaves a scenario to account for all the facts then known about their departure. Her loving descriptions throughout her manuscript of Stephen as the ideal husband and father render her reasons for leaving Australia unconvincing. Not only does she ask one to accept that she had been prepared to leave behind the best husband in the world, but also her own handicapped son, Ross, and Helen, the child she had come to mother and love. If her explanation is rejected, it leaves open the tantalising prospect that Magda was complicit in the surreptitious steps to flee Australia. If she was an accomplice in that subterfuge, one possible reason would be that she knew or suspected that her husband had committed a wicked crime. This, of course, does not imply she had any knowledge of his plans before the kidnapping. Alternatively, were her actions merely a device to avoid Gregor Weinberg taking steps to prevent his sons being taken overseas for an indeterminate period?

A more plausible explanation than the one provided by Magda is as follows: About six weeks after her return from Queensland to Sydney, Stephen came home from work and told Magda that he had been questioned by police about the registration on his Ford Customline. Stephen did not provide her with any further details of the police visit, and she did not enquire. However, it was unheard of for police to speak to a car owner at his workplace about something as mundane as car registration, and Magda strongly suspected that Stephen had given her a sanitised version of the police interview.

When, later that night, Stephen stunned her with the news that he wished to take the family on an extended trip to England at the earliest opportunity, Magda deduced that the police interview must have been far more serious than a mere discussion about a registration irregularity. She thought back to Stephen's sudden decision to send her and the two older children by plane to Queensland, while he remained in Sydney to drive up in the Customline. She knew only too well that the day she and the children had flown to Queensland was the day of Graeme Thorne's kidnapping. She had read the newspaper descriptions of the man of interest to police having a European accent, but she refused to contemplate that her loving husband, who was so adorable to her and their children, could be capable of committing such a contemptible crime. Stephen tempted her to go overseas by suggesting that Ross might be able to get some advanced treatment in London for his deafness – he had read about a new transistor device – and she might well be able to sell the musical compositions she had been writing so avidly over the years, which had repeatedly been rejected by Australian publishers. He assured her that they would return to Australia at some time in the future.

This sudden change of direction in their lives exacerbated Magda's recurrent fears about her husband. She found his desire to urgently leave Australia highly suspicious, and she became increasingly suspicious that his reason for wanting to go was much more serious than just a few creditors harassing him. She knew that it had something to do with the police interview, but she deliberately did not ask him for details, intuitively feeling that it was best if she did not know. Magda was truly conflicted by her desire to live with her husband and children in the land that had adopted her after the war and by her fear of crossing Stephen, coupled with her abiding determination not to undergo the ordeal of another divorce.

While she was scared of what Stephen might do if she refused to comply with his wishes, she also loved him dearly and considered that her marriage to him was far better than her previous one to Gregor Weinberg. Stephen had always been kind and generous to her, he had never spoken harshly to her or the children – even if he was often domineering – and she had every reason to believe that he had always been faithful to her.

In the end, she reconciled her conflicting emotions by deciding that the only way to stay married to Stephen and to allay her concerns for her safety and that of her children was to fully cooperate with him in whatever he wanted to do – even if that meant leaving Australia for a time. She also had to admit that the prospects of getting further treatment for Ross and selling her songs in Britain were particularly compelling.

***

Several days after booking the sea passages on the SS *Himalaya*, Stephen Bradley went to a second-hand furniture shop in Liverpool Street in the city operated by the firm AG Jones Auctions Pty Ltd, where he spoke to the proprietor, Mr Max Mauer. After a few days of negotiations, Mr Mauer agreed to pay £260 for all of Bradley's furniture and household goods that had been transferred by the removalists from the Clontarf house to a storage area. A few days later, the furniture and goods were delivered to Mr Mauer at his shop. Among the numerous items included in the sale were a vacuum cleaner, a standard lamp (which had its flex tied with a piece of string), and a dirty carpet. Bradley had no idea that in selling these items he was leaving evidence that could later be used against him.

Bradley returned to the shipping company and used the £260 to pay the balance of the fares for the whole family. He asked the booking clerk if he could store some paintings in his cabin on the ship, because they were very valuable and he was afraid they might get damaged in the cargo hold. He mentioned to the clerk that he had already made arrangements to send the family's Pekinese dog, Cherie, by air freight to England.

On 20 September, Bradley took his blue Ford Customline to Christy's Motor Auctions on Parramatta Road at Granville. He told the salesman that there was still £593 owing on the car, so an agreement was reached that he would be paid a mere £32, being the difference between what the vehicle was worth and what was still owing on his hire purchase contract. The next day, Bradley sold the Goggomobil, on which there was also a large amount of money still outstanding.

Before their departure, Magda and Stephen took other steps to sever all ties with Australia, telling a variety of people different stories in an attempt to camouflage their real intentions. The three children were told that they were going on an extended holiday with both their parents, and that the destination was a surprise they would be told about on the day of departure. On 23 September, Bradley withdrew his stepson Ross from St. Gabriel's, telling the headmaster, Brother John Regan, that the family was relocating to Brisbane. Brother Regan kindly gave him the name of a similar school in Brisbane and a letter of introduction to the headmaster. On the same day, Bradley went to Stewart's Veterinary Hospital at Rushcutters Bay and made arrangements to ship Cherie to an address in London. He also withdrew his stepson Paul from his local high school, telling the headmaster that they were moving to Victoria. The next day, Saturday 24 September, Bradley drove up to the Blue Mountains with Paul to see the boy's father, Gregor Weinberg, at his Leura guesthouse. He told Weinberg that the family were all going on a business trip to Melbourne for several days. Weinberg wanted Paul to stay with him for the weekend, but

Bradley put him off, telling him that he would see Paul the following week when they came back from Melbourne. There was no mention of the planned journey to England.

As the days drew closer to their scheduled departure, Bradley informed his employer at Nutt & Muddle that he was required to go into St Vincent's Hospital at Darlinghurst the very next day for an operation on an old spinal injury that might require some months for a full recovery. When his employer enquired how he had first received this back injury, Stephen told him it was 'from jumping out of an aeroplane some years ago in Hungary when he had to parachute from the aircraft'.

Bradley wrote several letters, which he kept to post when the *Himalaya* berthed in Melbourne on the afternoon of 27 September. One was addressed to the estate agent who had rented them the flat at Manly, advising him that they had vacated it. In partial payment of outstanding rent, Bradley included in the letter two vouchers for deposits he had paid to have the electricity and gas connected; however, the amounts outstanding to the utility companies were more than the value of the vouchers, so the agent was left out of pocket. Stephen asked Magda to write a letter to Gregor Weinberg, in which she explained that they had decided to go on an extended holiday – without saying where – which again he kept to post when they arrived in Melbourne. Stephen and Magda left several bills unpaid, including the telephone bill and twelve parking fines totalling £42 acquired by Madga over the previous twelve months.

Stephen and Magda Bradley had taken all the necessary steps to prepare for their family's departure on the *Himalaya* on Monday 26 September.

***

FLIGHT AND RUSES

On Sunday 25 September – almost six weeks after Graeme Thorne's body had been found – the newspapers all carried two pieces of highly sensational news. The first item was the launch the previous day in Newport, Virginia, of the USS *Enterprise*, the first atomic-powered aircraft carrier and the largest ship ever built at that time. The second piece of news – closer to home – was a notification to the public for the first time of the police search for an iridescent blue 1955 Ford Customline suspected to have been used in the kidnapping of Graeme Thorne, and a full description of the man seen in the vicinity of the car at the time. The *Sun-Herald* reported:

> *Moments after the car was first observed, a man was seen to leave the driver's seat and walk around to the Francis Street footpath. In this position he stood between the car and the approaching Graeme Thorne. Police have learned the same man was seen in Francis Street during the morning of either the Monday or Tuesday before the kidnapping . . .*
>
> *The Driver: Aged between 35 and 40, 5ft 7 in tall, stocky build, olive complexion, jet black hair which was very long and extended noticeably from beneath his hat. Some people have told police the man had a foreign appearance. He was dressed in a fawn gabardine overcoat which appeared to be very creased and wore a brown felt hat . . . Detectives are working ceaselessly to find the man.*[7]

***

Stephen Bradley read the article about the kidnapper and his car with considerable alarm and trepidation, acknowledging that the description fitted him to a tee. It supported his belief that someone in the passing car had provided the police

123

with a description of his vehicle. It also confirmed that he had made the right decision to leave Australia and thereby preclude the possibility of being asked to participate in a line-up in front of Freda and Bazil Thorne. His only consolation was that the very next day, Monday 26 September, he and his family were due to sail from Sydney on board the *SS Himalaya*.

***

One day after the publication of the information about the blue Ford Customline, Mr Neville Browne, a tenant at 49 Osborne Road, Manly, contacted the police to tell them that his neighbour, Mr Stephen Bradley, had a foreign accent as well as a car of the same description as the one they were looking for. Once again, the information provided was duly noted in a police running sheet, filed in the investigation archives, and given no special attention.

***

What Stephen Bradley did not know was that during the month that he had been making extensive preparations for his family's covert departure from Australia, a variety of highly skilled forensic scientists had been conducting minute examinations of the items that had been found on, and with, Graeme Thorne's body, and that these had revealed significant pieces of trace evidence that were gradually weaving a web of evidence to identify and trap the kidnapper.

10

LEAVES, SEEDS AND GENERAL VEGETABLE MATTER

The investigation of the kidnapping and murder of Graeme Thorne marked the beginning of a new era of forensic science in Australia. Never before had so many peripheral items of physical evidence from a crime scene been so intensively examined as they were in this case. Many items were of a kind that had not previously featured in forensic scientific examinations. The existence of this unheralded scientific exercise was not disclosed to the public at the time.

The autopsy on Graeme Thorne's body was conducted on 17 August 1960, the day after it had been found at Seaforth, by Government Pathologist Dr John Laing, with the assistance of Dr Clarence Percy, who had inspected the body at the scene where it had been found. Their findings enabled conclusions to be drawn as to the cause of death. Their examination disclosed that there was 'a patch of abrasions' on the right side of Graeme's neck, but no fracture of the hyoid bone, situated at the front of the neck and easily susceptible to injury in the event of strangulation. There were 'scattered surface haemorrhages' inside Graeme's lungs and upper air passages, consistent with asphyxiation. Graeme's stomach was empty, indicating that death had occurred 'at least some hours' after he had eaten his breakfast; however, because the body had been found a considerable time after his death, a more precise timing was not possible from the autopsy alone. Dr Laing found a wound to the back of Graeme's head with an underlying fracture of the skull, indicating the use of 'considerable force'. The battering of Graeme's head had caused a cerebral haemorrhage: bleeding from blood vessels within or around the lining of the brain, thereby indicating that Graeme had still been alive at the time of the blow. Over a period of time, this bleeding within the confines of the skull causes intense pressure on the brain stem, which controls breathing and heartbeat and, without medical intervention, will eventually lead to death. Both Dr Laing and Dr Percy concluded that Graeme's death had been due to either blunt force trauma to the head or asphyxiation, or both.[1]

In order to further the investigation, it was imperative for the police to know whether Graeme had been killed soon after his abduction or whether he had been kept prisoner for any substantial time. To advance this aspect of the case, certain parts of the body and clothing were sent to other experts to ascertain if they could assist.

Professor Neville White, the professor of plant pathology in the Faculty of Agriculture at Sydney University, examined under a microscope a yellow-green mould known as *Aspergillus repens* that had developed on the heels of Graeme's shoes. He discovered that this distinctive mould had reached what is known as the 'sex spore stage' of development. After examining the mean daily temperatures during the weeks between the kidnapping and the finding of the body, Professor White came to the conclusion that the shoes had not been walked on for at least four weeks prior to the body being found. Professor White also examined the socks Graeme had been wearing. Under the microscope, the professor found that they had decomposed from the actions of a primitive nematode – a type of worm. By assessing the number of nematodes on the socks – and again with knowledge of the prevailing temperatures – Professor White determined that the socks had not been walked on for somewhere between thirty-five and forty-five days prior to the body being found. As Graeme had been abducted forty days prior to the discovery of his body, these observations strongly suggested that he had been killed and his body dumped quite soon after his abduction. Deterioration of the body from blowfly larvae indicated death at least three weeks prior to the testing, which supported the estimates derived from the mould and the nematodes.

Other pieces of circumstantial evidence supported the scientific assessment of the timing of Graeme's death. His school tie was still as his mother had tied it just before he left home for school. His coat was still fully buttoned and two handkerchiefs in his trouser pockets were still folded in their laundered state. These additional facts, together with his untouched lunchbox, were indicative of his death having occurred several hours after his abduction. The information about the timing of Graeme's death was disclosed to Bazil and Freda Thorne in the hope that it might assist them to know that their son had not suffered for more than a few hours, however it was not disclosed to the public.

A few days after the autopsy, Detective Sergeant Alan Clarke of the Police Scientific Investigation Bureau carefully examined all of the items found with Graeme's body. His role was as the coordinating crime scene officer, however at the time there was no such position title. He minutely examined each item of physical evidence that had been found at Grandview Grove and made the decision whether it should be passed on to another expert and, if so, to whom.

Extensive enquiries were made about the picnic rug, which disclosed that it was one of approximately 3,000 of its kind manufactured by the Onkaparinga Company in Adelaide. This particular rug showed signs of considerable wear, and a number of its tassels were missing. From both Graeme's clothing and the picnic rug, Detective Sergeant Clarke scraped off tiny specimens of leaves, seeds and general vegetable matter. He took samples of soil from Graeme's coat, trousers, socks, shoes and the scarf that had been wrapped around his neck. Other officers in the Scientific Bureau found hairs on the rug and on Graeme's clothing, which were taken for further examination to Dr Cameron Cramp, a microbiologist at the Medico-Legal Laboratory at the Department of Health in Sydney.

After carefully examining the leaves, seeds and vegetable matter, Sergeant Clarke went to the vacant lot next to 16 Grandview Grove with a botanist from the Royal Botanic Gardens, who confirmed what Sergeant Clarke had suspected – that the plant material did not come from that lot. Sergeant Clarke concluded that it was likely to have come from the location where Graeme had been killed or where his body had been secreted after his death and before it was dumped.

Sergeant Clarke next consulted with another botanist at the Royal Botanic Gardens, Dr Joyce Vickery, to identify the type of plants that the leaves and seeds had come from. Dr Vickery called together all the botanists at the Botanic Gardens and with their combined knowledge they were able to identify the plant material as coming from two varieties of cypress: *Chamaecyparis pisifera* (Sawara cypress) and *Cupressus glabra* (Arizona smooth bark cypress). The former was quite widespread in Sydney, but the latter was rather uncommon. The combination of the two growing in close proximity to each other was likely to be rare.

When the Police Scientific Investigation Bureau officers examined the soil samples taken from Graeme's coat, trousers, the soles of his shoes, and from the knotted section of the scarf around his neck, they noticed that they included minute fragments of a pink-and-white, sand-like substance. One of the investigating police suggested that this might be mortar. Sergeant Clarke took the soil samples to Mr Horace Whitworth, the senior curator at the Geological and Mining Museum in George Street North in the city, who confirmed that the material was indeed limestone mortar. The even distribution of the pink-and-white mortar on the clothing indicated that Graeme's body must have been laid on its back in an area where the mortar was evenly distributed on the surface, suggesting an area under or near to the foundations of a building.

Dr Cameron Cramp conducted a close examination of the hairs found on the picnic rug and Graeme's clothing, and found both animal and human hairs. The animal hairs were microscopically examined and found to have the characteristics of dog hair. The human hairs were of three distinct types, including one that had been treated with a reddish henna rinse.

By the beginning of September 1960, with the identification of the two types of cypress tree, the pink-and-white mortar and the human and dog hairs, police had six significant pieces of information about the man who was most probably the kidnapper. They knew he:

- spoke with a foreign accent
- had the use of a 1955 blue Ford Customline
- had access to a building with pink-and-white mortar
- had access to a building near two varieties of cypress tree
- probably lived with a woman who used a red henna rinse and
- probably had a dog.

In mid-September, the police made the belated decision to focus their enquiries more intensely on the suburbs near to where Graeme Thorne's body and schoolbag had been found. Sergeant Clarke instructed two police officers, Detective Sergeant Mick Coleman and Detective Constable J. Shiel, to conduct a rigorous, street-by-street search of Seaforth and its environs, looking for houses made with pink mortar in combination with the two types of cypress tree. He provided them with a sample sprig from each of the two trees. The two officers conducted a concerted search of the streets of Seaforth and neighbouring suburbs, which occupied them for several weeks, with many sightings of one or two parts of the equation, but never of all three.

Finally, on 3 October, Constable Shiel went to the Balgowlah Post Office, which covered mail deliveries to Seaforth, Clontarf, Balgowlah and adjoining suburbs, and asked all the post deliverymen to keep an eye out when delivering the mail for a house with all three features. Later that very day, an observant postman noticed that number 28 Moore Street, Clontarf, had pink mortar in the brickwork of the foundations and both types of cypress tree in the garden. He immediately notified the police of his discovery, and Sergeant Coleman and Constable Shiel quickly attended the address, where they were thrilled to see that all three characteristics were present. For abundant caution, they asked Dr Vickery to attend the house to verify the identity of the trees, which she did.

Coleman and Shiel reported their findings to their superior officers. Police were given entry to the house by the new owner, Mr Palmer, and a more detailed inspection disclosed that there was easy access through an opening in the rear wall of the garage to a dark, damp alcove within the house foundations. Thankfully, Mr Palmer had not yet got around to cleaning the garage after taking possession of the house nearly three months earlier. Numerous fragments of twigs, seeds and leaves from the two cypress trees had been blown into the garage and the alcove. In the alcove, police could also see abundant fragments of pink-and-white mortar on the bare ground. It was quickly ascertained that the male occupant at the time of the kidnapping, Stephen Bradley, was a man with a foreign accent who had previously been interviewed as a Ford Customline owner. The police were dismayed, however, to learn that Bradley had departed Australia with his wife and children just eight days earlier.

All the characteristics of this house and its previous occupant matched the profile of the killer, and it was only two miles from where the body had been dumped. Surely, this could not all be mere coincidence! Only now did the police revisit the information that had earlier been provided by the Telfords about their neighbour in Moore Street and by Mr Browne about his neighbour in Osborne Road.

The following day, the police went to a Granville car yard, where they found Bradley's Ford Customline. Inside the boot, Detective Sergeant Clarke found a hairbrush with loose hairs, and there were more hairs on the floor inside the car. These were sent to Dr Cramp at the Medico-Legal Laboratory in the Department of Health for comparison with the hairs from the picnic rug. A close inspection of the spare-tyre well in the boot of the car disclosed soil and vegetable matter that appeared visually to be similar to what had been found on Graeme Thorne's clothing and the rug in which his body had been wrapped.

Subsequent testing of the car boot disclosed that if Graeme had been conscious and otherwise unharmed, and if his mouth had not been gagged, there was a sufficient intake of air into the boot to ensure his survival. However, with the scarf around his mouth and the boot lid closed, he was at risk of dying from asphyxiation. The blow to his head created a slow bleed which gradually reduced his capacity to breathe even further, causing Graeme to veer towards death.

On 5 October, Sergeant Clarke took numerous specimens of soil, twigs, leaves, seeds and mortar from the garage and the alcove of 28 Moore Street. He also took possession of a piece of twine he found hanging on the back fence, which appeared to be very similar to the twine that had been wrapped around Graeme's wrists and ankles. On the same day, the Goggomobil previously owned by Stephen Bradley was located and inspected. More hairs were found on the floor of that car, and they also were sent to Dr Cramp. The following day, Detective Sergeant Coleman and Detective Constable Shiel went to Mr Mauer's second-hand furniture shop and took possession of the vacuum cleaner and carpet that Bradley had sold. The vacuum cleaner bag and the carpet contained hairs of several types and colours, which were also forwarded to Dr Cramp.

On 7 October, Dr Cramp examined all of the hairs that had been submitted to him, and found both human and canine hairs. When he compared the canine hairs from Bradley's two cars with those found on the rug and Graeme's clothing, he discovered that both sets of hairs came from the same breed of dog.

On that same day, following information from neighbours at Clontarf that Bradley had owned a Pekinese dog, police were able to locate Cherie, who had been left at Stewart's Veterinary Hospital at Rushcutters Bay pending transfer to England. Dr Cramp collected comparison samples of hair from Cherie and from about ninety other dogs of varying breeds. He compared these to the hairs found on the picnic rug, looking at length, fineness, curve, colour and character. He concluded that it was highly probable that the dog hairs on the rug came from a Pekinese dog and that they were indistinguishable from the hairs taken from Cherie.

The human hairs, which had been found on the picnic rug, on Graeme's clothing and on the scarf around the boy's neck, were compared by Dr Cramp to hairs found in the boot of the Ford Customline, in the Goggomobil, in the vacuum cleaner bag, and on the carpet sold to Mr Mauer. The comparison enabled Dr Cramp to conclude that there were three types of human hair on the body and that they were indistinguishable from the three types of hair found in the Customline, the Goggomobil, the vacuum cleaner bag and on the carpet.

In addition, a red colouration found on several human hairs on the rug was consistent with a henna hair rinse that Magda Bradley had used. Bazil and Freda were kept informed of the progress of the investigation, but it was also explained to them that a difficult and protracted process lay ahead if Bradley was to be apprehended and brought back to Australia to face trial. None of these findings were disclosed to the public.

By this stage – only four days after the discovery of 28 Moore Street, Clontarf – the scientists had weaved a cogent, convincing, circumstantial case against Stephen Bradley. However, the police also wanted direct proof, as the combination of the two types of evidence would be virtually irrefutable. So, on 8 October police showed Freda and Bazil Thorne an array of photographs, which included one of Stephen Bradley. Both were readily able to identify him as the man who had come to their door purporting to be a private enquiry agent on 14 June, about three weeks before Graeme's abduction. This was the first piece of direct evidence, as opposed to circumstantial evidence, to link Stephen Bradley to the kidnapping. On the same day, Cecil Denmeade and his former fiancée – now wife – Dorothea, were shown the same array of photographs and they were able to say that the man they had seen getting out of the blue Ford was 'similar' to the photo of Bradley.

On 12 October, Sergeant Clarke went to the Bradleys' former flat at Manly and located a calico bag tied with string that appeared very similar to the string that had been tied around the picnic rug covering Graeme Thorne's body. Several days later, the Bradleys' former neighbour at Manly, Neville Browne – who three weeks earlier had tried to alert the police to his suspicions about Stephen Bradley – located some loose, processed film negative strips that had been thrown away in the garden behind the block of flats. He handed these over to the police, who printed them. One of the photographs showed Magda Bradley sitting on a rug that was remarkably similar to the one that had been wrapped around Graeme Thorne's body.

Also on 12 October, a police officer flew to Adelaide with the picnic rug to confirm with the manufacturers, Onkaparinga, that it had been made by them. He then flew to Melbourne, where he interviewed Jacob Fogel, who had been friends with Magda while she was married to Gregor Weinberg. Fogel identified the picnic rug as a gift he had given Magda in 1955 when her son, Ross, was born. By now, the police were convinced that they had successfully identified the owner of the rug that had been used by the kidnapper.

Several days later, Sergeant Clarke, along with colleagues from the Police Scientific Bureau, returned to the house in Moore Street, and again closely inspected the garage and alcove. On the garage floor, in among sweepings, they located a thread of woollen material that appeared to be identical to the threads of the tassels on the picnic rug; it should be remembered that the picnic rug wrapped around Graeme Thorne was missing some of its tassels. The noose was tightening even further.

A day or two later, Detective Sergeant Clarke took various pieces of evidence to Malcolm Chaikin, the Professor of Textile Technology at the University of New South Wales. These included: the picnic rug, the twine that had been tied around Graeme's wrists and ankles, the string that had been wrapped around Graeme's body to keep the rug in place, the calico bag with string from the Manly flat, the twine that had been found hanging over the back fence at Clontarf, the piece of tassel from the swept rubbish pile in the garage at Clontarf, and various other items. Professor Chaikin and a team of assistants conducted numerous examinations and tests on these exhibits, from which they concluded that the twine from around Graeme's wrists and ankles was identical to the twine found in the backyard at Clontarf; that the string from around the body was indistinguishable from the string on the calico bag; and that the thread from the garage was identical to the threads in the tassels on the picnic rug.

On 14 October, Mr Horace Whitworth, the curator of the Geological and Mining Museum in Sydney, certified that the pink-and-white mortar in the samples from the garage and alcove at Clontarf was identical to the mortar on the clothing and other items found on Graeme Thorne's body, and also to the material taken from the boot of the Ford Customline.

The police located the firm of removalists that had picked up the Bradleys' furniture from Clontarf on the day of Graeme's kidnapping. One of the men who had done the job that day, Gordon Barker, recalled that Stephen Bradley had not allowed them to go into the garage, which was locked, and instead insisted on bringing out various items from the garage himself.

A Clontarf real estate agent, Roy Burling, recalled that he had shown Stephen and Magda Bradley five homes in late June, and that one of them was at 16 Grandview Grove, Seaforth.

The voluminous and intricate scientific analysis of the trace evidence from the crime scene had convincingly established that Stephen Bradley was responsible for the kidnapping of Graeme Thorne. The scientific evidence implicating him now included: the pink-and-white mortar, the cypress seeds, the dog hairs, the human hairs, the twine, the string and the tassels on the picnic rug. As well as this matrix of scientific evidence, the police also had: the Ford Customline, the identification of Bradley by Freda and Bazil Thorne, the similarity of the man observed by Cecil and Dorothea Denmeade, the identification of the picnic rug by Joseph Fogel, the Bradleys' visit to Grandview Grove to see a house next door to the vacant block of land where the body had been found, and of course Stephen Bradley's European accent. The noose was now very firmly tied around Stephen Bradley's neck. It was just that he didn't know it.

***

On the same day that Dr Cramp was examining all the dog hairs in Sydney – 7 October 1960 – the SS *Himalaya* sailed from Fremantle into international waters of the Indian Ocean, bound for the next scheduled port – Colombo, the capital of Ceylon (now Sri Lanka).

11

INTERNATIONAL WATERS

The P&O-Orient Line was immensely proud of the SS *Himalaya*. It had first gone into service in 1949 and was one of their new, impressive passenger liners in the post-war period, designed to make up for their massive losses during the Second World War. It was not only a splendid and luxurious liner, but also the fastest and largest ship that P&O had ever owned, having a top speed of 25 knots. She was able to cut the time of the trip from the United Kingdom to Bombay by five days and the overall voyage to Australia from thirty-eight days to just twenty-eight.[1] She carried 758 first-class passengers and 401 in tourist class. The voyage from Sydney to England involved brief stopovers in Melbourne, Adelaide and Fremantle, and then the six-day Indian Ocean leg across the equator to Colombo. From there, the journey proceeded via Bombay,

Aden, the Suez Canal, Port Said, Marseilles and Gibraltar to Southampton.

Stephen, Magda and the three children, Paul, Helen and Ross, had the most wonderful time on board the SS *Himalaya*. It had been a long time since they had all been together for such an extended period of time. When they berthed in Melbourne, Adelaide and Fremantle, Stephen insisted that they all stay together on board the ship and not disembark for the few hours that passengers were permitted to go on-shore. They played deck games; they consumed voluminous amounts of food and drink; once the ship headed north from Fremantle, the weather warmed up and the children spent numerous hours playing in the open-deck swimming pool. Never before had they felt such togetherness as they did on this voyage. Stephen was more relaxed than he had been for many months, and Magda seemed to respond positively to the lack of tension emanating from her husband. The children were excited to be on an ocean liner for the first time and pleased to have both their parents' undivided attention.

***

When the *Himalaya* berthed at the three Australian ports en route, Stephen was unable to dispel a sense of unease, and this was why he was reluctant to disembark with the other passengers who were eager to do some sightseeing. Only when they sailed out of Australian territorial waters was he able to fully relax, convinced that he had put Australia and his past behind him, and that a new start in England would enable them to lead a more prosperous life. He believed that it was unlikely that he would ever have to account for what had happened to Graeme Thorne, because now that he was gone, the police could hardly get the direct identification evidence that could link him to the crime. In any event, he would be able to get occasional Australian newspapers in London, and if it looked like the police were close to making an arrest, he could easily convince Magda to go with him to one of the many countries with warm climates that lacked an extradition treaty with Australia.

***

On 8 October 1960, the day after the *Himalaya* left Australian territorial waters, the Deputy Commissioner of Police, Mr Norman Allen, notified the Department of External Affairs in Canberra and the Australian High Commissioner in Ceylon of arrangements already in train to obtain a provisional warrant – designed to justify the holding of a suspect pending a formal extradition request – for the arrest of Stephen Bradley in Colombo. The warrant, charging Bradley with the murder of Graeme Thorne, was issued by a chamber magistrate in Sydney that night and transmitted via Interpol to Ceylon. The Australian warrant had no force outside Australia, but several days later a Colombo magistrate issued a locally enforceable provisional warrant for Bradley's arrest. This was the first step towards having Bradley taken off the *Himalaya* and extradited back to Australia to face trial. Detective Sergeants JH (Jack) Bateman and J Coleman were directed to proceed to Colombo to facilitate the whole process, but due to a faulty plane engine, they did not arrive until 14 October, well after the *Himalaya* had docked and departed. Even in the absence of the Australian police, however, the Ceylonese police were content to arrest Bradley on the local provisional warrant.

By the time the *Himalaya* arrived in Colombo on the afternoon of 10 October, Captain Hugh Slinn had already known for some days that a suspected kidnapper and murderer was on board his liner. The police in Sydney had contacted him by radio to ask him to keep Stephen Bradley under observation. Captain Slinn kept a discreet, but watchful eye on his male passenger and satisfied himself that neither the vessel nor its other passengers were at risk from this man.

***

When the *Himalaya* berthed in Colombo, Magda was desperate to get off the ship, as she was suffering from restlessness, having already been on board for fourteen days, and she was dying to see the capital of exotic Ceylon. The children also were anxious to disembark, because they had heard stories about the wonderful gifts that could be bought very cheaply. Stephen, however, was wary about leaving the ship at all. Magda put it down to nervousness about a foreign country, but when she suggested this explanation to Stephen, he laughed and offered the lame excuse that he just wanted to get to England as quickly as possible.

The *Himalaya* had been in port for barely half an hour, and passengers had not yet been allowed to disembark, when uniformed members of the Colombo Harbour Patrol came on board. Stephen Bradley was buying some curios from native men who had come onto the ship, when a page boy called him to the ship's Purser's office. As he approached the office, he saw a group of men waiting and, with a skip of his heartbeat, instantly knew that they were police. The Harbour Patrol officers placed him under arrest. He was allowed to go briefly to his cabin to pack a few of his personal effects in a battered, brown suitcase. As he was doing so, Magda and the children arrived at the cabin, which now contained some very officious-looking men, most of whom were clearly local police in uniform. The officers read out some papers, but Magda didn't understand what they were saying. Fear and panic seized her, but she managed to keep them in check so as not to unduly scare her children. Stephen asked her to remain on board the ship with the children and to continue their journey, saying that he would rejoin them when the misunderstanding had been cleared up. Magda nodded supportively, but deep down she knew perfectly well that she would be continuing this journey to England without him. As Stephen was escorted out of the cabin carrying his suitcase, Magda wondered whether she or their children would ever see him again.

***

Stephen Bradley was taken to the Ceylon Harbour lock-up, where he was kept overnight. The following morning he appeared briefly in the Colombo Magistrates Court, from where he was transferred to the Magazine Remand Prison, Colombo's main, high-security gaol.

In Sydney the following day, the news of Stephen Bradley's arrest for the murder of Graeme Thorne was splashed across

Bazil Thorne after his television appearance, pleading for the safe return of his son.

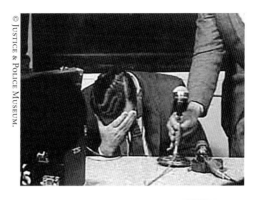

POLICE DEPARTMENT,
SYDNEY.
8th July, 1960.

KIDNAPPING

Have You Seen This Boy?

No. 1.   No. 2.

Your co-operation is urgently sought in locating GRAEME FREDERICK HILTON THORNE, 8½ years of age, who was kidnapped in the vicinty of his home in Edward Street, Bondi at about 8.30 a.m. on Thursday, 7th July, 1960, whilst on his way to school.

The boy is described as 8½ years of age, tall for his age, fair hair well oiled and making it appear brown, fair complexion, heavy build, dressed in grey Scots College uniform with facings of the College colours, being navy and gold, short trousers, light blue shirt, College tie, grey pullover, long socks, black shoes, grey serge cap with Scots College badge of unicorn on front. The uniform worn by Thorne is the same as that shown in photograph No. 2 above.

If you have seen this boy since 8.30 a.m. on Thursday, or have any information of his possible whereabouts, please contact the Police by ringing telephone 2222 or B030 or contact your local Police direct. A GOVERNMENT REWARD OF £5,000 HAS BEEN OFFERED IN CONNECTION WITH THIS MATTER.

The police reward notice.

V. C. N. Blight, Government Printer

C. J. DELANEY,

Commissioner of Police.

Freda and Bazil Thorne.

The Thorne home at
79 Edward Street, Bondi.

The general store at
the intersection of
Wellington Street and
O'Brien Street, Bondi,
near the location of
Graeme Thorne's
abduction.

Magda Bradley.

Stephen Bradley.

The Bradleys' residence, 28 Moore Street, Clontarf.

Stephen Bradley's Ford Customline.

Police and civilians ready to search near the Wakehurst Parkway, where Graeme's school case had been found.

Magda Bradley and the rug.

The garage and entrance to the alcove at 28 Moore Street, Clontarf.

The location of Graeme Thorne's body under a rock in Grandview Grove, Seaforth.

The peeled apple found in Graeme Thorne's lunchbox.

The funeral service for Graeme Thorne at St Mark's Church, Darling Point.

Stephen Bradley is escorted by police after his arrest in Colombo.

Extradition proceedings in the Magistrates Court, Colombo.

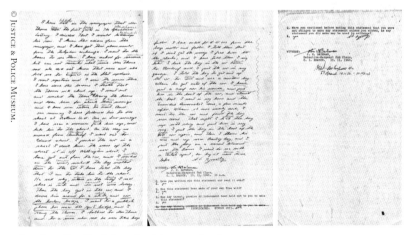

Stephen Bradley's handwritten confession.

Police arrive at the Darlinghurst courthouse with the exhibits for the trial.

The public queuing for entry during Stephen Bradley's trial at Darlinghurst Courthouse.

Frederick Vizzard QC, Public Defender, who represented Stephen Bradley at his trial.

Magda Bradley visits her husband at Long Bay Gaol.

A gaol photograph of Stephen Leslie Bradley two days after his trial in March 1961.

every front page and was the first item on every radio and television news broadcast. The *Daily Mirror* breached the *sub judice* rules by publishing a photograph of Stephen and Magda, which caused fury among police, because it meant that any further identification would be tainted by the public dissemination of the photo. As a result, the Attorney-General commenced contempt-of-court proceedings against the newspaper.

***

Stephen Bradley was severely shaken by the events of 10 October, when he was forcibly escorted from the *Himalaya* and placed into custody at the Ceylon Harbour lock-up. He was particularly disturbed that his wife and children had been forced to witness his humiliation. Surely, he thought, the police could have done it in a more respectful manner that would have allowed him to maintain his dignity. Once in custody, he had a chance to consider his position and think about what options might await him. He was determined that he would admit to nothing and would challenge the arrest at every opportunity. He was not going to make things easier for whoever had caused his family trip to be disrupted. He felt so sorry for Magda, knowing that she would now have to cope with the children on her own so far from home.

The next day, during his first appearance in the Magistrates Court, he was astounded at how many journalists from many parts of the world were in the courtroom, and he realised that this attention in Colombo would translate into extensive publicity in the Australian papers, as well as on radio and television. He was concerned that if the newspapers published his photograph – and their cameramen had taken many at the dock as the police led him away from the ship – Bazil and Freda Thorne, or the woman living above them, might recognise him. He kept reassuring himself that the police in Australia could not have any cogent evidence against him. Identification by Bazil or Freda or the woman upstairs could hardly be enough to prove his involvement in the kidnapping, and his ownership of a Ford Customline was something he shared with numerous other people. He had got out of so many scrapes in the past, and he was confident that his street-smart, winning personality would get him out of this one.

***

By the time of Stephen Bradley's first appearance in the Colombo court, the *Himalaya* was already sailing away from Ceylon bound for Bombay in India. Magda was terribly distressed to be separated from her husband. She pretended to be calm for the sake of the children, who couldn't understand why their father and stepfather was no longer on this exciting journey with them, but in reality she was anything but calm. How would she cope on her own with three children in England? How would she survive financially without Stephen's support? Was Stephen really the monster who had snatched Graeme Thorne off a street in Bondi and murdered him in an attempt to get money from his parents? Was he callous enough to do such a terrible thing to Graeme's poor parents? Was he responsible for his previous wife's death? Did she really know this man at all?

For Stephen's daughter, Helen, and stepsons, Paul and Ross, the startling arrest in Colombo was the beginning of an increasingly traumatic period of their lives. Their idyllic holiday on-board ship had been disrupted and they couldn't fail to notice Magda's tension and worry. They tried to enjoy themselves, but Stephen's absence hung around them like a thick fog.

***

When, about a week after the *Himalaya* sailed from Sydney, Dr Frank Laszlo in Melbourne learnt that Stephen Bradley and his wife had precipitously departed Australia without notifying family and friends, he was enraged – not because of anything to do with the murder of Graeme Thorne, but because his former son-in-law had taken away Frank and his wife Ilse's beloved granddaughter, Helen. The now sixty-six-year-old Frank Laszlo had never liked his son-in-law, especially after his daughter Eva had suddenly died in a suspicious car accident. Over the years he had always harboured a secret belief that somehow, in some way, his son-in-law had been responsible for Eva's death. Frank had never said anything about his suspicions directly to Stephen, because to have done so would have ensured that Frank and Ilse would lose contact with their granddaughter. Even so, after Magda came on the scene, it was a rare event for Frank and Ilse to have substantial contact with Helen, and after the Bradleys moved to Sydney there was even less interaction. However, Frank and Ilse still dearly loved Helen.

When the news first emerged on 11 October that Stephen Bradley had been taken off the ship and arrested in Colombo for the murder of Graeme Thorne, and that the New South Wales government was seeking to extradite him, Dr Laszlo saw an opportunity to retrieve his granddaughter. He ascertained from the Union Steamship company offices in Melbourne that Magda and the three children had remained on the *Himalaya* bound for England. By that time, the ship was already on its way to Bombay.

Dr Laszlo immediately sought legal advice from a specialist firm of lawyers in Melbourne about his chances of forcing Magda Bradley to return Helen to Australia and to hand over custody of the child to Frank and his wife. After all, Magda had no blood relationship with Helen; neither had she formally adopted the child. With Stephen now locked up in a Ceylonese prison, Frank Laszlo held the view that Magda had no legal right to the custody of his granddaughter, that he and Ilse were now the child's next of kin and the obvious ones to take care of her. Frank was advised to obtain an emergency *ex parte* order from a court in Melbourne, and then seek to enforce it overseas. His lawyers advised him that to have any chance of success, he should take steps to enforce the court order in a country that had a British common-law system of justice. Frank was determined to act as soon as possible, rather than waiting until Magda and the children arrived in England. There was insufficient time to obtain a Victorian court order and convey it by air to Bombay before the *Himalaya* left, but there *was* enough time to get it to Aden, a small British colonial outpost on the southern tip of Yemen.

Frank Laszlo's solicitors obtained an urgent court order from the Victorian Supreme Court making Helen a ward of the court and requiring the return of the child to that State.

Frank secured the services of a firm of solicitors in Aden and caught the next plane, armed with multiple copies of the order. He arrived in Aden several days after the *Himalaya*, but in the meantime his solicitors had obtained from the local Supreme Court an interim *habeas corpus* order that prevented the child from leaving the jurisdiction pending a further court order. When served with this order, Magda refused to leave Helen on her own in Aden, so all four of them disembarked.

***

When the *Himalaya* berthed in Aden at 6am on 15 October, Magda was at a very low ebb, being still traumatised by the arrest of her husband in Colombo. As soon as the ship docked, she was called to the Purser's office. Expecting to receive some mail or news from Stephen, she hurried excitedly to that part of the ship, where the Purser handed her the court papers he had been given by a local firm of solicitors acting on behalf of Dr Laszlo. The papers required Magda to produce Helen to the Court that very morning. The *Himalaya* was due to leave Aden at noon that day. Magda was firm in her resolve to resist her husband's former father-in-law's application. Helen was terribly upset at the threat of being separated from the only mother she had ever known, and became increasingly clingy with Magda. When they arrived at the court, Magda was told that nothing could be done until Dr Laszlo arrived in several days' time. Being determined to oppose the application and not prepared to leave Helen with strangers in Aden, Magda returned to the ship, packed up their belongings and disembarked with all three children. The local employees of the Orient Steamship Company assured Magda that once she sorted out her legal problems, she and the children could embark on the next P&O ship that passed through the port bound for England, and that there would be no additional charge. They took up residence at a cheap hotel in Aden, where the local papers reported that their first outdoor venture was to the pool at the Royal Airforce Swimming Club.

Several days later, at a hearing in the Supreme Court of Aden, Dr Laszlo was represented by a senior barrister. Magda appeared with a legal aid solicitor. The newspapers reported:

> *Dr Laszlo arrived at the court this morning with his lawyer, Mr Westby Nunn. Mrs Bradley dressed in a smart black hat and a black and white striped frock, conferred with Mr Horrocks [her solicitor] before and after the case was heard in the chambers of the Chief Justice. She said later: 'If the welfare of the child is at stake, she should be mine. I love her as mine and have cared for her since she was a baby.' Mrs Bradley met Dr Laszlo for the first time today.*[2]

***

When Stephen Bradley heard about Frank Laszlo's attempt to wrestle Helen away from Magda, he was incensed at the effrontery of a grandparent trying to take a child away from the only mother she had ever truly known, and he was sure that Helen would prefer to stay in Magda's care. He immediately sought advice from his counsel in Colombo, and at his suggestion, an affidavit was prepared and forwarded to Magda in Aden informing the Court there that he, as the sole surviving parent, had authorised Magda to take the child to London.

Surely that would be the end of the matter! However, some time later, Stephen changed his mind about where he thought Helen should reside. He reasoned that if he was extradited to Australia, Helen's dependency on him would provide a convincing argument for his release on bail to look after her. So, he countermanded his earlier instructions and communicated his wish that Helen be transferred to a convent in Sydney to await his arrival and release, at which time he could resume his parental responsibilities. According to the newspapers, Bradley's solicitor in Colombo, Mr De Silva, announced:

> *Stephen Bradley wants his wife Magda and her two sons to go to London and his daughter Helen to return to Sydney if he is extradited. Mr De Silva said that Bradley wanted Helen 'kept in a convent in Sydney until such time as his trial is over'. Mr De Silva said he would cable Mrs Bradley today setting out Bradley's request. He said he did not think Dr Laszlo or a court would object to Bradley's desire to have his daughter remain in a convent temporarily.*[3]

***

At the hearing in Aden before the Chief Justice Mr Justice Le Gallais, Dr Laszlo applied for an order of the court that custody of the child be immediately handed over to him so that she could be returned to the State of Victoria where a final custody order would be made. He alleged that Magda's real plan was to take Helen to live in Hungary. Magda's legal aid solicitor, though young and inexperienced, was keen and bright, and he pointed out that none of the parties, including Helen, had the required residency status in Aden that would give the court jurisdiction to make any order affecting this child. The Chief Justice agreed and dismissed Dr Laszlo's application, ordering him to pay Magda's legal costs and her hotel bill.

Frank Laszlo returned to Melbourne empty-handed and bitterly disappointed, but still determined to seek custody of his granddaughter when another opportunity arose. He told reporters on his return to Australia:

> I must have new evidence to place before the court before I can resume the struggle for Helen. At the moment I am too tired to think of any new moves. I must consult my legal advisers in Melbourne. But I will resume the battle as soon as I have something to work on.[4]

***

After the hearing, Magda and the three children remained in a cheap hotel in Aden waiting patiently for the next P&O ship bound for England. Their every move was shadowed by reporters, who repeatedly asked Magda if she had had advance knowledge of her husband's kidnapping plans, so it was impossible for them to relax. Helen became even more fearful that she might be wrested away from Magda, despite assurances from her stepmother that she would never let anyone take the girl away. During that time Magda received a letter from Stephen in which he urged her to continue their journey to London. The P&O Company agreed to allow them to transfer their tickets to the SS *Strathmore*,[5] which was due to arrive on 4 November. Magda and the children remained in Aden for more than three weeks before they boarded the *Strathmore*, bound for Tilbury on the River Thames near London.

✳✳✳

The procedures for an extradition of a suspect from an overseas country to Australia are extremely complex and highly technical.[6] A small error or omission in the documentation can result in the whole process being thwarted. In cases where there is an extradition treaty between Australia and the foreign country, that agreement establishes the steps that are required for an extradition order to be made. However, in 1960, there was no extradition treaty between Australia and Ceylon. The extradition of Stephen Bradley, therefore, depended to a large extent on some old, colonial-era legislation and the goodwill of government authorities in Ceylon. An application for extradition requires an initial hearing in Australia where all the evidence is presented to a magistrate or coroner, who is required to collate and authenticate the prosecution case and then certify that there is sufficient evidence of a criminal offence to warrant the extradition. The magistrate's finding is then transmitted to the local State authorities who endorse the request for extradition, and then relayed to the Federal Department of External Affairs, which advises the Governor-General whether or not to make the formal request for extradition. The request is then sent to the appropriate government department in the foreign country, which then commences proceedings in its own magistrates court to assess whether the police brief from the overseas country warrants an extradition order being made.

Both court hearings fulfil an important role in screening the strength of the case against the suspect.

The first part of the process of extraditing Stephen Bradley involved an extradition hearing in Sydney. On 17 October 1960, Magistrate A Hodgson opened the hearing at the Central Court of Petty Sessions in Liverpool Street.[7] The proceedings were extensively covered by the media. The *Sydney Morning Herald* reported:

> *When the hearing began spectators, predominantly elderly and middle-aged women, jostled for good positions at the rear of the courtroom and defied police requests to leave some seats vacant. A crowd of about 300 stood in Liverpool Street, outside the court, to watch figures in the case leave during the luncheon break.*[8]

Sixty prosecution witnesses were called over three days by Sergeant Don Goode, appearing for the police. As is usually the case in the initial stages of an extradition hearing, Stephen Bradley was not represented, so there was no cross-examination of the witnesses. The witnesses included Freda Thorne, who tearfully identified Graeme's school case, schoolbooks and raincoat, and confirmed that she had peeled an apple for his lunch and wrapped the skin back around the fruit, as she always did. When shown the tie found on Graeme's body, she said, 'That was the way I tied Graeme's tie that morning'. She identified photographs of Stephen Bradley as being the man who had come to her home on the evening of 14 June enquiring about a Mr Bognor. On the third day of the hearing, Magistrate Hodgson ruled that the police had made out a *prima facie* case against Bradley and that the evidence raised 'a strong, probable presumption of guilt' for the murder of Graeme Thorne.

The next step involved the papers being relayed to the State Government of New South Wales. All the witnesses' statements and evidence that had been presented to the Magistrates Court in Sydney were collated into an extradition brief, and each page was signed by Magistrate Hodgson and the New South Wales Minister of Justice, the Honourable Norman John (Jack) Mannix.

The brief was then forwarded to the New South Wales Executive Council, consisting of the Governor, Sir Eric Woodward, the Minister of Justice, and the Attorney-General, the Honourable Robert Reginald (Reg) Downing. After Sir Eric had signed the papers, the next step involved their transmission to the Federal Government in Canberra. The physical task of transporting the papers was delegated to Detective Sergeant Brian Doyle, who had been assigned the task of travelling to Ceylon with the extradition brief. In Canberra, Doyle had to deal with the Department of External Affairs, the Attorney-General's Department and the Commonwealth Crown Solicitor's Office. The final signature obtained was that of the Governor-General of Australia, Lord Dunrossil. Finally, Doyle returned to Sydney and obtained authenticated copies of the relevant legislation from the Clerk of the New South Wales Parliament. All of this was accomplished in an unprecedentedly short three days, and on 21 October Sergeant Doyle boarded a plane for Colombo with a suitcase full of certified documents, exhibits and a formal request from the Commonwealth of Australia to the Government of Ceylon for the extradition of Stephen Leslie Bradley.

Doyle's departure was covered by every news organisation in the country. The whole nation was on edge lest the man who was suspected of committing this vile crime might evade justice by having slipped away from Australia just a few days before the police could identify him. Bazil and Freda Thorne were desperate that the man who had so cruelly murdered their son might slide away from the grasp of the law.

When Sergeant Doyle arrived in Colombo, he served on Bradley's solicitor a copy of the formal request signed by the Australian Governor-General, the extradition brief and the exhibits. The original documents were formally presented to Mr Justice Sansoni in the Supreme Court of Ceylon. The judge made a finding that the provisions of the Ceylonese *Fugitive Offenders Act*, 1881, had been complied with, setting the scene for an extradition hearing in the Colombo Magistrates Court.

***

When Stephen Bradley was served with the extradition papers containing the statements and evidence of more than sixty witnesses, he was astounded by the size of the brief against him. He pored over the evidence, reading each statement carefully and marking many with his comments. It came as a genuine shock to him to read in the post-mortem report that Graeme Thorne had sustained a fractured skull. He had previously thought that the boy must have died from a lack of oxygen in the boot – something that he had not anticipated before the kidnapping. He realised immediately the significance of this new information in relation to the murder charge on which the police were seeking to extradite him. As he worked his way through the brief, he became overwhelmed at the extent to which the police had gone to secure a case against him. In a sense he felt that they had persecuted and victimised him by going to so much effort to 'stitch him up'.

In the Magazine Remand Prison, Bradley was in custody with five men who had been charged with the 1959 assassination of the Ceylonese Prime Minister, Solomon Bandaranaike. One of the prisoners, Ossie Corea, who had at one time been a Ceylonese Customs and Excise Inspector, was alleged to have supplied the gun used in the shooting.[9] Bradley became particularly friendly with Corea and spent more time with him than with anyone else. After going through the brief, Bradley gave the papers to Corea, who had offered to read them and – with the benefit of his training as an inspector – provide an opinion on the case against Bradley. True to his word, over a number of days Corea read the brief, and then ventured the opinion that Bradley had no chance of beating the murder charge. Bradley quickly discounted this view, rationalising that his gaol friend came from a country where prosecution evidence was meekly accepted in the court system, whereas in Australia the courts had a healthy scepticism of police.

Bradley recognised that if he was to extricate himself from his current, dire situation, he had to change tack. He prided himself on his readiness to adapt to altered circumstances – a quality that derived from his traumatic experiences during the war. The former inspector's advice had convinced him that it was useless to deny that he had been involved in the abduction, but he could use an admission of that as an opportunity to provide a convincing defence that the boy's death had been a terrible, unforeseen accident. Bradley had read the newspaper articles explaining that there was no offence for kidnapping on the statute books of New South Wales, so he was optimistic that if he could avoid responsibility for Graeme's death he might receive a light sentence for some minor offence for taking the boy away. Perhaps he would be joining Magda and the children in a shorter time than everyone had imagined. This became his overriding plan of action.

***

Soon after Bradley's arrest in Colombo, a Queen's Counsel, Mr Diyasena Sudhira Jayawickrema, and a solicitor, Mr Anthony De Silva, offered to act for him without any payment (*pro bono*). They advised their client not to speak to the Australian police who had arrived in Colombo, and Bradley readily accepted their advice. The extradition hearing in the Colombo Magistrates Court began on 31 October 1960. Sergeant Doyle was the only witness, and through him the entire extradition brief was tendered. Mr Jayawickrema QC argued that the evidence did not establish a strong presumption of guilt, as required by the *Fugitive Offenders Act*, but the Magistrate, Mr Amerasinghe, found otherwise, and made an order recommending Bradley's extradition. Although Bradley had a right of appeal, he elected not to exercise it, as the conditions in the Magazine Prison were oppressive and the food not to his liking. Bradley instructed Mr De Silva to send a cable to his solicitor in Sydney, Mr Richard Holt of Gilbert M Johnstone & Co, warning him of his impending arrival in Sydney. At the conclusion of the fifteen-day appeal period, the Governor-General of Ceylon, Sir Oliver Goonitelleke, signed a formal order directing the prison authorities to release Stephen Bradley into the custody of Detective Sergeants Bateman and Doyle.

The progress of the extradition proceedings and the conditions under which Stephen Bradley was held in Colombo were the subject of enormous public interest in Australia. The *Sydney Morning Herald* reported details of his gaol cell, the prison security, his diet and even the books he had borrowed from the gaol library. The reports included:

Bradley's thick-walled cellblock is one of the coolest places in Colombo, which is sweltering in pre-monsoon temperatures in the nineties. But warders say he seems to relish sunshine and spends most mornings sunbaking.[10]

***

Sergeants Bateman and Doyle had to conduct extensive negotiations with the British airline company BOAC (British Overseas Airways Corporation), because the airline was reluctant to take on-board a prisoner who was suspected of committing a violent offence and could pose a risk to other passengers or to the safety of the plane. The airline felt that the main risk was that Bradley, in a fit of violence, might break one of the plate perspex windows of the plane, causing a sudden, catastrophic depressurisation. The airline finally agreed to take him on-board but they insisted on several requirements: Bradley had to sit in an aisle seat with one of the two police officers between him and the window, and the other officer on the opposite aisle seat; Bradley's hands were to be cuffed together at all times while the plane was in the air, with another set of handcuffs attaching him to the buckle of his seatbelt; the detectives were to remain awake at all times while the plane was in the air and could not leave Bradley at any time during the journey; Bradley was not to wear shoes in the plane; while he was allowed to eat, he was not permitted to have a knife while there were other passengers about. Only upon acceptance of these conditions did the airline agree to transport Stephen Bradley back to Australia to face trial for murder.

12

CROSSING THE DIVIDE

At 7.20am on 18 November 1960, Detective Sergeants Doyle and Bateman arrived at the Magazine Remand Prison in Colombo and, after signing a receipt for Stephen Bradley's person and another for his belongings, they formally took possession of their prisoner. They were escorted by local police on the thirty-mile trip to Colombo airport, where Bradley and his escorts were taken to a special private lounge to await the arrival of the BOAC Comet from India, which was to transport them to Australia. At Colombo airport, Bradley made it clear that he did not wish to discuss with the police anything about the crime with which he had been charged. Once in the aircraft, according to a *Herald* correspondent:

Bradley sat quietly reading newspapers and eating chicken and salad sandwiches on the 5 hours and 40 minutes journey from Colombo to Singapore. He hung his woollen Bermuda jacket over the back of his seat and kicked off his shoes. During a 45 minute stop in the Malayan capital, Kuala Lumpur, Bradley was served with fried fish, chips, peas, bread rolls, iced water and fruit. When Bradley visited the washroom, his handcuffs were unlocked unobtrusively and one of the detectives casually followed him to the door, where he stood until Bradley emerged. When a sari-clad hostess gave Bradley a form which, under Australian quarantine regulations must be completed by passengers, Sgt Doyle instructed Bradley to write his address as 'care of CIB, Sydney'.[1]

The police had chosen this particular flight because it was the only one between Colombo and Sydney without any overnight stopovers in foreign countries. This flight did have landings in Kuala Lumpur and Singapore, but they were only brief. The police escorting Bradley back to Australia had obtained special permission from the airline and the Australian Civil Aviation Department in Canberra to remain on the plane during these stopovers. The reason for this unusual procedure was that the police and the Australian authorities feared that if Bradley disembarked from the plane in a foreign country, his lawyers could insist upon another extradition hearing in that country. While he remained on the BOAC plane, he was technically under the British flag and not amenable to be served with any local legal documents. Arrangements were made with Qantas employees working at each of the two stopover airports to come onto the plane and cater to any needs of the escorting police or Bradley.

It was only while the plane was on the ground and all the other passengers had disembarked that Bradley was permitted to eat hot food with a knife and fork and to move within the plane.

Despite all of the intricate planning and arrangements that had been made for the long flight back to Sydney, an unforeseen and unforeseeable event occurred during the stopover in Singapore that threatened to bring the whole exercise to a standstill. A traffic-handling superintendent of Malayan Airlines, Mr R Tedd, came aboard the plane to check Bradley's passport. Not wanting to get off the plane, the police insisted that the officer take the passport away to check it. About an hour and a half later, when the plane was due to depart, the superintendent and the passport were nowhere to be seen. Detective Sergeant Doyle made a calculated decision that the plane should take off, even though they did not have Bradley's passport. The next landing was at Darwin, and Doyle was confident the absence of the passport would present little, if any, problem when they arrived. It was later ascertained that Mr Tedd had wandered off and forgotten that he had the passport. The Customs Department in Singapore made sure that the passport was forwarded to Australia on the next plane.

***

Detective Sergeant Jack Bateman had been in the CIB since 1945, and he prided himself on having a 100 per cent success rate in solving murders. He was known among his colleagues as 'Father Confessor' because of his ability to befriend criminals and convince them to admit to their crimes. He was a brilliant and utterly professional investigator who would use his intelligence to identify crooks, give them time to talk, and then use the information against them in court. Detective Sergeant Bateman described his reaction on meeting Bradley for the first time:

> *I was prepared for an ogre dripping blood – a man I could loathe on sight. Instead I met an intelligent, personable, well-spoken man who seemed suave, mild and inoffensive. How could he have done it?*[2]

On the flight from Colombo to Singapore, neither Bradley nor the two police officers said much. However, on the flight between Singapore and Darwin, Bradley's mood seemed to change for the better. Perhaps something about the proximity of the Australian mainland caused him to relax as he began to chat with Sergeant Bateman about his experiences in the Colombo gaol system, telling him that he had lost a stone in weight during the thirty-eight days he had been in custody. Bradley then moved to more personal topics, explaining how the Germans had nearly killed him in Hungary during the war and describing the agony he had gone through when his second wife had been killed in a car accident in Melbourne. Sergeant Bateman began to feel sympathy for his prisoner and the hardships he had seemingly faced in life. So friendly did they become that Bateman asked Bradley to sign his autograph book – and Bradley complied. After the plane landed in Darwin, and then took off for the long flight across Central Australia to Sydney, Bradley's mood improved even further. It was as though the closeness of his home city brought him some relief and comfort. What lay in store for him once he landed seemed, in that moment, irrelevant.

They were about forty minutes away from Sydney, many thousands of feet in the air above the Great Dividing Range which follows the eastern seaboard about 70 miles inland, with Bradley handcuffed to his seatbelt, flanked on both sides by two burly police officers and approaching the destination where his fate would be decided, when he unexpectedly began to speak about the charge he was facing. He introduced the topic to Sergeant Doyle in a seemingly innocuous fashion:

'Who will interview me in Sydney?' he asked.

'Perhaps Bateman and I. Perhaps no one,' replied the detective. There followed many minutes of silence.

Bradley said: 'I am pleased to be back in Australia', followed by another lengthy period of silence. Then, completely out of the blue, Bradley astounded his escort and said: 'I have done this thing to the Thorne boy. What will happen to me?'

Always the utter professional, Detective Doyle put on his formal policeman's voice and said to his prisoner: 'In view of that, I have to warn you that anything you say, even on the plane, may be taken down and used in evidence against you. Do you understand that?'

'Yes,' said Bradley. 'I know. I have wanted to talk to tell you.'

Sergeant Doyle then called over Sergeant Bateman and said in a voice loud enough for Bradley to hear: 'He tells me he has done this thing to the Thorne boy.'

Bateman said: 'All right, we will be back in Sydney shortly, and you can tell us about it then, if you want to.'

Many less experienced police officers would have encouraged Bradley to tell all he knew right then and there. But Sergeants Bateman and Doyle had been involved in too many criminal trials in which oral confessions had been disputed and aggressive defence counsel had alleged impropriety or fabrication during vigorous cross-examination. They were determined that this case would proceed by the book and that no defence counsel would help Bradley squirm out of his confession by making false allegations that it was a 'police verbal'. Too many juries in the past had been left in doubt when it was the word of one police officer, or even two, against the word of the accused.

The journey to Sydney continued in silence.

***

Stephen Bradley had been instructed by his legal counsel in Colombo not to talk to the two police officers, which from his point of view made the long plane journey a bore. Between Singapore and Darwin, it was Sergeant Bateman who began chatting with him. Bradley immediately sensed that the officer was attempting to ingratiate himself, and so he decided to play along with him in a teasing fashion. It amused him that Bateman was unaware that he had seen through the officer's blatantly obvious tactics. Bateman asked him about his origins, so Bradley fed him the usual stories about his miraculous escapes during the war. Then they moved to his early years in Australia, and Bradley gave him a melodramatic account of his misery after his wife Eva's death in a car accident in Melbourne. The officer then faked an interest in how he had been holed up in the Magazine Prison, so Bradley gave him an accurate account of the atrocious conditions there. The most laughable part of their interaction was when Bateman asked him for his autograph – as though he were a film star. How could he refuse such fake flattery dressed up as a serious request? He joined in the game and sarcastically wrote, 'Good luck, Jack, until I see you again. Leslie Bradley'.

During the flight from Darwin to Sydney, Bradley couldn't help but have a bit of fun at the officers' expense. The men were obviously intent on extracting a confession from him, and Bradley couldn't resist giving them a small taste of what they so clearly wanted – just to see their reaction – and then to pull back, leaving them frustrated. After all, he was giving the police nothing that they weren't going to get later during a formal recorded interview, when he would advance the defence he had been planning during the weeks he had languished in Colombo. He was quite surprised by the officers' calm, officious reaction when he dropped the bombshell. Instead of pumping him for more information, Sergeant Doyle gave him the traditional warning and both officers refused to discuss the matter further. Bradley was unimpressed by their pretentious professionalism, and disappointed that it put an end to the entertaining game he had been playing with them. Did they really think they had cajoled him into a confession against his better judgement?

⋆⋆⋆

At 8:07am on Saturday, 19 November 1960, the BOAC Comet arrived at Kingsford Smith Airport in Sydney. Stephen Bradley was taken off the plane through the crew's gangway. The *Sydney Morning Herald* reported that about 200 people watched in silence as he disembarked and was whisked away in a police vehicle to the central police station in the city. The paper stated:

Twelve police and four detectives guarded the edge of the tarmac as the giant BOAC Comet pulled in at 8:07am. Eight other police stood on watch in the doorways of the international terminal lounge and on nearby footpaths and roads. Normal customs formalities for Bradley and Detective Sgts Bateman and Doyle were completed in the airline itself. One of the largest batteries of TV, movie and Press cameras ever seen at the airport recorded the scene.[3]

***

On board the P&O liner SS *Strathmore*, Magda and the children had a difficult time dealing with Stephen's absence. The majority of the passengers were Australians who recognised them as soon as they embarked in Aden. While some people were kind to them, others clearly snubbed them as though they were lepers, so Magda largely remained in their cabin and avoided contact. Whenever the ship berthed – at Suez, Port Said, Naples and Marseilles – numerous reporters came on board wanting to interview and photograph her. In Marseilles, Magda was pursued by reporters as she made her way to a dockside telephone where she tried unsuccessfully for many hours to make a long-distance call to Australia.

On the very same day that Stephen Bradley was driven through the heavy concrete entrance portal of the Central police station in Sydney, Magda Bradley arrived with the three children on the *Strathmore* at the port of Tilbury on the Thames River, just 25 miles from London. The synchronicity and dissonance of both members of this couple arriving at their destination at the same time, but on opposite sides of the globe and in vastly different circumstances, was not lost on the media of either continent. In order to give the reporters the slip, the ship's crew had arranged for Magda and the children to disembark at the Tilbury docks before the other passengers. However, word of the ruse quickly spread, and in no time Magda was surrounded by a bevy of more than thirty newspaper reporters from around the world, who again assailed her with questions suggesting advance knowledge of the kidnapping, which she assiduously ignored. Her seventeen pieces of luggage were quickly loaded into a taxi and she and the children were then driven at high speed to London, where she booked into a small, nondescript hotel near Regents Park, thinking that she had evaded the media pack. As soon as they had completed the formalities at the hotel, she sent a telegram to Stephen in Sydney: 'The children and I have arrived safely. Keep smiling.'

Within hours, the newspapers had discovered Magda's location and were camped in the street outside the hotel, causing the proprietors to complain to her about 'all these Pressmen hanging about'. Magda is reported to have said:

> *I'm sure even Princess Margaret doesn't have as many as that*
> *following me. I am hoping their interest will die down and*
> *I do not intend to see any more newspapermen. I realise now I*
> *should have got off the ship in the normal way and talked to*
> *the Press there. All the weekend I will stay in my flat.*[4]

However, the children were very restless after the long sea voyage and in deference to their wishes she took them for a walk in Regents Park, where news photographers were constantly snapping at them. When she asked one of the reporters for information about Stephen, she was shown a newspaper report about his departure from Colombo. On reading it, she remarked:

> *Poor Steve, how he must be suffering without me. I'm sure I could help him such a lot if I was in Sydney with him. It was his wish that I come on with the children, although there were times today when I wished I was back in Australia. Steve and I did not have time to say much to each other when he was arrested. Before he left the boat he said to me, 'Don't worry, darling. Look after the children.' Please tell Steve we are all well.*[5]

When asked by the reporters whether she would be interested in any approaches from Hungarian sympathisers in London, she replied:

> *I may have been born in Hungary, but I am now an Australian with a British passport and free to come and go as I please. Anyway, I don't need any help. We are quite well off.*[6]

In fact, Magda was not well-off at all – either financially or emotionally – and she did reach out for help. On the second day after their arrival, she rang her Uncle Leslie, an orthopaedic surgeon who lived in London just a few blocks from where they were staying. She explained to him that although she was not in need of money, she would appreciate moral support and advice about the children's schooling – particularly Ross's. Her aunt then intervened and took over the phone, emphatically telling Magda that they were very sorry but she should not disturb them with her worries, insisting that Magda should not get too close to them because they could not afford to have their names in the newspapers. Magda begged her aunt to allow her to see her uncle, because she was desperate and lonely in a big, foreign city, but her aunt refused. A few days later, Magda wrote a plaintive letter to her uncle Leslie, requesting contact and advice. He replied with an envelope containing merely a newspaper cutting about Stephen and a list of flats and agents, with a few impersonal words written by hand on the edge of the cutting. Magda was devastated by the rejection from one of the very few members of her family who had survived the Holocaust.

***

Meanwhile, at the Central police station in Sydney, after being briefly placed in a holding cell, Stephen Bradley was brought into an interview room at the CIB with Sergeants Doyle and Bateman. He felt a mixture of emotions at this point. He was relieved to be back in Australia and no longer in custody in a third-world country. He was concerned about his wife and their children, but he trusted Magda to do the right thing and look after them well. His solicitor, Mr Holt, had not yet arrived, but was on his way. Bradley had had a lot of time while in custody in Colombo to think about what he would, and would not, say to the police once he arrived in Sydney, and so he had not the slightest reluctance to be interviewed. Bradley realised that whatever he told the police in this interview would feature prominently at his trial, so now was the time to weave into his story some vindicating facts that would exonerate him for the murder, diminish his overall culpability and provide support when he came to be sentenced. He did not need to wait for a solicitor to advise him before speaking to the police, because he knew better than any lawyer what his defence would be.

By this stage, Stephen Bradley was convinced that Graeme Thorne's death had been a tragic accident – and not his fault – and so he was in no way driven by guilt to unburden himself to the police. Rather, his decision to speak to them was a calculated one that he had made earlier in Colombo. While incarcerated, he had realised that it was in his best interests to admit that he had taken Graeme from Bondi, that he had made the ransom call to the Thornes' home that morning, and that he had kept the boy prisoner during the day with no intention of harming him. He would explain that he had secreted Graeme in the boot of his car and, having dealt with the removalists, returned to the car to find – to his horror – that the boy was dead. He had then been forced to dispose of the body, which he did in a rather haphazard way because he was so disturbed by this unexpected turn of events.

After disposing of the body, he had made a further call to the Thornes' home, and then accepted the inevitable termination of the ransom venture. He would explain to the police that if everything had gone according to plan, Graeme would have been safely home and tucked up in bed on the same night as his abduction. He was convinced that he could convey to the police his lack of responsibility for Graeme's death and how it had all been a tragic misadventure for which he was not to blame. Surely, they would understand that to successfully carry out his plan to get the ransom money it had been in his best interests to keep the boy alive. He would tell them that he was still mystified as to how or why Graeme had died, but presumably the boy had hit himself on the head within the confines of the boot. In the absence of any direct evidence, how could the police prove otherwise? He would make a point of not showing any remorse for the boy's death, because that would be interpreted as guilt.

He had gone over this story in his mind many times as he whiled away the hours of confinement in Colombo between extradition hearings and as he waited to be handed over to the Australian police. Now that he was in police custody in Sydney, if he was to delay communicating these exculpatory facts and chose instead to wait until his trial before disclosing them, it would no doubt be suggested by the prosecutor that he had invented them purely for the benefit of the court hearing. It would therefore be best to advance his carefully crafted version now.

***

Sergeant Doyle began the interview session by again giving Bradley the traditional caution, and then commenced to question him:[7]

Doyle: You said on the plane you did this thing to the Thorne boy?
Bradley: Yes. I have put him in the boot of the Customline before the furniture men came. I didn't see him again until it was dark and he was dead. I have thrown his things away near Bantry Bay and put his body on a vacant allotment.
Doyle: Was it you who rang the Thorne home demanding £25,000 and threatening to feed him to the sharks if they did not pay?

Bradley: Yes. But I did not know it was a policeman until I was in the Magazine Gaol [in Colombo].
Doyle: Did you ring again?
Bradley: Yes, but I read the big write-up in the afternoon papers at Balgowlah and I got very frightened, so I have not said much and I have hung up quick.
Doyle: The boy had a fractured skull. Did you hit him?
Bradley (emphatically): No, I did not hit the boy.
Doyle: What did you use the scarf for?
Bradley: I put it in his mouth to stop his calling out noise – not on his neck as the newspapers say.

Doyle then asked him questions about the previous visit to the Thornes' home. Bradley admitted that he had gone to their home posing as a private investigator, but he could not remember using the name Bognor. Feeling embarrassed to admit that the real reason for the visit was that he had been unable to contact them on the phone number provided by the exchange, he offered a flimsy explanation: 'I have wanted to see both the mother and father. I don't remember what name I used. Mrs Thorne sent me upstairs. I went up to that flat in chance Mrs Thorne watched me.'

Doyle then quizzed Bradley on the interview that he had conducted with him at the Nutt & Muddle factory on 24 August. Bradley explained: 'It was all lies. What I have told you today is the truth.'

At this point Sergeant Bateman took over the questioning, asking Bradley to start at the beginning and tell the whole story. This was all Bradley needed to launch into an exhaustive explanation of what had happened and how Graeme Thorne had accidentally died. He related his version in a matter-of-fact way, as though he were speaking about a book he had read or a film he had seen. He began:

It is a long story. I read in the paper where Mr Thorne won the Opera House. His address was in the paper: 79 Edward Street, Bondi, and I wanted money. I went out to Edward Street to see number 79, and three or four mornings I went out to Edward Street to see what the boy did each morning. Each time he has walked down and went to the school with a lady in the car. One morning I followed them to the school at Bellevue Hill. One night I went out to the house and spoke to Mrs Thorne. I saw Mr Thorne at the same time. I wanted to know them both. Mrs Thorne has sent me to the flat upstairs. I went up to the flat in chance Mrs Thorne watched me.

Bradley then moved to the day of the kidnapping:

Then the next was the kidnap. I went out there in the Custom-line between 8 and 8.30. The boy came down, and I have told him that the lady is sick and that I am to take him to school. The boy got in the car. He sat in the front with me.

At this point Bradley painted an extraordinarily benign picture of the kidnapping that neither of the two police officers believed:

I drove him around Bondi and Kings Cross for a while and then over the bridge. I keep telling him that I am to pick up some other boys too. I drove over to the Spit and I rang up from

a public telephone box. I rang Mrs Thorne for the £25,000.
Then I drove him to the house in Moore Street. I drove the car
into the garage. I got out and walked to the back near the boot,
and I told him to get out, and that I would now then take him
to see the other little boy. He got out and I pushed him into
the boot and closed the door. The door locks automatically.
The furniture men arrived a few minutes later. It was after
my wife and children have gone on their holiday. They flew
to Hayman Island [sic], you know. The furniture men were
there all day.

Bradley knew that what he was about to say was the decisive
part of the interview and would play a critical role in the
outcome of his case:

Several times I went into the garage and carried out some
parcels for the furniture men, but I did not let them go in there.
I did not speak to the boy again, but I hear the noise of him
hitting his shoe like this …

At this point, Bradley lightly kicked three or four times with
the tip of his shoe against the leg of the table in the CIB interview room. He then continued:

The furniture men were there all day. I read the big news
write-up in the papers. I bought the afternoon papers at
Balgowlah and I got very frightened. Very late in the after-
noon, just on dark, I went to the car. The boy was dead – quite
dead. I got him out and tied his legs with string to carry him
easy, and I put him under the house. Later I got him out and

wrapped him in the rug and put him back in the boot. I drove over to near Bantry Bay and I have thrown his cap and case and things away. Then I have come back and put him on the vacant allotment next to the house the estate agent showed me to buy. Then I ring up again.

Sergeant Bateman then quizzed Bradley on some of the details of this account:

Bateman: Do you say that you did not go to the boy from the time when you say you first pushed him into the boot before the furniture men came until it was dark?
Bradley: Yes.
Bateman: The boy had a fractured skull. Did you hit him with something?
Bradley: No, but I think he hurt his head on the spare tyre.
Bateman: Did you pull the boy into the car at Bondi?
Bradley: No, I have told him the lady is sick, and he got in the front with me.
Bateman: Did the boy complain or protest when you did not take him to the school?
Bradley: No, I keep telling him that I am to pick up some other boys too.
Bateman: What about the scarf and the twine?
Bradley: I put the scarf around his mouth to stop his call out noise before I push him into the boot. The string came later.
Bateman: The rug was your own?
Bradley: Really Weinberg's and my wife's, but call it ours.
Bateman: Was your wife associated with you in this matter?
Bradley (emphatically): No, she and the children had gone.

Bateman: Were you associated with any other person in this matter?

Bradley: No, I was on my own.

When Bradley was informed that there were witnesses who claimed they could identify him in a line-up, he told the police that he did not want to participate in such a procedure, saying: 'Please don't line me up. I am the man who has done this thing, so don't bring the people to see me. There is no need.' He was, however, prepared to assist the police by showing them the route he had taken with Graeme in the Customline, and where he had disposed of the boy's body and belongings.

Sergeant Bateman then asked Bradley whether he was prepared to make a written statement about the matter. This was a standard request after an oral police interview that was generally answered in the negative, because most interviewees felt that they had done quite enough in answering questions orally. Bradley, however, as an educated man, readily agreed to create a written account in his own words. He was given a pen and paper and he wrote out in his own handwriting a two-page confession as follows (using Bradley's spelling):

I red in the newspaper that Mr. Thorne won the first prize in The Operahouse Lottery. So I desided that I would kidnap his son. I knew ther adress from the newspaper, and I have got their phone number from the telephone exchange. I went to the house to see them. I have asked for someone but cannot remember what name. Mrs. Thorne said she did not know that name and she told me to enquire in the flat upstairs.

I went upstairs and I seen the woman there. I have done this because I though that the Thornes will check up. I went out and watched the Thorne boy leaving the house and seen him for about three mornings and I have seen where he went. And one morning I have followed him to the school at Bellevue Hill. One or two mornings I have seen a womman pick him up, and take him to the school. On the day we moved from Clontarf I went out to Edward Street. I parked the car in a street I don't know the name of the street it is off Wellington Street. I have got out from the car, and I waited on the cornor, untill the boy walked down to the car.

I have told the boy that I am to take him to the shool. He sed why, where is the lady. I sed she is sick and can not come today. Then the boy got in the car, and I drove him around for a while, and over the harbour bridge. I went to a public phone box near the spit bridge and I rang the Thornes. I talked to Mrs. Thorne and then to a man who sed he was the boys father. I have asked for £25,000 from the boys mother and father. I told them that if I don't get the moneys I feed him to the sharks, and I have told them I ring later.

I took the boy in the car home to Clontarf and I put the car in my garage. I told the boy to get out of the car to come and see another boy. When he got out of the car I have put a scarf over his mowth, and put him in the boot of the car, and slamed the boot. I went into my house and the Furniture Removalist came, a few minutes after. When it was nearly dark, I went to the car and found the boy was dead.

That night I tied the boy up with string and put him in my rug. I put the boy in the boot of the ford car again, and them I throw his case and toys out near Bantry Bay, and I put the boy on a vacant lotmount near the house I went to see with a Estate Agent, to buy it some time before.

Bradley duly signed this statement and his signature was witnessed by Detective Sergeant Bateman. Following this, Detective Inspector Windsor, an independent officer, was called into the room to ask some formal questions to verify with Bradley that his written confession had been made voluntarily.

It was only after this written confession had been completed that Bradley's Sydney solicitor, Mr Richard Holt from the law firm of Gilbert M Johnstone and Co,[8] arrived at the CIB and came into the interview room. In Bradley's presence, Sergeant Doyle said:

Mr Holt, as you probably are aware, we have brought Bradley back from Colombo this morning, and later on he will be formally charged before a Magistrate with the murder of Graeme Thorne. He has written out in his own handwriting quite voluntarily and freely a full statement in connection with the Thorne matter.

Looking at Bradley, Sergeant Doyle then asked him: 'Is that correct?' to which Bradley replied: 'Yes.' The statement was then provided to Mr Holt to read, and the police left the room to allow the solicitor to confer privately with his client. About ten minutes later, Mr Holt invited the police back into the room. Sergeant Doyle then said:

He has told us that he is prepared to go with us and point out where he put the boy's body, where he picked him up from, and so on, and he has told us to that he does not wish to be lined up for identification.

Mr Holt was then given access to a telephone in order to consult with a barrister. On returning to the interview room, arrangements were made for Mr Holt to communicate with the police later that day about his client's further assistance to the police.

***

During the oral interview, when Stephen Bradley advanced the explanation that Graeme Thorne might have hit his head on the spare tyre, he couldn't help but notice the looks of incredulity on the faces of the two detectives, and he realised just how lame the excuse really was – and that he could do better. By the time he came to make the handwritten statement, he had had time to think of another possible explanation: that he had accidentally hit the boy's head when he slammed the boot lid shut; and so he added that detail about closing the boot in his written version. The police clearly had no evidence to prove exactly how the boy had sustained the head injury, and so they were entirely reliant on his account. How could they prove that he had deliberately hit the boy, as opposed to his version of an accidental injury?

Bradley did not hesitate to make a written statement when asked by the police, because as far as he was concerned it was a way of ensuring that the police did not corruptly add anything to their account of their conversation with him in order to strengthen their case for court. He had no reluctance to acknowledge the voluntariness of his confessions when Inspector Windsor came in, or to confirm it when Mr Holt arrived. After all, this was his exculpatory version that he would rely on at court to demonstrate that he was not responsible for Graeme Thorne's death.

***

Later that day, Saturday 19 November, Stephen Bradley appeared in the Central Magistrates Court and was formally remanded in custody to appear at the Coroner's Court for an Inquest into the death of Graeme Thorne. One of the journalists present during this brief first appearance in court described him as follows:

> *He was short and pudgy. As a young man he probably had a good physique. Now he looked soft, well fed, as though he indulged himself in all the good things of life. Olive skinned, with dark hair thinning out, a round face with a slightly porcine look, but with no hint of malice. He moved well, despite the bulk he had gained.*[9]

Although Bradley had expressed a reluctance to participate in a line-up, the following Monday, 21 November, he consented to the police conducting an identification parade in which Freda and Bazil Thorne were given the opportunity to identify the man who had come to their home some weeks before their son had been taken. This procedure was a rather hollow and facile exercise, in view of the fact that both of them had identified a photograph of Bradley more than a month earlier and that the

Daily Mirror had already published a photograph of both him and Magda.[10]

∗∗∗

The Thornes avidly followed the progress of Stephen Bradley's extradition, and were gratified when he finally arrived back in Australia. They were confidentially informed that he had confessed to the police and that he might well plead guilty to the murder, which would save them from the ordeal of a trial. When the day came for Bazil and Freda to attend the CIB to identify him, they were conflicted in their emotions. On the one hand, they both relished the opportunity to contribute to the prosecution case against him, however they also felt revulsion at acknowledging the very existence of the vile creature who had deprived their son of his life and ripped away all joy from their lives. When the time came for them to enter the small room at the CIB where the identification parade was to occur, they felt nauseous at the idea of being in the same space as him. When they laid eyes on the man responsible for so much misery and loss, they were shocked at his 'ordinariness' and deeply offended at his seemingly arrogant attitude. They could not fathom how a man in his predicament, who was so obviously guilty, could be so coldly confident, rather than cringing in shame at what he had done.

As expected, Freda immediately identified Bradley in the parade. When instructed by the police that she had to go up and touch the man she was identifying, she vehemently refused to have any physical contact with the person responsible for the death of her son, indignantly pointing at him several times and saying emphatically, 'That is the man who came to my place.' Bazil also immediately recognised Bradley, and he also would not touch the man who had been responsible for causing so much anguish to his family, saying, 'No. I will not touch him, but that is him there.' After leaving the CIB, Bazil and Freda were overcome by intense hatred and anger towards the man they had just identified. Never before in their lives had these inherently benevolent people held such powerfully negative sentiments about anyone or anything. How were they to cope with such feelings that threatened to overwhelm their intrinsic personalities?

***

Bradley's reasons for permitting the identification parade were twofold; first, he thought that if he refused, it could be taken as a sign of guilt by the jury at his trial. Second, he thought that it was worth taking a gamble that the Thornes would fail to positively identify him. He had lost such a lot of weight in the remand prison in Calcutta that it was possible that they just would not be sure. In that event, his counsel could surely make headway at the trial on the issue of identification. When the police lined him up with some hapless volunteers from the street, he deliberately adopted a haughty attitude, thinking that Bazil and Freda would be looking for someone cowering after a lengthy period in police custody. When first Freda and then Bazil nominated him as the man who had come to their home, he was unperturbed because they refused to touch him as the police regulations specified, so the whole process would probably be ruled invalid by the trial judge. Surely, their reluctance to touch him would be seen as uncertainty on their part.

**

Later that day, three other witnesses were given an opportunity to identify Bradley in a line-up: Mrs Lord, Mr Denmeade and Mrs Denmeade. Mrs Lord identified Bradley, while Mr and Mrs Denmeade, who had also previously been shown photographs of him, said that he looked like the man they had seen at Bondi on the morning of the kidnapping.

Also that day, Stephen Bradley accompanied two police officers, Detective Sergeants Don Fergusson and Roy Coleman, in a police car to retrace his movements with Graeme Thorne on 7 July. He identified where he had parked his car on the corner of Francis Street. He pointed out the place in the park opposite the Thornes' home from where he had conducted surveillance of their household. He took the police on the route that he claimed to have taken with Graeme: from Bondi they drove along Old South Head Road towards Centennial Park, where Bradley became disoriented and claimed not to be sure which streets he had taken in the area. He stated to the police: 'I cannot remember the streets now, but we drove around here and we came out into Anzac Parade near Moore Park.' He directed them through suburban streets to Anzac Parade by a route that was considerably longer than the most direct one – avoiding Centennial Park. He then indicated the streets to the city and over the Harbour Bridge, then through Neutral Bay and Mosman Junction to the Spit Bridge area, where he pointed out the public phone box from which he had first telephoned Mrs Thorne. He again insisted that Graeme had remained quietly seated in the car while he made this call. Throughout this journey, Bradley remained calm, matter-of-fact and unemotional. Once again, he gave the impression that he was re-enacting a scene from a book he had read or a film he had watched, rather than a disturbing, real-life drama that had resulted in the tragic death of a young boy.

The police then drove Bradley at his direction to his former home in Moore Street, Clontarf. Here, for the first time, he became quite agitated, saying that he did not want to go into the garage because 'That is where I done it.' The police accompanying him were convinced that this sudden display of emotion was prompted by self-pity and a realisation of how far he had fallen from grace, rather than any acknowledgement of the offence that he had wrought on Graeme Thorne.

Still in the police car, which was parked outside 28 Moore Street, Bradley told the police that when he drove into the garage Graeme was still sitting next to him, and that it was only when they were inside the garage that he had forced him into the boot. He confirmed that he had then supervised the removalists. When asked what he had done with Graeme after the removalists had finished, he replied:

I went back to the garage about dark, and the boy was dead. That is when I put him under the house.

Bradley then accompanied the police to the Wakehurst Parkway, and pointed out the two locations where he had thrown Graeme's school case and other objects into the bush. Later he directed them to the vacant allotment in Grandview Grove where he identified the large rock under which he had dumped Graeme's body. He also identified a phone box at the corner of Seaview Street and Upper Beach Street, Balgowlah, where he had made the second phone call to the Thornes' home.

When they returned to the CIB, Sergeant Fergusson showed Bradley the picnic rug that had been found wrapped around Graeme's body, which Bradley identified as belonging to his wife. He also identified the scarf that had been found around Graeme's neck as one of his own.

***

Bradley had no qualms about accompanying the police when they requested he show them the route he had taken with Graeme Thorne. All he had to do was to keep to his story that the boy had remained calm for the duration of the journey to Clontarf. He was never going to tell them about the period in Centennial Park, because he could not think of a satisfactory reason for having driven there – at least, not one he was prepared to disclose. After going past the park, he became slightly disoriented when he realised that he was not directing them by the shortest route from Bondi to the Harbour Bridge, but he quickly corrected himself, taking them to Anzac Parade near Moore Park, which was a slightly longer route, but still perfectly acceptable. He had no hesitation showing them the phone box he had used to make the first call, because it would be futile to deny this aspect of his involvement in the kidnapping. When they arrived at his old home, however, Bradley surprised himself when he became quite emotional and nostalgic, remembering all the good times he, Magda and the children had had in the short period they had owned that house. Out of embarrassment, he feigned an unwillingness to go inside the garage because of what had happened to the boy, but in reality he felt no guilt at all for his death, because it had, after all, been an unfortunate, unforeseen and unpredictable accident. He still believed that Bazil and Freda were partly to blame, because they had recklessly involved the police at such an early stage, and then the police had unwisely kept the media thoroughly informed. He still was firmly of the view that if everyone had behaved sensibly and predictably, Graeme Thorne would have been home safe and sound on the night of his abduction.

***

After the re-enactment of the events of 7 July, Stephen Bradley was transferred to the remand section of the Long Bay Gaol. Due to the nature of the crime with which he had been charged, and to the fact that most people in Australia had already made up their minds about his guilt, Bradley was at risk of serious harm from other prisoners. A great deal of hostility and belittlement was directed towards him in the gaol from prisoners and gaolers alike. Because of the high level of antagonism, he was kept in segregation away from most other prisoners and constantly accompanied by prison warders when out of his single cell. In fact, he ate his meals with the warders. Within a few weeks, however, he had used his amiable nature to make himself quite popular with his gaolers. Compared to his incarceration in Calcutta, this was the Long Bay Hilton.

13

REMAND, REVERSAL AND REUNION

In the few weeks between his confessions to the police in mid-November 1960 and the Coronial Inquest that began in earnest on 5 December 1960, Stephen Bradley's position on his responsibility for the kidnapping of Graeme Thorne completely reversed. Because of this change of tack, his solicitor, Mr Richard Holt, was forced to withdraw from representing him because he was now a potential witness for the Crown, having heard his client admit in front of the police that his confession had been made freely and voluntarily.

Stephen Bradley qualified for legal aid, and he was assigned Frederick Vizzard, the Public Defender of New South Wales to defend him, instructed by a solicitor from the Public Solicitor's office. Fred Vizzard, then in his late fifties, had been the State's only Public Defender since 1946,[1] and there was not another barrister in Sydney who knew more about criminal law than he did. According to Chester Porter QC, who practised alongside him in many cases:

Fred was a bachelor, with a strong Catholic faith and an enormous sympathy for his fellow humans, especially those for whom he appeared: the less fortunate, the friendless, the unlucky. Whereas some subsequent Public Defenders wisely adopted a philosophical attitude to their inevitable losses, he felt each one. When he defended Stephen Bradley for the shocking murder of Graeme Thorne in 1961, he believed his client to be innocent – the only person in Sydney with that belief. Fred felt for each of his clients, worthless though others might think them.

He was a very careful, meticulous advocate, cautious about asking the adventurous question, hardly ever putting a client in the witness box. In those days Judges and Crown Prosecutors tended to treat accused persons in the witness box with little courtesy and less fairness. He was a superb advocate on pleas of guilty for persons with shocking records. I remember his sub-mission: 'The Prisoner has paid for those past convictions; he should not be punished again for the same offences.'

Of all the many fine advocates who have been Public Defenders, few tried harder or more effectively than this able, but extremely modest man. Some counsel who appeared for hopeless, friendless, villainous clients believed that they were entitled at least to sympathy from their counsel. Fred was one of those, but he gave more than sympathy. He gave first class advocacy.[2]

***

Just three days after Stephen Bradley's arrival in Sydney, a brief preliminary hearing of the Inquest into the death of Graeme Thorne opened at the City Coroner's Court in George Street North before the Coroner, Mr CS Rodgers, in order to allow a single witness who was going overseas to give his evidence before departing. The main Inquest hearing was adjourned until 5 December.

***

We do not know exactly when or why Stephen Bradley came to change his story and to repudiate the truthfulness of his confessions to the police, but it certainly happened while he was in custody and before the Inquest. This sort of sudden about-face is not unusual in accused persons who are remanded in gaol while they await their committal proceedings or trial. In the prison community there is a hierarchy of 'gaolhouse lawyers' who are only too willing to express their views about the best way to defend a case, often based on personal experience in multiple court appearances. The more trials that a prisoner has undergone, the more his opinion is valued – no matter what the outcome of his cases. It was in all probability in this context that Bradley came to realise the futility of his denials of responsibility for the death of Graeme Thorne.

***

When Stephen Bradley first arrived at the remand section of Long Bay Gaol, he was placed in a protection wing because the gaol authorities recognised that he was at risk of serious harm from other prisoners. Prisoners have their own hierarchies of status and morality, and one who has harmed or killed a child is very much at the lower end. If one believes prisoners, the gaols are full of innocent people, but when it comes to a child killer, protestations of innocence are useless to protect the offender from attacks – both physical and verbal – by other prisoners.

The protection wings in the gaol system are designed to offer a safer environment to prisoners at risk of harm from their fellows, but in reality they are merely a parallel gaol system in which there is a reduced level of violence, because everyone there is fearful of becoming a victim. The warders in protection are no more able to guarantee safety than they are in the normal gaol population. The protection wings contain a greater proportion of 'VIP prisoners' who are of a higher calibre in terms of education and life experience, due to their former positions in society – as police officers, prison officials, government employees, lawyers, doctors, accountants, financiers and other professional people who have fallen seriously foul of the law. The protection wings also house most of the prisoners known as 'rock spiders' – those who have preyed sexually on children. Even in the protection areas, the rock spiders are shunned by other prisoners. One will also find in protection the most hated prisoners of all, who are known as 'rats' – those who have 'turned' and agreed to give evidence for the prosecution. The real aristocracy of the prison population – the safe-breakers, the bank payroll robbers and those who have taken the police on high-speed car chases – would never be seen in a protection wing.

When Stephen Bradley first arrived at the protection wing at Long Bay Gaol, he was placed in a cell close to the warders' office, because he was considered to be particularly at risk of harm. Within a few days, though, he had made contacts with other prisoners and even with some of the warders. His congenial personality soon won him social acceptance from other prisoners and respect from the warders, who considered him a model prisoner with whom they could share a joke without fear that he might unexpectedly become violent or abusive. Prisoners' conversations at Long Bay – like inmates around the world – inevitably turn to everybody's favourite topics: what are you in for; did you do it; when is your next hearing date; which lawyer do you have representing you; what is your defence; have you made any admissions to the police? Countless hours of the day, which would otherwise pass at a grindingly slow pace, are spent discussing the strengths of prosecution cases and the merits of proposed defences. Stephen Bradley's conversations were no different.

When Bradley felt safe and confident enough to discuss his own case with a few of his fellow prisoners, he was surprised by their reaction. They were aghast that he had confessed to his involvement in the kidnapping, both orally and in writing; that he had taken the police on a run-around to the various locations involved in the crime; and that he had agreed to participate in a line-up. They were particularly scathing when they heard that he had admitted in front of his own solicitor to the voluntariness of his confessions, pointing out that Mr Holt would now have to withdraw from representing him. It was during these conversations that it was explained to Bradley by one of the 'VIP prisoners', who seemed to know more than the others about the law, that even if the prosecution could not prove exactly how or when Graeme Thorne had come to die,

191

he, Bradley, would in all probability still be found liable for the death and convicted of his murder.

When Bradley protested that the prosecution had to prove beyond a reasonable doubt that it had not been an accident, the other prisoners laughed uproariously and said that he clearly did not know how juries worked. They told him that any jury of ordinary people would be so horrified at the kidnapping that they would hold him responsible for whatever happened to the child while in his 'care'. The VIP prisoner also mentioned the probability that the Crown would rely on 'felony murder'. When he expressed ignorance of this, the prisoner patiently explained to him that if an offender commits a crime that carries a penalty of life imprisonment, such as intentionally causing grievous bodily harm that results in a death – even an accidental one – the perpetrator can be convicted of murder, although no death was intended. When Bradley self-right-eously declared that he had not inflicted grievous bodily harm on the child, the prisoner raised his eyebrows and retorted, 'So, how did he get his cracked head?'

The advice of his gaol colleagues – particularly the ones who had once been part of high society – convinced Bradley that his defence of an accidental death would not stand up against the evidence, leaving him no option other than a total denial or capitulation. The realisation that his previous defence was doomed caused Bradley to go into a great depression. It was the long-term prisoners – the ones who had spent much of their adult lives in and out of gaol, the ones who knew the tricks the police could get up to, and the ones who were well versed in manoeuvres to jerk a miraculous acquittal out of the jaws of an impending conviction – who bucked him up and gave him some hope of a way out of his morass. Any confession, they explained, even a written one, can be challenged. In fact, at trial the accused gets two chances to knock out a confession – one in front of the judge by requesting that he exclude it from the evidence, and another by challenging its veracity in front of the jury.[3] Juries, they explained, know that police fabricate confessions, or forcibly extract them through 'biffs', threats of violence or, most insidiously, by threatening to charge family members unless the suspect gives them the confession they want. 'What kind of threat?' asked Bradley. 'Ask yourself what sort of threat would cause you to admit to something you haven't done,' they told him.

After much thought and many more conversations with his 'gaolhouse lawyer' friends, Bradley came up with what he considered to be a most credible story of intimidation by the police to explain his willingness to comply with them. They had threatened him that unless he fully cooperated and confessed to the kidnapping, they would haul Magda back from England in a similar fashion to the way they had dragged him from Colombo, and charge her with complicity in the kidnapping. Upon her arrest, the children would be taken away from her, and they would undoubtedly end up in an orphanage in London while she languished in gaol. Surely, any father would understand the intense pressure that such coercion would place on him to comply with the police.

Bradley's fellow prisoners had also explained that his counsel did not need to win over every member of the jury. In fact, he only needed to convince a single one of them, because the requirement for a unanimous verdict meant that one vote in his favour in the jury room could thwart the whole process.[4]

It was unrealistic to hope for an acquittal, but a hung jury would be as good a victory – especially if the Attorney-General decided that there was no point putting him on trial again.

Bradley had faith in his own ability to convincingly mount his defence to a jury of his peers, and a belief that, with the help of solid counsel like Mr Vizzard representing him, he could convince some of the jurors to his point of view. His main concern was that a jury of twelve ordinary, Anglo-Australians would inevitably be biased against a man like him, who had come from Eastern Europe, who spoke with an accent, and who had been married three times. He had met this kind of prejudice on numerous occasions and been able to overcome it with his charm and intelligence, and he was confident that, if he had an opportunity to project his personality in the courtroom, he would be able to overcome it again. It went without saying that he would need to give evidence in his own defence, so that he could charm that one juror he needed to win over. He made a mental note to tell his counsel to make sure there were some women on the jury. He rarely failed to enchant someone when he set his mind to it, and he was sure that this time he would once again work his magic.

***

A week or two after Bradley's incarceration at Long Bay and prior to the inquest, Fred Vizzard went to see his client at the Long Bay Gaol, accompanied by his instructing solicitor, Mr Pat Smith from the Public Solicitor's Office. Vizzard had already been supplied with copies of all the statements and Bradley's written confession, and he had read the whole brief very carefully. He recognised that he was to represent the most hated man in Australia, but as the State's only Public Defender he was accustomed to such situations. He took very seriously the right of any person accused of crime to be represented by the barrister of their choice, and the duty of that barrister to do his best for the client.[5] Bearing in mind the confessions, he was fully expecting his client to acknowledge his guilt and instruct him to plead guilty, appealing to the mercy of the court on sentence. There was not the slightest suggestion in the brief that Bradley was suffering from any mental illness, so a psychiatric defence was out of the question.

Vizzard met his client in a small, airless cubicle in which a dividing window separated the two lawyers from their client, so communication was laboured and tiring. Vizzard had been in these cramped conditions at Long Bay on numerous occasions, and it never ceased to amaze him how relieved his clients were to see him, even in this insalubrious environment. *This* client, however, was different, maintaining a confrontational and haughty attitude. To Vizzard's surprise, Bradley insisted on his innocence and gave an account of being pressured by the police to cooperate and confess. Vizzard was quite used to receiving unexpected instructions from his clients, and his general approach was to accept them and advance them in court. Such is the role of the professional advocate! In this case, however, he could not resist probing his client just a little to test his resolve to pursue this surprising defence. He asked Bradley to acknowledge that he would stand up in court to say that he had been coerced, and Bradley confirmed that he was ready, and indeed keen, to face his accusers and be cross-examined. Vizzard could see that Bradley was adamant that this was to be his defence, and so, in the best traditions of the Bar, he assured his client that he would do his best for him. As their discussions continued, and Bradley outlined his and Magda's histories, Vizzard could not help feeling that this charming man, who had a family of his own, who claimed innocence so firmly, and who had suffered so much trauma in his life, was incapable of committing such a heinous crime as the one he was charged with.

***

Fred Vizzard's belief in Stephen Bradley's innocence was his default position that he adopted with all his clients who professed their innocence. This approach in a defence counsel has advantages and disadvantages. The main benefit is that the barrister can genuinely appear to the jury to hold a passionate belief in his client's innocence, rather than merely being a paid mouthpiece. The principal detriment is that it tends to blind the barrister to the inherent weaknesses in their client's case, and permits them to mount arguments that defy common sense and have little appeal to a jury. In the author's experience, the best defence barristers are those who have a healthy scepticism for their clients' assertions and focus on the need for counsel to maintain integrity and credibility in front of the jury if they are to succeed. However, many people facing trial for serious crimes prefer to have a barrister who believes them without qualification, rather than one who is more mindful of the intricate tactics required to conduct the defence case effectively.

Stephen Bradley was quite content to be represented by Fred Vizzard. He believed that his own charm and intelligence, supported by Vizzard's unquestioning belief in Bradley's innocence, would ultimately win the day and convince the jury to acquit. But first, there was the Coroner's Inquest to deal with.

***

On 5 December 1960, the Coronial Inquest opened in Court 3 of the Central Court of Petty Sessions in Liverpool Street, Sydney. The court sat all that day, and then again on 13 and 15 December. Public interest in the hearing was intense, with queues of people jostling to get into the courtroom at the beginning of each day and after each adjournment. The Coroner was assisted by a Police Prosecutor, Sergeant Don Goode. Fred Vizzard appeared for Stephen Bradley.

This type of Coronial Inquest has a dual function. It enables the Coroner to make a formal finding in relation to the cause of death of a person, but if the Coroner finds that there is sufficient evidence to warrant a finding that a particular person was criminally responsible for a death, he can refer the case to the Attorney-General and the Clerk of the Peace,[6] so that the person can be put on trial for homicide. In this situation, the Inquest hearing also functions as a substitute for committal proceedings. The purpose of committal proceedings is to ensure that there is a sufficient body of evidence to warrant the matter being sent to one of the superior courts for trial by jury. It also provides an opportunity to disclose the prosecution's evidence to the accused person, so that they know the case against them and are able to prepare their defence at trial. Committal proceedings, as well as an Inquest, are generally not the occasion when the defence presents its case. In fact, in most instances, the defence does its utmost to conceal what its tack will be if the matter goes to trial. This was the approach taken by Vizzard during the Inquest into the death of Graeme Thorne.

The only hint of his client's defence that Vizzard gave during the Inquest emerged when he cross-examined Sergeants Doyle and Bateman to suggest that Bradley had made his confessions under duress. He suggested that the police had threatened to haul Magda Bradley back from England to charge her, and that they had used this as a lever to extract a confession from Stephen Bradley. It became clear during the Inquest that Vizzard would also challenge the validity of the scientific and pathological evidence. Dr John Laing, the government forensic pathologist, gave evidence that Graeme had died from asphyxiation or a skull fracture, or both, and that the head injuries could not possibly have been caused by some movement of the boy himself inside the boot of the Customline. Dr Laing was of the view that the fracture to Graeme's skull had been caused by considerable force from a solid, blunt object.

Magda Bradley's friend, Jacob Fogel, gave evidence about the picnic rug he had given her many years earlier. When shown an image of the rug in a photograph – one of those printed from the discarded negatives found by Mr Browne in the garden at Manly – Fogel admitted to Vizzard that all he could say was that it was the same colour and pattern as the one he had given his friend. Public interest was considerably heightened on 15 December when Bazil and Freda Thorne gave evidence.

***

Bazil and Freda Thorne were not permitted to come into the courtroom to listen to the proceedings before giving their evidence, so when they were finally called they were frustrated because they were determined to hear every bit of evidence that they could. They believed that their presence in Court was not only on their own behalf, but also as representatives of their darling son who had so cruelly been deprived of his life. They were there to witness justice being done for Graeme, and if that meant hearing gruesome details of his confinement in a car boot, or the brutal circumstances of his death after a blow to the head, or the disgustingly disrespectful way in which his body had been discarded, that was just something that they had to endure for his sake. They believed that only by going through this torturous process could they begin to properly grieve for their son, and only when the course of justice was completed could they finally start to repair their lives. They were keen to assist in any way they could to see that justice was done. The sight of Stephen Bradley in the depersonalised environment of the stark, wooden dock in the middle of a courtroom was easier to deal with than the identification parade, when they had been in a small room at the CIB. It was abundantly apparent that, with the exception of the defendant and his counsel – as well as the Coroner, who remained appropriately impassive – the whole courtroom was sympathetic to them.

***

Vizzard treated the Thornes in the witness box with considerable respect and consideration for their loss. The only area in which he challenged them was their identification of his client as the man who had come to their home on 14 June. On the same day, Dr Cameron Cramp, the microbiologist, gave evidence of his analysis of the hairs found on the rug. At the end of that day, the Coroner found that there was a sufficient case against Stephen Leslie Bradley to commit him for trial to the Central Criminal Court – the venue for all murder trials since the 1860s.

Following the Inquest, on Christmas Eve 1960, while Fred Vizzard was holding the Bradley brief, he was appointed a Queen's Counsel. He was now to be known as Fred Vizzard QC. Some hypothesised that his appointment was to create the impression that the State was providing the accused with a defence barrister of the utmost calibre, so that in the event of his conviction, nobody could claim that he had been denied a fair trial.

***

Magda Bradley and the three children found a suitably modest place to stay in London. There was a considerable amount of publicity in the English papers about the case in Sydney, and she followed the reports of the Inquest with great interest and much trepidation. She found the task of being a single parent arduous and she feared for their financial future. Although she and Stephen exchanged letters, his were short and full of expressions of love and concern, but they did little to alleviate Magda's fears for their family's future. Although she had told the newspaper journalists when she first arrived that she had sufficient money at her disposal, that was a blatant lie, and she was forced to work to keep the wolf from the door.

Luckily, she found an excellent school for deaf children, where Ross was able to board during the week.

As she whiled away the weeks and months in London, Magda wrote a manuscript about her life with Stephen, in which she expressed the great love they shared and her longing to be reunited with him. She wrote:

> *You really do not know Stephen Bradley as I do. Steve is not a criminal and he can't be a murderer. No one will ever make me believe it. His nature is so soft and gentle and there is no trace of any cruelty in him. He has never been violent with me or anyone else, and I have never even seen him losing his temper. Of course, he has his own little faults and weaknesses as we all have, but no worse than anyone else. I remember and appreciate the happiness that only he was able to give me since my childhood. For so many years the war, with all its horrors, used to come back to me in my dreams. In these nightmares I used to see time and time again 40 of us sealed up in a railway carriage without water for days. I used to breathe again the heavy air and hear the screams of 1944 when we were taken to Auschwitz. But since I have known Steve I have learnt to laugh again and enjoy life as it is lived by others who were never in a concentration camp.*[7]

She also wrote of what he had told her of his life as a child:

> *Gradually he told me many things about his life and it didn't take me long to realise that he had had a very unhappy and lonely childhood, sadly lacking in love and affection. Whenever he had a little bit of happiness, something always happened to*

him and he was lonelier than ever. He always wanted someone who would love him and care for him, and he was prepared to give himself and devote all his life to that person. I think our union was a lucky one, as we both wanted the same things out of a relationship – understanding and affection – and we both found what we were looking for in each other. Of course, I can really only speak for myself, but I feel that I made Steve happy too.[8]

Finally, she wrote of the devastation that his arrest and charging had had on her:

Here I am in London, in the middle of my dream town, but with my tired eyes and soul I am far from being able to enjoy it. I have thought about coming to London for years. I always wanted to see all those beautiful things I had read so much about. I wanted to see snow fall again, and the spring in the English countryside. I wanted to show my children and see with them the remarkable old buildings – the history – England – and I had also hoped so much that London might bring me a chance to be recognised as a songwriter. But my dreams have turned out to be a terrible nightmare. My songs have been lying in a drawer for long months. I have lost my energy to enjoy, see or try for what I wanted in the first place. My dreams have finished in the fog. I'm not myself any more – my unwritten songs slowly dying in my heart, my soul wrapped around with sadness and frustration. Since I have known that my husband's trial will be on March 20 I spend my days in agony and I can only pray to the good God to help us and help the jury to see the truth. I try hard these difficult days to control my feelings while I am at home with the children. I don't want them to realise that these coming days will be a landmark for our whole future. I try to pretend so as not to worry them too much, but I have to admit that I am not as brave as some people think. I feel exhausted and sick with worry. Only with Steve's help and encouraging letters am I able to hold on to myself. My poor husband who is brave enough to try and help me from the gaol with his letters and even with poems that he has written for me. He is really suffering for himself and worrying about me and the children all the time, yet he still gives me all the help and encouragement not to crack under the terrible strain. He reminds me that God always helped us in the past when we most needed it, and I know how right he is. The good Lord only knows all the answers, and only He knows why we have to suffer so much.[9]

On 5 December 1960 – the day that the Coronial Inquest began in Sydney – Magda Bradley was visited at her London home by Chief Inspector Amos Gibson, a detective from Scotland Yard, and Superintendent Ron Walden, who was the head of the CIB in Sydney. Naturally, when she saw them at her door, she suspected the worst – that they were there to arrest her and take her back to Australia – and she feared for what would happen to their children. She allowed the visitors to come into the lounge room, where they all sat down and Superintendent Walden politely suggested that she make them all a cup of tea. While she made tea in the kitchen, she furiously thought about the impossibility of making suitable arrangements for the children if the police were going to take her away immediately. Surely, if the police arrested her now they had an obligation to make appropriate provisions for the care of the children. Then, suddenly, it occurred to her that those arrangements might involve Paul, Helen and Ross being placed in a government orphanage in which they would be treated abominably and emotionally neglected, and where they would desperately miss their mother. She began to weep at the thought of her children being deprived of their mother after the dreadful experience they had already suffered, seeing their father arrested on the ship in Colombo.

Composing herself as best she could, she brought the tea to the two men, and sat down to hear what they had to say. She was enormously relieved when Superintendent Walden told her that they were there to try to convince her to return to Sydney as a witness in her husband's trial. Their tone was respectful, apologetic and imploring, as they explained that they wished to take a written statement from her now in anticipation of her return to Sydney to give evidence. Magda suddenly realised that it was she who had the upper hand in this negotiation. She confidently told the two police officers that she would think about their request and get back to them. They left her home in a deferential manner, after providing her with Chief Inspector Gibson's business card and a request to call him at her earliest convenience.

Magda Bradley took her time to get back to the two police officers. Eventually she agreed to go to Scotland Yard to be interviewed by Superintendent Walden. The resulting statement was completely supportive of her husband and did not mention any of her suspicions about him. Over the weeks and months since they had been separated in Colombo, believing that she had an overwhelming duty to be loyal to Stephen and to support him under any circumstances, she forced herself to believe that the accusations against him were groundless. She knew that he would be totally alone while incarcerated and awaiting trial in Sydney, and that they would both be subjected to vile and vituperative articles in the newspapers. She, at least, had her freedom and the children, as well as one or two new friends in London. Stephen only had her – 10,000 miles away. Magda wrote a letter to the Public Solicitor, Mr Hawkins, and offered to return to Australia to support Stephen.

***

Magda Bradley's police statement was sent by airmail to Police Commissioner Delaney, who immediately forwarded it to the Public Solicitor, Mr Hawkins. The statement was not of any use to the prosecution, but it was of great value to the defence. Mr Hawkins arranged for the English Legal Aid Office to obtain a second statement from Magda with further supportive material. Magda let Mr Hawkins know how impoverished she was, and how inconceivable it was for her to afford a return airfare to Australia. She also made it clear that if she returned to Sydney, all three children would have to accompany her. As a result, Mr Hawkins made an application to the Attorney-General, Mr Reg Downing,[10] for payment by the government of airfares for Magda and the three children, stressing how crucial it was to the defence case to have her available at the trial. The application was considered at length, and finally granted, but only eight days before the trial. This meant that Magda and the children had to hurriedly make arrangements to fly to Sydney in time for the beginning of the trial on Monday, 20 March 1961.

The children were incredibly excited at the thought of an international flight, but they were also well aware that the reason for the journey was because Stephen was in trouble and Magda needed to be near him. They had witnessed numerous instances of Magda becoming annoyed or distressed when reporters had asked her questions, and they feared that once back home this would only be exacerbated.

Just before leaving London, Magda agreed to be interviewed by a journalist working for the Sydney *Daily Mirror* newspaper. The paper described her situation in these words:

In her London flat yesterday, Mrs Bradley told the Daily Mirror *that she wanted to fly to Sydney as soon as possible to comfort her husband … 'I feel my husband needs my comfort.' It is understood that she is worried over any possible custody action involving the children … 'London seems very lonely. I feel very dispirited' she said. She smoked continuously and frequently swept her fingers through her blonde shoulder length hair. As she talked, the children played in front of the television set in the small lounge. Mrs Bradley invited the* Daily Mirror *representative into the hallway of the flat on the top storey of a high terrace house in south-west London. She was wearing a pink and white-spotted woollen dressing gown, flowered silk pyjamas and mule sandals. Her fingernails and toenails were painted pink. She broke off the interview to attend to her youngest child, who is a boarder at the School for Deaf Children during the week, but comes home at weekends. Mrs Bradley said she was living on savings, but she hoped to get money from the articles she had written about her two marriages and from music compositions, including one she had composed before leaving Australia.*[11]

It was not until 8.45 on the morning of Sunday, 19 March 1961 – the day before the trial was due to begin – that Magda and her three children arrived in Sydney. A squad of twenty police officers was on hand at the airport to control the crowds. At the Customs Office a copy of the banned book *Lolita*[12] was confiscated from Magda's luggage. On exiting the customs area, she spoke briefly to reporters and paused for photographs. She was then driven to the Gresham Hotel, an upmarket establishment in the city, where the two younger children were picked up by friends who would look after them during Stephen's trial. Paul was to stay with his father.

As the trial was due to start the next day, Magda immediately met with Mr Vizzard for a three-hour conference in his Phillip Street chambers in the city. Immediately after that meeting, with the personal approval of the Minister of Justice for an unscheduled gaol visit on a Sunday afternoon, Magda made a poignant trip to see her husband at Long Bay, spending about an hour with him.

***

The reunion of Stephen and Magda Bradley at Long Bay Gaol was highly emotional, but also stressful and stilted. They were relieved to be finally together after four months apart, but they were only too aware of how much still lay in front of them before they could ever hope to be rejoined as a family. They also suspected that their conversation was being overheard through a hidden listening device, so they were careful not to discuss the crime with which he had been charged or the evidence that each of them would give. As they were both acutely aware that the late-afternoon visit would be restricted to an hour, they were simultaneously rushed and somewhat lost for words. They were unable to express their deep emotional connection – perhaps because of the artificial and confined environment. They both desired to bridge the gap between them, but the impending trial, the hostile surroundings and the fear of their privacy being intruded upon by unseen observers made it impossible. Without it being said, both of them instinctively sensed that their relationship was at a crossroad.

When Magda returned to the Gresham Hotel that evening, she telephoned the two older children, who asked her about Stephen. All she could tell them was that she had visited him in a government place, where he was quite comfortable, but unfortunately unable to leave, and that he had told her how much he loved them. That night, Magda locked herself in the bathroom and quietly wept for the woeful situation of her divided family. She had read excerpts from the inquest in the English newspapers, including Stephen's confessions to the police, and she suspected that the prosecution case against her husband was overwhelming. She knew only too well that there was no way that Stephen could have been coerced or tricked by the police into making such damaging admissions unless they were based on the truth. Rather, if anything, he would have minimised his involvement and painted himself in the best possible light. She admitted to herself that not even a threat to bring her back to Australia and charge her with a criminal offence would have induced him to admit to a contemptible crime he had not committed – he was too street-smart for that. She believed that to keep her emotional equilibrium she had to maintain the appearance of an unshakeable belief in Stephen's innocence, no matter how much evidence the prosecution threw at him.

***

Two days after her arrival in Sydney, Magda Bradley was forced to leave the Gresham Hotel for more modest accommodation, because the New South Wales Government were paying her an allowance of only £5 per day, and so the People's Palace – a Salvation Army hostel – became her temporary new home. Each time Magda ventured out of the People's Palace she was confronted by vituperative barbs from people who recognised her in the street, in shops, or on the bus. This wounded her every time, and resulted in her going out as little as possible. Magda realised that, no matter what was the outcome of the trial, she would be forced at its conclusion to return with the children to London if she was to have even a semblance of normal life.

14

JUSTICE IN ACTION

The Supreme Court trial of Stephen Leslie Bradley for the murder of Graeme Thorne began on Monday, 20 March 1961 in the Central Criminal Court[1] at the Darlinghurst Courthouse at Taylor Square in Sydney. It was in this historic sandstone building that almost every murder trial since the 1860s had been held. Behind the courthouse was the old Darlinghurst Gaol, which since the 1920s had been converted into the East Sydney Technical College and the National Art School. Bradley faced trial only for murder, because, as has been explained, at the time there was no offence of kidnapping under the laws of New South Wales. Public interest in the trial was at an unprecedented intensity, and queues of people waiting to gain access to the public galleries in the courtroom began forming outside on Oxford Street at about 6am on the first day of the trial. A bench in the public gallery was reserved for family and close friends of the Thornes. The newspapers reported that this was the first murder trial in the State's history in which women could be selected to serve on the jury.[2] It was also noted that it was just short of eleven years since Bradley's arrival in Australia.

When the trial got under way, the jury selection process had to be temporarily interrupted because of the noisy scramble of people trying to get into the courtroom to watch. Each time there was an adjournment – for morning tea or lunch – the jostling for seats and standing positions began anew. The accused arrived by truck in a secure laneway at the back of the courthouse. The dock in the Central Criminal Court is situated in the centre of the courtroom, so that during the proceedings an accused is seated facing forwards towards the judge, with the result that those in the public gallery at the back of the courtroom cannot see their face. Access to the court for the accused is through a trapdoor at the back of the dock, which conceals a steep, stone staircase coming from the underground cells and passageways beneath the courthouse. This means that the only opportunity that the public ordinarily gets to see the face of an accused is when they come into the dock and when they stand up to leave via the trapdoor and stairs. Whenever Stephen Bradley came into or left the courtroom, those in the public gallery would strain to catch a glimpse of him – particularly the women, who seemed to have a strange fascination for him. Some of them were overheard making comments about his charisma and sex appeal. Although Bradley was only 5 feet 6 inches, with a stocky build, he had an almost full head of dark hair, an olive complexion and an air of irrepressible optimism – all of which combined to make him quite handsome.

***

Some women are irresistibly attracted to the 'bad boy' image of male criminals. The more serious or bizarre the crime, the more fascination they elicit. There are even some women who are willing to devote themselves to a serious relationship with an incarcerated prisoner – necessarily limited to correspondence and weekly gaol visits – and occasionally even to marry them. Such a personal connection necessitates an unqualified accept-ance of the prisoner's protestations of innocence, especially in the face of a conviction. These relationships rarely survive for long after the release of the prisoner, because their appeal lies in the forced incarceration of one and the freedom of the other. Indeed, part of the benefit of these liaisons to the females is that they are left alone for most of the week to pursue their lives unencumbered by the demands of a normal relationship, but with the illusion of being in one. The saying goes that 'absence makes the heart grow fonder', and enforced absence due to incarceration is no exception. Stephen Bradley had many of the features that attracted the attention of such women. He was thirty-four years old; he was reasonably good-looking; he was articulate and irrepressibly self-confident; and his crime, which was unique in the annals of Australian legal history, had attracted the attention of the nation, making him, in the eyes of some, an infamous superstar and the ultimate 'bad boy'.

***

The public gallery of the Central Criminal Court consisted of two levels at the back of the court. The lower level, with tiered seating, was split into three sections, divided by the two entrances from the expansive courtyard outside. The upper level, again tiered, was reserved only for men and spanned the entire width of the courtroom. In total, the gallery accommodated a maximum of about a hundred people if they sat cheek by jowl. At least twice that number would queue for access each morning, and when an especially interesting part of the trial was about to occur, possibly three times the number would clamour to get in. Those who were unsuccessful were often rude to the Sheriff's Officers tasked with keeping control.

The trial was presided over by Mr Justice Clancy, who was assisted by an Associate, his daughter Margaret. The prosecution was conducted by Senior Crown Prosecutor, Mr WJ (Bill) Knight QC[3] and his junior counsel, Crown Prosecutor Vincent (Vin) Wallace,[4] instructed by Mr William (Bill) Job,[5] a solicitor from the Clerk of the Peace Office. Stephen Bradley was represented by Fred Vizzard QC, who was instructed by Pat Smith from the Public Solicitor's Office.

A large panel of citizens had been summonsed for the selection of a jury. The twelve jurors, whose names were randomly plucked out of a box by the Judge's Associate, ended up being all male – much to Bradley's discontent. The women on the panel were so few in number that none of their names were called. The selected jurors were required to remain at the courthouse in the care of the Sheriff's Officers for the duration of the trial. Two upstairs dormitories, of a standard akin to a boarding school, were provided at the courthouse to accommodate the jurors overnight. They were kept entirely isolated from newspapers, television reports and the radio. Any telephone contact with family had to be under the supervision of a Sheriff's

Officer. The trial took place over eight days – at the time one of the longest criminal trials in New South Wales.[6] This required the jurors to remain together over the intervening weekend in the care of Sheriff's Officers, who did their best to occupy their charges by taking them on escorted scenic drives, being careful to keep prying members of the public at a discreet distance.

The Crown case relied heavily on the forensic scientific evidence and the oral and written confessions of the accused, as well as the identification of Bradley by Freda and Bazil Thorne and Mrs Ford. Because of the heavy reliance on diverse categories of forensic science, the trial of Stephen Bradley was one of the most complex in New South Wales up until that time, and it exemplified the sophistication and value of modern forensic science in the detection and prosecution of serious crime.

Bill Knight's case was that although Bradley had admitted responsibility for the kidnapping of Graeme Thorne, his explanations of what had happened to the boy during his captivity were largely self-serving, unreliable and contradicted by the evidence from the autopsy. In his opening address, Knight suggested that Bradley had put 'a lot of gloss' in his admissions to the police in order to paint himself in the best possible light, telling the jury that it was quite fanciful that the boy would have sat quietly in the car when they pulled up on the Harbour Bridge to pay the toll and, even more improbably, when they stopped at the telephone booth on the Spit Road. Knight also suggested that another improbable aspect of the accused's version was his claim that it was at Clontarf that he had first put a cloth around Graeme Thorne's mouth, and that he had imprisoned him in the boot of the car while the boy was still in a conscious state. Knight described as 'too silly for words' the notion that Bradley would have allowed Graeme to remain in that state while the removalists were moving around the Clontarf house.

The most dramatic part of the first day's proceedings came during the testimony of Freda Thorne. She gave evidence slowly and purposefully of her identification of the photograph of Stephen Bradley as the man who had come to her home three weeks before the kidnapping and the confirmation of that identification during the police line-up. She became teary when describing Graeme's departure on the morning of his abduction. In cross-examination, Mr Vizzard suggested to her that her identification of his client was incorrect and that she had been influenced by seeing other photographs of Bradley prior to being asked to identify him. In a fit of pique and frustration, Freda Thorne shot back at him: 'I don't care what you say!' Pointing at the accused in the dock, she shouted, 'That's the man who killed my boy,' and then slumped into her chair, buried her head in her hands and began weeping profusely. According to a journalist:

> Graeme Thorne's mother, Mrs. Freda Thorne, dramatically accused Stephen Leslie Bradley of having 'killed her boy' as she sobbed and trembled in the Central Criminal Court witness box today. She caused a stir among jurymen and in public galleries as she broke down after a tense silence, emotionally pointed to Bradley and sobbed: 'I don't care what you say, this is the man who killed my boy.' Bradley, who has pleaded not guilty to the boy's kidnap-murder, sat calmly and showed no reaction to Mrs. Thorne's outburst.[7]

For Vizzard, this emotional, heart-wrenching outburst in front of the jury was a tactical catastrophe, and he did his best to edge back from the precipice by lamely saying to Freda, 'I don't want to upset you, you understand that?' Whatever connection Vizzard may have had with the jury prior to that moment would have been completely dissipated by feelings of sympathy for Freda and Bazil and revulsion for the accused.

After a short break, Freda was able to continue with the questioning, however within minutes she broke down again, and, with Mr Vizzard's assent – and to his relief – she was excused from giving further evidence.

***

Freda and Bazil remained in attendance during the remaining days of the trial. Like many family members of murder victims, they desperately wanted to know exactly what had happened to their son and, having missed most of the Inquest, felt that this was their only chance. They hoped – even expected – to see some signs of remorse – deep, intense remorse – emanating from the person who had killed their son. Surely, a man with children of his own – and they had been led to believe that he loved them dearly – could not maintain the pretence of arrogant innocence for too long. They would surely be able to see through his bravado to the hidden regrets beneath. Perhaps it would be better if he kept up the pretence, because the jury would see through it, loathe him and be only too ready to convict.

If Bazil and Freda thought that the trial would provide them with any credible answers about what had really happened to Graeme, they were sorely disappointed. Stephen Bradley's defence at his trial was that he was in no way involved in the kidnapping or death and that his confessions were false and had been coerced from him by devious and unscrupulous police officers using unfair and unethical tactics, such as lies, harassment and duress.

***

Fred Vizzard QC strenuously cross-examined the two police officers, Detective Sergeants Brian Doyle and Jack Bateman, who had obtained Bradley's confessions (oral and written). It was suggested to them that they had denied a request by Bradley for a solicitor. Vizzard alleged that the police had told Bradley that his wife was implicated in the crime, and that he had better confess or she would be in terrible trouble. It was put to them that they had promised Bradley that if he made a statement admitting to the crimes, his wife would be protected and able to remain in England to look after the children. It was alleged that they had taunted Bradley that unless he confessed, Gregor Weinberg would get custody of the children. Vizzard put to them that although Bradley's police statement had been written out in his own hand, it had been dictated to him by the police, who had deliberately inserted language errors in order to make it sound more genuine. Both police denied all these allegations. When Detective Doyle was questioned, he reminded Vizzard that the accused had told his solicitor, Mr Holt, in their presence in the interview room at the CIB that he had confessed freely and voluntarily. Vizzard retorted rhetorically that all his client was trying to do was to save his wife from any trouble with the police, and that if he had told

Mr Holt the truth in their presence, his wife would have been in severe jeopardy.

Bill Knight QC called a host of expert scientific witnesses, who wove a web of damning evidence implicating Stephen Bradley in the kidnapping and death of Graeme Thorne. Two witnesses refuted the suggestion that the boy could have accidentally died from lack of oxygen in the boot. These two experts gave evidence that they had conducted a test using a similar Ford and had ascertained that a sufficient amount of air would enter the boot to enable a person confined in it to maintain life. If anyone had been locked in the boot of the Ford, they would not have been suffocated to death over a period of eight hours. The Senior Crown Prosecutor also called the forensic pathologist, Dr Laing, who gave evidence about the dual causes of death. In his view, in order to cause the severe fracture to Graeme's skull it would have been necessary to apply 'a good force'. Dr Laing insisted that it was quite impossible that the boy could have done the injury to himself while in the boot.

Cherie, the Bradleys' Pekinese dog, made a surprise appearance at the trial. After discovering Cherie at the veterinary surgery of J Stewart and Sons in Rushcutters Bay, the police arranged for the dog to be looked after until the trial by the surgery kennel manager, Mr Victor Drury. Just six days before the trial, on Wednesday, 15 March, Drury and his wife were walking the dog in nearby Rushcutters Bay Park. A couple of drunks frightened the dog, which ran onto the busy roadway adjoining the park, where it was killed by passing traffic. Cherie's body was retained and, at the request of the police, sent to the Australian Museum, where it was hurriedly stuffed and preserved without the use of any chemical processing, so that the colour of the dog's fur would not be altered. The preserved remains of Cherie were tendered in evidence at the trial by Bill Knight QC, so that the jury could see for themselves the appearance of the dog hairs.

On Monday afternoon of the second week of the trial, having called seventy-eight witnesses, the Senior Crown Prosecutor closed his case, and the defence case began.[8]

The response by an accused was – and generally still is – the most keenly awaited part of a trial – both by jurors and by observers in the public gallery. One of the most important decisions to be made in a criminal trial is whether or not the accused goes into the witness box to give sworn evidence like all the other witnesses. At that time there were two other options: to make an unsworn statement from the dock,[9] or to remain silent. Unlike the question-and-answer format utilised with other witnesses, a 'dock statement' consisted of an unprompted, unstructured monologue in which the accused was able to give their version of events, with very few restrictions on what could, or could not, be said. An accused was not required to take an oath to tell the truth in a dock statement, and he or she was not subject to cross-examination on it by the Crown Prosecutor. The dock statement was therefore the preferred choice of most defence counsel, as it effectively avoided the main risk of giving sworn evidence in the witness box – of being decimated during an effective cross-examination by the prosecutor. The two principal tactical disadvantages of a dock statement were: firstly, that the defence counsel lost the opportunity to make an opening address to the jury; and secondly, that the jury might think that the accused had failed to give sworn evidence because of a fear of the truth emerging during cross-examination, despite being told by the judge not to reason in this impermissable way.

***

Fred Vizzard QC knew only too well that one of the most important functions of a defence counsel during a trial was to contribute to the decision of whether the accused should give sworn evidence, make an unsworn statement from the dock, or do neither and remain silent. Vizzard had a reputation for rarely putting his client in the witness box, as he had seen the damage that a good cross-examination could wreak on the defence case. In this trial, however, where the defence was mounting a positive case of coercion by the police, there were additional considerations and the decision was a particularly complex one. During a number of conferences at the gaol, including a lengthy one the week before the trial, Vizzard, as he always did, advised his client of the advantages and disadvantages of each option – and then strongly suggested that no decision be made until shortly before the commencement of the defence case. Most of his clients were only too pleased to delay making a decision of this magnitude, but Stephen Bradley was different. Right from the first time they discussed it, he insisted that he wanted to give sworn evidence like all the other witnesses, so that the jury would be able to scrutinise and evaluate him in exactly the same way as the others.

The ultimate choice that Stephen Bradley made – with the benefit of advice from Fred Vizzard QC – was an unusual one, but not unprecedented. Bradley both delivered a dock statement and gave sworn evidence in the witness box. This allowed the prosecutor to cross-examine him on any topic, including the contents of the dock statement.

At the commencement of the defence case, Vizzard stood up and announced to the court that his client would make a statement to the jury. He then turned to his client and quietly said to him, 'Make your case slowly'. No one in the courtroom was surprised at this election, and no one at that time, except Vizzard, his solicitor and their client, knew that he would also be giving sworn evidence. The advantage of this combination was that Bradley had an opportunity in his dock statement to give his version of events unimpeded and without interruption. Of course, the contents of the statement had been extensively discussed and rehearsed beforehand with Vizzard. Bradley then entered the witness box, thereby throwing himself open to cross-examination and refuting the unstated accusation that he had remained in 'coward's castle' – the dock – in order to avoid his version being tested by the prosecutor.

Vizzard's decision for Bradley to take both these courses was based upon his client's wishes and the barrister's belief in his innocence, but also on Vizzard's assessment that Bradley was an impressive public speaker and an intelligent man who would make a formidable impression on the jury. Vizzard was also confident that his client would be able to sustain his account and maintain his cool under what was likely to be a withering cross-examination by Bill Knight. He was right on both counts. One of the police officers, who sat right through the defence case, gave this assessment:

Never have I seen a more plausible performance under such an ordeal. He never batted an eyelid.[10]

Both in his dock statement and when giving sworn evidence, Bradley maintained the stance of an aggrieved, honourable citizen who had been the subject of a monstrous, unfounded allegation. In the dock, he was eloquent and articulate, with hardly the trace of an accent. It was clear to experienced court watchers that it had been thoroughly rehearsed. Bradley was the antithesis of the typical criminal and when he spoke it was impossible to imagine him committing these horrendous crimes. He had taken a cue from some of the professional police witnesses who gave evidence against him and from time to time would look across at the members of the jury, particularly at those who, by their body language, seemed the most inclined to favour him. He knew that he only needed to win over one of them to his cause for a guilty verdict to be avoided, so he was constantly on the lookout for the slightest indication of body language to suggest an individual juror's receptiveness to him.

The news reporters noted that Bazil and Freda Thorne listened to the statement 'intently, but without any apparent emotion'.[11] That was because they had been warned by the solicitor for the Crown that any outburst or reaction might result in the judge asking them to leave the courtroom. They were so intent on hearing every word of the proceedings that they assiduously obeyed these instructions.

***

Bradley's version of events in his dock statement was a complete denial of any involvement in the kidnapping or death of Graeme Thorne:

I never been to 79 Edward Street, Bondi, and I had nothing to do with taking away that little boy. I was not at Francis Street, Bondi, on 7th July or prior in that week.

He attempted to explain the argument with Magda the previous night:

The previous day – on the 6th July – we had some argument – my wife – because we had to move quickly, and no place to go. My wife got overtired and nervy and angry, as sometimes she does, and she said she was tired of it all and would fly up to Surfers Paradise and leave me to finish the packing. I was annoyed with my wife. I thought it was very unreasonable to go off suddenly and leave me to finish packing. We have the argument, and often we don't talk for a day or so.

He maintained an alibi for the morning of the kidnapping:

On the 7th July we were moving. I got up about 7.30 and continue the packing of the night before. Somebody was helping with the packing – probably Paul. That is the eldest boy. After a while I told him that I was going out to Balgowlah to get some wires. Paul often gets the children's breakfast, as my wife was up late on the 6th July, and when she goes to bed late, she usually sleeps in. I very seldom have breakfast, if ever. I went to Balgowlah. I went in the Customline. The other car – the Goggomobil – was not home ... I went to the hardware store in Sydney Road next to two banks there. That is where I got the wire.

Then I went across to a paper shop and bought a paper and I came back across and went to a delicatessen and bought some cigarettes. I was still annoyed with my wife, and I sat in the car a while and read the paper. About 10 o'clock, I drove home to Moore Street. When I got home my wife and family had already left. They were booked on the 11.45am plane to Coolangatta.

Shortly after, the removalists arrived. During that morning, while the removalists were there, I received a phone call from my wife from the air terminal. I told her that the removalists were there and I had been to Balgowlah and got some wire. I wanted to make up with my wife, and drove up to Surfers Paradise to spend a few days with the family.

Clearly, if this version of events was accepted, there had simply not been enough time for Bradley to have driven to Bondi and kidnapped Graeme Thorne. He next sought to give an account of the interview with Detective Sergeants Doyle and Fergusson at Nutt & Muddle on 24 August. He admitted being questioned about his ownership of the Ford Customline but he denied that he had been asked anything about the Thorne kidnapping or a prior visit to the Thornes' home. He also denied telling Sergeant Fergusson that he had seen Magda and the children off on the morning of 7 July. He asserted that he had told the sergeant that it was in the Customline that he had gone to the hardware store at Balgowlah.

He attempted to explain the surreptitious planning of the bookings made on the P&O ship to leave Australia:

In April 1960, we applied for passports. My wife was advised that she has much better chance to sell her songs and musical compositions in England than in Australia … She made a booking for herself and the eldest boy, Paul. She wanted to take him for company, and also give him a trip.

I was not keen to go to England. It was intended that the little girl Helen and Ross would stay with me. I did not want to be separated from my wife. We decided we would all go. We changed the booking from one to two cabins. On the 26 September 1960, we sailed.

To explain his confessions at the CIB, he asserted that police officers had threatened to arrest Magda in England and bring her back to Australia to face charges. He told the court that an hour after the flight had left Colombo Sergeant Doyle began the process of intimidating him with threats:

Sergeant Doyle told me there were two men sent to Aden to question my wife, but they decided against it and decided to wait until she gets to London, where they can arrest her and take into custody in Scotland Yard. They talked about it all the time. I was also told that Mr Walden, the chief, is in London and they are going to fix her. It was suggested they could arrest her and take into custody and bring her back, and she was implicated in this thing. I knew she had nothing to do with it. Neither did I. I didn't tell them anything.

On the leg between Darwin and Sydney, according to Bradley, the intimidation had intensified:

I was very confused and worried. He [Sergeant Doyle] said Mr Walden and Scotland Yard were arresting my wife and taking her into custody, and the only way to help is if I admit to it. He said, 'The only way to help your family is if you admit it or confess to it.' I am not quite sure about the words he used, but he also said, 'If you don't admit to it you get your whole family in a jam.'

I was very confused and worried. I did not make any admission to the police they say I did. I was very worried about my wife. It brought back old memories of how she has been in Auschwitz – a terrible concentration camp. Her father and mother were killed, or put in the gas chamber. She was blinded in one eye through beatings. I felt that if she has to go through that ordeal as I have she will never stand it. I love my wife and family and I was prepared to do anything to help them.

By the time he was placed into the interview room at the CIB, Bradley asserted, he was utterly confused and overwrought, as he had had only about an hour's sleep during the whole flight. He maintained that he had asked to see his solicitor, Mr Holt, but that Sergeant Bateman had said to him, 'You know what lawyers are. They don't come on Saturday.' The process of intimidation then intensified a number of notches:

Sergeant Doyle told me, 'The only way to help the family is if you make a statement – admit to it.' I said, 'How can I make a statement? I don't know anything about it.' They shouted at me, 'You bastard, you did it. Who was with you? If you don't tell us, there is a pack of wolves outside that is going to tear you apart,' pointing to detectives walking outside the room. I was in a bad state. It is not correct to say that I was clear and collected. I was in such a state of shock, I just did what they said. One of them said, 'You had better write it down.' Sergeant Doyle gave me a piece of paper and he said, 'You had better write it down. That is the only way to help your wife and family.'

Bradley claimed that the police had dictated the contents of the statement to him, and that he had only participated in the run-around in the police vehicle to the various locations involved in the kidnapping and the disposal of the body after Detective Sergeant Fergusson had threatened him by saying: 'We can take you out. We have the power to.'

He gave this account of the run-around:

We drove to Wellington Street, Bondi, where Sergeant Fergusson pointed to a place. He said, 'This is where the Thornes live.' I said, 'I would not know.' … Then they drove to Clontarf, where I identified my home at 28 Moore Street, Clontarf, but I did not say – I did not ask not to be taken into the garage, and during that trip I never admitted anything to do with this boy.

Bradley acknowledged that his family had owned a rug similar to the one found wrapped around Graeme Thorne, but he claimed that it had disappeared around Christmas 1959. He alleged that Sergeant Fergusson, on showing him the blanket, had said: 'That is yours. Of course it is. I would like to wrap it around your head and smother you.'

After Bradley finished his dock statement, everybody expected him to sit down. When he remained standing, the judge quizzically asked him: 'Is that all you wish to say, Bradley?', whereupon Mr Vizzard stood up, moved to the dock and whispered something to Bradley and the police officer guarding him in the dock. The police officer then unlocked the gate of the dock and escorted Bradley to the witness box at the front of the courtroom, causing a hum of commentary and conjecture in the public gallery at this strange departure from the usual practice. Mr Vizzard then made the announcement: 'I will now tender the accused as a witness, and he will give evidence on oath.'

A Sheriff's Officer administered the oath to Bradley, who calmly sat in the witness box, seemingly keen to confront his accusers.

There was a marked difference between Bradley in the dock and in the witness box. While he maintained his equilibrium and calmness at all times, his language skills were clearly not as proficient when giving sworn evidence as they had been during the dock statement, and his accent was more pronounced. This was highly relevant to the issues in the trial, because one of the allegations from the defence was that the police had deliberately inserted language errors into the confessions to make them appear more genuine. Vizzard first asked Bradley to confirm the correctness of his dock statement, thereby giving the contents of the unsworn statement the same status as evidence on oath. He then asked Bradley several questions about the scarf and the rug, and then requested that Bradley explain why he and Magda had told various people different lies about where they were going before they left Australia. Bradley explained that the reason for the lies was that they did not want Paul's father,

Gregor Weinberg, to know that they were going overseas, because Gregor had previously objected to them taking Paul to Canada. Vizzard ended by asking his client the crucial question: 'Do you swear on your oath that you had nothing to do with the taking of that boy away from his home?' To which Bradley answered, 'I do.' Vizzard then abruptly sat down.

***

It hardly ever happens that an accused person breaks down during cross-examination and admits to their crimes. The best that a cross-examiner can hope to achieve is to elicit the manifest absurdities and inconsistencies in the account that an accused maintains. Sometimes this merely consists of putting to the accused the factual scenario that they have asserted in a way which highlights the absurdities or inconsistencies in it. At other times, the cross-examiner leads the accused down a path of logic towards an irresistible conclusion pointing to guilt, in the hope that the accused will either deny one or more of the (provable) facts, or refute the logical conclusion which the jury will inevitably accept. Either way, the accused loses credibility before the jurors in a way which will assist them to reject the defence case and ultimately accept the prosecution case. In a sense, when cross-examining an accused person, the Crown Prosecutor is acting as a soundboard (like the soundboard of a piano, which does not create the notes, but gives them clarity and vibrancy), so that the jury can make an assessment of whether the accused is being forthright, credible and reliable, or is vacillating, lying or otherwise resisting the emergence of the truth. Often, the jury's impressions derive as much from the demeanour of the person being cross-examined as from the content of their answers.

The preparation of a cross-examination therefore requires a careful dissection of the defence case to identify the manifest absurdities and inconsistencies – big and small. The next task is to order the questions on each topic in a way that anticipates every escape route that the accused may take to avoid the point being made. It is as though the cross-examiner is gradually enclosing the accused by building a fence around him, so it is important not to close the gate before all the pieces of the fence are in place. Having constructed a thorough plan, it is vital for the cross-examiner not to be overly dominated by his or her preparation, as it is crucial to focus on the answers given in court, because unexpected responses will sometimes contain nuggets of gold that need to be mined. The cross-examination of an accused by the Crown Prosecutor is the most dynamic, unpredictable and challenging aspect of advocacy in the whole criminal trial process.

***

Bill Knight QC unleashed a ferocious, penetrating cross-examination on Bradley, hoping to rattle him into making mistakes and contradicting himself.[12] Bradley was clearly prepared for such an onslaught and maintained a calm and confident demeanour; however, his accent and his language errors were more pronounced and more frequent than during his evidence-in-chief. One prominent journalist described his evidence in the witness box as follows:

He was confident, unshaken by the probings of counsel. He treated the Crown Prosecutor guardedly, but not with fear. There was a suggestion of impatience, an impatience at having to go through the rigmarole of cross-examination, rather than anxiety in the way he stood, slowly bringing his open hands together at the fingertips, then suddenly pulling them apart again. He was cunning, but not cunning enough. When he spoke he lapsed into his normal idiom, ungrammatical at times and quite different from the fluency of the dock statement.[13]

The positions that Bradley took on some factual issues raised in the cross-examination were so fanciful that not even he could provide convincing reasons why the jury should accept them. Foremost among them was the allegation that threats from the police had caused him to confess to these terrible crimes. Knight pointed out that in all the voluminous papers with which he had been served in Colombo there was not a single allegation that Magda was implicated in the kidnapping. Knight put Bradley's handwritten confession in front of him and read out the section about the car trip with Graeme from Bondi to Clontarf. The cross-examination continued:

Knight: When you wrote that, you realised that that was something that was extremely serious, didn't you?
Bradley: Had I realised, I would not have written it.
Knight: Do you say you just wrote this in a trance, in effect?
Bradley: I would not know what to call it, but I was in a state of shock, I can tell you that.

Knight then continued:

Knight: [Reading from the handwritten statement] 'I have asked for £25,000 from the boy's mother and father.' When you wrote that, even if you were not thinking very clearly, you realised that you were writing down that you had committed a very serious crime, didn't you?

Bradley: The whole statement is pointing to a very serious crime.

Knight: But that was a very serious matter that you were writing when you wrote that sentence, wasn't it?

Bradley: Yes, it would be.

Knight: You realised it at the time?

Bradley: No.

Knight: [Reading] 'I told them that if I don't get the boy – if I don't get the moneys – I feed him to the sharks.' You realised when you were writing that, that it was a very serious thing to write?

Bradley: I told you that if I had realised it, I would not have written it. I was very strongly induced to write this.

Knight: I am not worried about whether you were induced. I'm worried about whether you were conscious when you wrote it?

Bradley: I would not say, in the real sense.

Knight: You realised when you were writing that, that if you wrote it, there was no hope for you not to be convicted of this crime, didn't you?

Bradley: Well, it is very hard to answer the question. At that time, when I was writing that, I was prepared to take the blame.

By eliciting the manifest absurdities in Bradley's story, Bill Knight's cross-examination painted him as evasive and unwilling to come to grips with the powerful case against him. Bradley agreed that he and Mr Holt had spent a period of some hours alone at the CIB over the weekend after making his confessions, but he had no satisfactory explanation to give as to why he had not told Mr Holt that the admissions had been forced from him.

The cross-examination ranged over a variety of topics, including the rug, the string, the twine, his lies at Nutt & Muddle, the fact that he and Magda had been looking at expensive houses, the argument with Magda overheard by neighbours the previous night, the departure from the Clontarf house on 7 July, the sudden decision to leave Australia after the police interview at Nutt & Muddle, and many other matters. Bill Knight QC asked Bradley what he had been doing between 23 June, when he left Nutt & Muddle, and 7 July. Bradley's reply – 'Generally packing and resting' – was most unconvincing. Towards the end of his cross-examination, Knight put these penetrating questions to Bradley, which contained fundamental allegations:

Knight: It was on the night of the 6th that you told your wife that you were going to kidnap Graeme Thorne, wasn't it?
Bradley: No such thing happened.
Knight: That was the reason why your wife refused to be associated with you on that day, wasn't it?
[No answer].
…
Knight: She [Magda] did not travel back to Sydney [from Queensland] in your Ford, did she?

Bradley: No.

Knight: I am putting to you the reason she did not want to be associated with your Ford was that she knew your Ford was going to be used [sic][14] in the kidnapping of Graeme Thorne?

Bradley: No.

...

Knight: You knew Centennial Park well?

Bradley: No.

Knight: You did take the police, on that day when you were running around with them, you did take the police close to Centennial Park, didn't you?

Bradley: I did not.

Knight: Did the car that you were in get close to Centennial Park at any time when you were going with the police?

Bradley: It could have been, I do not remember exactly.

Knight: Would it appear to you to be silly for a man, if he was kidnapping a boy, to drive him sitting up in the car in the front seat to the tollgate on the Sydney Harbour Bridge and pull up to pay the toll with the boy sitting alongside him in the front seat of the car? Does that appear silly to you?

Bradley: You are asking my opinion?

Knight: Yes.

Bradley: Yes, I think it is definitely.

Knight: And then to pull up at a phone box and leave the boy sitting in the motorcar while someone who had just kidnapped him went and made a phone call, a demand for ransom. That is just silly too, isn't it?

Bradley: Yes.

Knight: It could not happen, could it?

Bradley: I don't know that.

Knight: I am suggesting to you that you took this boy into Centennial Park and that he was in the boot of the car from the time it came out of Centennial Park and when it went over the Harbour Bridge?

Bradley: Definitely not. I never saw that boy.

...

Knight: Was there any coincidence in the fact that you were interviewed by Detective Sergeant Doyle and Detective Sergeant Fergusson on the 24th August, and your wife booked her passage to London on the 25th?

Bradley: Definitely not.

At the conclusion of Knight's cross-examination, Vizzard asked his client several clarifying questions in re-examination, and then Bradley returned with his escorting police officer to the dock, where he sat down and looked around the courtroom with an air of assured confidence that he had done a good job at convincing everyone of his innocence.

*** *

As Stephen Bradley walked back to the dock after giving evidence, he was proud that he had admitted nothing under the gruelling barrage of questions from the Senior Crown Prosecutor of New South Wales. He was sure that very few, if any, accused people would be able to say that to themselves after such an ordeal. Knight had tried again and again to trick him into inadvertently admitting something that would demonstrate his guilt, but he had been wise to the prosecutor's tactics and had never slipped up. He was also pleased that he had kept cool and calm at all times, despite many provocations and considerable disrespect towards him. Surely the jury would think that a man with that degree of composure would be incapable of committing such an impulsive and ill-considered crime. He was gratified that he had been able to convey to the jury his emotional attachment to his wife and their children, so that they could appreciate the pressure he had been under while at the police station during his questioning. As he was giving his evidence he noticed two jurors leaning forward in their seats, seemingly anxious to hear every word he uttered. It was on those two that he focused as he occasionally turned to the jury to address his answers directly to them, as he had seen the police officers do when giving evidence at the Inquest and the trial. He hoped that these two jurors would champion his cause when they came to deliberate their verdict in the jury room. He was convinced that his decision to expose himself in the witness box had been the right one.

***

Bazil and Freda Thorne were very distressed at Bradley's dock statement in which he denied responsibility for the kidnapping and death of their son. They were only too aware of the holes in his version, and they felt that it was unfair that he was able to advance it without being questioned, while all the other witnesses had been through rigorous cross-examinations to test their accounts. They were particularly concerned at Bradley's assuredness during his dock statement, thinking that it might sway some of the jurors to have a reasonable doubt about his guilt. Bazil and Freda stared repeatedly at the jurors to see if they could divine what they were thinking about Bradley's denials, but none of them would give anything away by their body language. Perhaps that was because Mr Justice Clancy had told the jurors they were judges of the facts.

When Bradley went into the witness box after his statement, Bazil and Freda were shocked, because Knight QC had confided that it was his expectation that the accused would make a dock statement, so as not to be cross-examined. Knight elaborated that very few accused got into the witness box and he lamented not being able to exercise his cross-examination skills more often. As Bazil and Freda listened to Bradley's evidence-in-chief in answer to questions from Vizzard QC, they wondered what the defence counsel had up his sleeve, and they were taken by surprise when he suddenly sat down after a few desultory questions. Within a few minutes of Knight QC beginning, they could see why he was the Senior Crown Prosecutor of New South Wales. This was a man with the precision of a skilled surgeon wielding a scalpel. He had a command of the exchange and a penetrating force to his questions that was quite intimidating, even for an observer. It was not only that he was overtly aggressive in manner – it was also that one could palpably feel the penetrating impact of the logic inherent in his questions.

After Bradley had finished giving evidence, Bazil and Freda asked to have a few brief words with Knight, and he willingly gave them his attention. Even though the cross-examination had gone well for the prosecution, they were worried that Bradley might have pulled the wool over the eyes of some of the jurors with his pathetic denials. They knew that the verdict had to be unanimous, and they feared he might be able to thwart justice with a hung jury. They did not want to have to bear another trial, where they would have to give evidence again. However, Bill Knight reassured them that in his opinion – based on decades of experience in criminal trials – the jury were highly unlikely to be fooled by Bradley's denials. Despite this, Bazil and Freda spent the rest of the trial worrying that Bradley's glibness might gain him a hung jury or an acquittal, in which case justice for their son would be delayed or even denied.

***

A Crown Prosecutor is not meant to have any emotional investment in whether or not a conviction results from a trial. So long as the prosecutor has presented the evidence in the best light and has competently analysed and presented the evidence in both opening and closing addresses, the verdict is a matter for the jury. Whatever the final outcome, justice is done! This attitude of enviable objectivity and professionalism is one for which every conscientious Crown Prosecutor strives, however the reality is that the criminal justice system in Australia – based on the British system – operates in an adversarial environment in which the two sides are represented by opposing counsel, so that most prosecutors take pride in the quality of their work and see a proper conviction as tangible evidence of it. In some cases, of course, the proper verdict is an acquittal, and a Crown Prosecutor can take equal pride that justice has been done in such circumstances. The Crown Prosecutor represents the community, which has a justifiable interest in seeing the conviction of the guilty and the acquittal of the innocent. The whole system proceeds on the basis that it is better to have ten guilty men go free than one innocent man be wrongly convicted. The Crown Prosecutor is not in court to achieve a conviction at all costs. Rather, he or she is there to see that justice is done.

Despite his awareness of the proper role of a Crown Prosecutor, Bill Knight was so utterly convinced of Stephen Bradley's guilt that he firmly believed that an acquittal would be a travesty of justice – not just for Graeme Thorne and his family, but also for the community at large. He was quietly confident that Bradley's performance in the dock and the witness box had failed to make a dent in the vast body of evidence against him. While Bradley may have succeeded in not making any obvious mistakes or admissions, he had been ineffective at convincing anyone in the courtroom of his innocence – except his own counsel. Of particular note, his language errors in the witness box when pressed during cross-examination were quite similar to those in the disputed confessions. In light of how confidently Bradley had withstood the onslaught during Knight's cross-examination, Bradley's assertion that he had succumbed so readily to the police threats was unconvincing. The reasons he advanced for selling Clontarf and suddenly leaving Australia were unimpressive. His story about the picnic rug having vanished from his home was convenient and contrived. He completely failed to account for the vast bulk of scientific evidence against him, and he had not convinced anyone that Freda and Bazil Thorne's identification of him was mistaken. Overall, Bill Knight was pleased with his cross-examination of Bradley and maintained his confidence that justice would be done.

✳✳✳

Vizzard next called Paul Weinberg, who supported his step-father's alibi, claiming to have helped Stephen to put labels on furniture before seeing him leave the Clontarf house at 8.30 on the morning of 7 July. If true, this would preclude Bradley having been at Bondi at the time of the kidnapping. Paul also said that the family had had a rug similar to the one in court, but it was torn and had disappeared around Christmas 1959. In cross-examination, Paul inadvertently told Knight that the rug was not at Clontarf when the family was packing up to go to Surfers Paradise because it was kept in the Customline. He admitted in cross-examination that he had not had any reason to think back to the events of 7 July until he was asked about them in London in February 1961 – seven months later. Paul Weinberg gave the clear impression that he was trying to tell the truth, but there were severe doubts about the accuracy and reliability of his recollections.

Great excitement was evident in the courtroom when Vizzard next called Magda Bradley.

***

By the time Magda Bradley came to give evidence, she had a fair idea that her husband faced an almost irresistible case against him. Although she was not permitted to enter the court before giving her evidence, she had read the newspaper summaries of the evidence given by the Crown witnesses, so she knew there was a mountain of evidence against him and that there were weaknesses in his planned response. She was also only too aware of public opinion, fanned by the newspapers, that she had known beforehand what Stephen was planning and perhaps had even given him encouragement. While she acknowledged to herself that the evidence against Stephen was all one way, she still refused to accept that the man she had loved and lived with so successfully for years was capable of committing such an atrocious crime. She decided that he was entitled to her absolute loyalty and support in attempting to beat the charge at this trial, but that if he was convicted she would then put distance between them and create a new life for herself. But first, she had to give evidence to bolster his slim chances of an acquittal.

The odds were so heavily stacked against Stephen that Magda felt justified stretching the truth to give him some hope of an acquittal. Surely the police had engaged in similar massaging of the evidence in stitching together such a strong case, so she believed she was just slightly redressing the imbalance. She had no qualms about doing this, because she firmly believed that Stephen was innocent, despite the weight of the evidence against him, so she was only attempting to avoid an injustice being perpetrated against him.

***

Magda Bradley's arrival in court caused a loud murmur from the public gallery. Her appearance was described as follows:

> She entered wearing a black tailored suit and a black, turban style hat. Bradley smiled at her as she entered the witness box.[15]

Fred Vizzard QC began his examination-in-chief of Magda Bradley by asking about her experiences as a prisoner in

Auschwitz concentration camp in the Second World War. She showed the court the camp number tattooed on her left arm, and told everyone that both her parents had died in the camp and that her left eye had been injured in the year she had spent there. She gave evidence that the picnic rug in which Graeme Thorne's body had been wrapped was similar to the one Jacob Fogel had given her, but much more worn and faded. When shown the scarf from around Graeme Thorne's neck, she denied that her husband had owned one like it. She provided an innocent explanation for why she and Stephen had argued the night before she left for Surfers Paradise, explaining that after furiously working at packing up all their belongings on that day, she had become fed up and angry with Stephen because it was all so rushed and they had nowhere to live after their return from Queensland. She maintained that it had been *her* spontaneous decision to let Stephen finish the packing on his own, while she and the children flew to Queensland. At her insistence, Stephen had rung the airline to make a booking, but he could not get seats before mid-morning the next day. She attempted to explain why she had called a taxi to go to the airport on the morning they flew to Coolangatta, rather than waiting for Stephen to return home, stating that she was still angry with him from the argument the night before, and that she knew when he returned from the hardware store he would have to wait for the removalists.

She told the court that Stephen had informed her that the police had visited him at his workplace, telling her that the enquiry related to the registration of the Customline. In an attempt to explain her initial booking of ship passages only for herself and Paul, she said that it had originally been her idea to go to England to see if she could sell her songs and stories, thinking that Stephen and the other two children would stay in Australia until she had achieved a measure of success. However, when they discussed it further, they both did not want to be apart, so they decided to all go overseas together. It then became their hope to get some treatment for Ross while they were in England, and this eventually became a major reason for their trip.

Magda Bradley's cross-examination by Bill Knight QC took place on the seventh day of the trial. When the court doors were opened that morning, dozens of women rushed for seats, and several, caught in the crush, had to be helped by court officers. The public gallery was even more crowded than on previous days and the court officers had to force their way through spectators standing at a side door to allow witnesses to enter the court. The Senior Crown Prosecutor squarely put to Magda that when she left Sydney for Surfers Paradise it was because she had had advance warning of what her husband was planning to do. He suggested:

> *I put it to you that you wanted to leave that night [6 July] because you did not want to be in Sydney when your husband did something the following morning. You wanted to be in Surfers Paradise the following morning?*

And this:

> *I put it to you that you knew your husband could not drive you to the terminal because you knew he was somewhere in the Bondi area at the time?*

Magda denied both of these suggestions. She asserted that it was a mere coincidence that the very day after police had interviewed her husband at work she had booked a passage for herself and one of the children to go to England. She explained why she and Stephen had lied to people about where they were going, insisting that she knew that her ex-husband Gregor Weinberg would disagree with Paul going abroad. She admitted that she had written him a misleading letter, which was posted in Melbourne.

**

Magda Bradley had been dreading giving evidence in court. She knew that there was an undercurrent of hatred against her in the community that had been encouraged by the newspapers, and she anticipated that the atmosphere in the courtroom would be hostile towards her. When she entered the court-room, she was surprised by the looks she got from the public gallery, where both men and women were clearly interested in her appearance. She was sure that she had not disappointed them! As she walked past the dock to go to the witness box, she threw a glance at Stephen, who lovingly smiled back at her. Her evidence-in-chief proceeded smoothly, as she had carefully gone over the questions beforehand with Vizzard QC in his chambers, so there were no surprises. When the time came for the cross-examination by Knight QC, she was surprised by his aggressive attitude, and looked to the judge to rein him in, but nothing happened. At this stage, she felt overwhelming antagonism from the courtroom, and she found it hard to focus on the questions, as though her brain had gone to mush.

From time to time, she looked across at Stephen, hoping to gain strength from a friendly face, but he was quite aloof and poker-faced. No doubt Vizzard had told him not to interact with her in front of the jury. Towards the end of the ordeal, Knight put some monstrous allegations to her, as though she were the one on trial. What could she say except to deny them? When it was over, she felt that she had done her best for Stephen, although she recognised that it hadn't amounted to much, compared to the weight of the evidence against him. If she had given him some hope that he might be acquitted and thereby lightened his burden, then it was worth having made the long trip from England.

***

Vizzard's next witness was Dr Alexander Fraser from the Division of Animal Genetics at the CSIRO, who gave evidence about the dog hairs that had played a prominent part in the Crown case. Dr Fraser claimed that although the hairs were similar to those of the Bradleys' Pekinese, they were not sufficiently unique to be able to say that they were the same. This evidence was identical to the position that had been taken by the Crown's dog hair expert, Dr Cramp, prompting Justice Clancy to say to Mr Vizzard at the conclusion of this evidence:

> There is no mystery about it, Mr Vizzard. He is saying what Dr Cramp said.

Before closing his case, Fred Vizzard QC tendered copies of the Sydney *Daily Mirror* newspaper from 11 October, which contained the offending photograph of Stephen and Magda Bradley.[16] The relevance of this was to explain the unreliability of the line-ups that had been held six weeks later on 21 November, by demonstrating that the witnesses who claimed to have identified Stephen Bradley had previously seen his photograph in the newspaper, thereby rendering their identification unreliable.

The evidence having concluded, what now remained was for Vizzard and then Knight to give their closing addresses, and then for Justice Clancy to sum up to the jury. The traditional wisdom at the time was that the Crown Prosecutor had a distinct advantage in the order of addresses, because his was the last word that the jury heard from the opposing parties, and they would therefore be more likely to remember it and be influenced by it.[17]

Fred Vizzard commenced his six-hour closing address by asserting that no man had ever come before a court in a more prejudicial atmosphere than Stephen Leslie Bradley, thereby making it very difficult for justice to be done.[18] He claimed that the identification witnesses were of no value because of the earlier publication of Bradley's photograph in the newspaper. He told the jury that it was no exaggeration to say that more miscarriages of justice had occurred through misidentification than from any other cause. He valiantly tried to account for the scientific evidence, labelling it as purely circumstantial and suggesting that some people would overestimate its value. At times he was rebuked by Mr Justice Clancy for misstating the scientific evidence. Vizzard made particular mention of the fact that there had been no pink mortar on the rug, which would be inexplicable if Graeme Thorne's body had been wrapped in it and placed under Stephen Bradley's Clontarf house. He attempted to deal with the seeds from two types of cypress tree by reminding the jury that witnesses had agreed that garden clippings had been dumped on the allotment where the body had been found. He suggested that the Bradleys had very good reasons for not disclosing their travel plans or their real reasons for leaving the country, and he stressed that the Bradleys had obtained their passports a long time *before* Bazil Thorne had won his lottery prize. He criticised the Crown Prosecutor for inconsistency in conceding that Magda Bradley was not implicated in the plot, but then suggesting to her that she knew in advance about her husband's plan. Pounding the Bar table, Vizzard submitted that Bradley had been induced to sign his confession because of fear that his wife would be arrested in London, and he advanced the view that it would have made no sense for Bradley to complain about the threats to his solicitor shortly afterwards, because that would have resulted in his wife being dragged back to Australia. He attempted to deal with the identification of Stephen Bradley as the man who had called at the Thornes' home three weeks before the kidnapping by advancing a rather unconvincing argument that the jury could not be certain that the person who took Graeme Thorne was the same person who had called at their home. In a particularly lame submission, he suggested:

The person who called at the Thornes' or the person who kidnapped the boy might have looked very like Bradley and might be of the same race, for all we know.

He reminded the jury of the alibi evidence from Paul Weinberg, and concluded by saying to them: 'Unless you reject the evidence of Bradley, Paul Weinberg and Mrs Bradley, you cannot possibly convict.'

Bill Knight QC began his closing address to the jury early on the afternoon on the eighth and final day of the trial, Wednesday, 29 March 1961. He pointed out that circumstantial evidence can be immensely powerful, depending on the case. In this instance, he suggested, the circumstantial evidence, including all the scientific material, was overpowering. He submitted that Bradley's confessions were an important part of the prosecution case, and suggested that the jury would assess their authenticity by noting that Bradley had sought to minimise his culpability:

> [Bradley's confession was] the least blameworthy explanation that he could give of all the circumstances. He tried to make up the most innocent statement of what he had done that he could think of at the time, and this is it.

He said that because the confessions minimised parts of the crime, it was highly improbable that they had been coerced from Bradley or dictated by the police. He pointed out that Bradley had withstood a vigorous cross-examination, with questions being fired at him for more than an hour, without crumbling or becoming disoriented, and thereby had shown himself to be the sort of man who would not easily buckle under threats from the police. Knight pointed out that although the identification parades had taken place after the publication of Bradley's photograph in the newspaper, Freda and Bazil Thorne and the Denmeades had all originally picked Bradley from an array of photographs they had been shown by police three days *before* the photo of Bradley had been published. He submitted that for the defence case to be correct, approximately seventy Crown witnesses, including seven police officers, would have been required to perjure themselves, which was manifestly absurd. He suggested that Magda Bradley's journey to Surfers Paradise on 7 July occurred because of her refusal to become involved with Bradley's plan for a kidnapping and her desire to secure an alibi for herself, and that Magda had rung for a taxi to get to the airport because she knew that her husband was not going to be available to take them. Knight alleged that Paul Weinberg was mistaken about seeing his stepfather on the morning of the kidnapping. Knight concluded his address in just under two hours – less than a third of the time Vizzard had taken – by saying to the jury:

> *The whole of this case is so overwhelming that there cannot be the slightest shadow of a doubt that the accused is guilty of the crime of which he stands charged.*

Mr Justice Clancy commenced his summing up after lunch, informing everyone in the courtroom that he would be sending out the jury that same afternoon, even if that meant they would retire to consider their verdict after the usual 4pm recess, when courts normally adjourned for the day. He explained to the jurors the various categories of murder and the difference between murder and manslaughter. He told them that murder is when a person kills someone intending to kill or do grievous bodily harm, or when acting with reckless indifference to human life. Manslaughter, on the other hand, occurs when a person accidentally kills someone while doing something that is unlawful and dangerous, but without the state of mind required for murder. He explained to the jury the significance of circumstantial evidence. He summarised each of the different categories of scientific evidence. He pointed out that both Mr and Mrs Thorne had seen a photograph of Stephen Bradley in the press on 11 October, which was prior to the identification parades, however he also noted that they had first identified the accused from photographs on 8 October. Mr and Mrs Denmeade had also been shown police photographs before the press image was published.

It was not until 4.27 that afternoon that Justice Clancy finished his summing up and sent the jurors out to consider their verdict. Fred Vizzard QC then complained that the judge had not reminded the jury that in addition to making an unsworn statement from the dock, Bradley had given evidence on oath and been cross-examined. The judge testily refused to bring the jury back to remind them of this. Vizzard then protested that the judge had not properly and fully put Bradley's defence to the jury, asking the judge to remind them that the accused's defence was that he was not at Bondi and had called evidence to prove that he was at home until he left at 8.30am to go to the hardware store. Although Mr Justice Clancy considered that the jurors would be well aware of this, he agreed that to be on the safe side he would remind them of it. The jury were brought back into the courtroom for the judge to refer to this aspect of the defence case, and then sent back to the jury room to continue their deliberations. At 5.43pm, the jurors returned to court at their own request so they could have read to them the medical evidence about the cause of Graeme's death. They then returned to the jury room to resume their deliberations. Nobody knew how long it would take for the jury to reach a verdict. If necessary, they would be locked up overnight to resume their deliberations in the morning.

At 6.15pm, on the judge's order, the court was cleared for dinner until 7.30pm. By then, it was well past the copy deadline for the next day's morning newspapers, so if there was a verdict that night, it was likely that the afternoon papers the following day would get the scoop.

***

As Magda Bradley had not been allowed in the public gallery until she had completed her evidence, the prosecutor's closing address was her first opportunity to hear a comprehensive account of the case against her husband. She was deeply shocked at the strength of the evidence, and realised that a conviction was almost inevitable. After the jury retired, she spoke to a few journalists, who made it clear that they thought that a conviction was likely. Greatly stressed, she decided that she could not bear to hear the verdict when the jury returned or to witness the deflation when her husband realised that they would not be reuniting soon. Without informing Stephen or his counsel, she left the courthouse, telling a journalist that she had 'not given up hope'. She told journalist Tom Prior, who was working for the *Daily Telegraph*, that she had heard enough and didn't want anyone shoving a microphone in her face. Prior told her that his newspaper had a flat available on the other side of Taylor Square where she could wait for the verdict if she liked, promising to come and inform her of it. After a lot of thought, Magda agreed to wait there.[19]

15

LAST EMBRACE

As Stephen Bradley sat in the underground cell beneath the courtroom where his trial had taken place over the previous eight days, he had several hours, punctuated by a sandwich, in which to contemplate his prospects while he waited for the verdict that would determine the rest of his life. He was realistic enough to accept that the prosecutor's closing address had been persuasive, and that his own barrister's entreaties to the jury, although longer than the prosecutor's, had been less cogent. He was convinced, however, that his primary obstacle in securing a favourable outcome was not so much the evidence against him, but rather the prejudice that Anglo-Saxon jurors would harbour, even subconsciously, against a foreigner like him. His origins, his accent, his faulty English, his olive complexion, his history of multiple marriages – they would all raise the kind of bigotry that he had so often encountered in his everyday life since arriving in Australia. Why should it be any different with a representative sample of citizens on a jury? His own barrister had acknowledged this hurdle in his closing address to the jury.

The more he thought about it, the more convinced he became that prejudice would be the real reason for the jury to convict him. It would be prejudice if they ignored his alibi evidence or the fact that he and Magda had applied for passports well before the kidnapping. It would be prejudice if they overlooked the fact that there were numerous homes in Sydney that had wind-blown seeds from two types of cypress, or Onkaparinga blankets, or blue Customlines, or Pekinese dogs. These were all very interesting facts, but how could they use them to implicate him in the kidnapping, except by suspending logic and rationality and substituting them with prejudice? The newspapers had begun the process of vilification months earlier by constantly drawing attention to his foreign origins and his unorthodox family situation, and they had exacerbated the situation by relentlessly reminding readers of these irrelevant factors up to, and even during, the trial. His barrister had drawn attention to the background of prejudice in the media, and had unrealistically asked the jurors to put it aside. As if jurors could simply put their preconceived notions into a box and place it under the jury room table, leaving them free to deliberate without bias! He was convinced that he could not get a fair trial against the background of this protracted denigration, and that his foreignness would inevitably intrude into the jury's consideration of his case.

***

In the jury room, right from the beginning there was not a single juror who accepted Stephen Bradley's denial of involvement in the kidnapping and death of Graeme Thorne.[1] The only question was whether his actions amounted to murder or manslaughter. Ten of the twelve jurors were convinced that it was murder, while two thought that it could be manslaughter. It was only after the medical evidence was re-read to them, indicating that 'a good force' would have been necessary to fracture Graeme's skull, that the jurors in the minority swung around and joined the others in a unanimous verdict. No one in the jury room was concerned by Bradley's origins, his appearance or the number of his marriages. The only reference to his accent was during discussion about the identity of the man looking for Mr Bognor.

After deliberating for three-and-a-half hours, the jury returned to the courtroom at 7.49pm on the eighth and final day of the trial – Wednesday, 29 March 1961. The atmosphere was electric and a pin drop could be heard as the accused and then the foreman were requested to stand. Then the foreman was asked the critical question by the judge's associate: 'How say you: is the accused Stephen Leslie Bradley guilty or not guilty on the charge of the murder of Graeme Frederick Hilton Thorne?' The foreman replied with the one word that almost everyone in the courtroom was hoping for: 'Guilty'. The associate then recited the time-honoured words signifying unanimity: 'So says your foreman, so say you all.'

As soon as the verdict was announced, pandemonium broke out in the public gallery, with clapping, whistles, catcalls and cries of elation. One woman screamed, 'Feed him to the sharks!' It was quite clear from these spontaneous outbursts and from the body language of the prosecution team that the verdict met with the approval of almost everyone in the courtroom. Bazil and Freda Thorne initially restrained their emotions, but when Bazil put his arm around Freda, she was unable to contain herself any longer and began to weep. It was as though Graeme's death had only now been officially acknowledged. Stephen Bradley stood with his hands firmly clenching the rail of the dock in front of him, his face showing no emotion. Fred Vizzard appeared devastated by the verdict.

After what seemed like several minutes, a Sheriff's Officer called out for silence, and Mr Justice Clancy asked Bradley if he had anything to say before passing sentence. Normally, at this point prisoners either choose to remain silent, or at most say something predictable, like, 'I am not guilty, your Honour.' Stephen Bradley, however, took advantage of this invitation to deliver the following lengthy, rambling speech:

Yes, I have two things to say. I never had an opportunity to say anything until I came to this Court. It was the first time anybody heard me say anything.

One thing I would like to say. I do not accuse anybody, but I would like to say as a matter of fact I knew before I came to this court that I would be convicted of the crime which I did not commit, and why I was more or less convinced because of a certain human emotion – what you call prejudice. Prejudice is the same or similar as jealousy. That is a human emotion. It is a very dangerous one – extremely so. It affects your mind to that extent that you cannot – you are unable to judge things really with the full facts. You are forced by these emotions more or less to back up that emotion and it more or less controls your mind.

And I think that one of the main factors – it was given very bad publicity in the newspapers. Everybody read about it. Although Your Honour instructed the jury for them to forget about it – but it is impossible. It is impossible.

Anyway, I am not saying – accusing the jury, who are very good citizens. They tried to do their best. They have been influenced by this very powerful emotion.

Anyway, I could tell you a lot of other things, but I don't think they would alter the fact, and cannot alter the fact – the fact that the jury has decided on a certain verdict, and naturally it is your duty to pass sentence according to the law. That is all I wish to say.

His Honour Mr Justice Clancy said nothing in response to Bradley's rationalisation of the verdict, thereby demonstrating his contempt for Bradley's claim of prejudice, and he proceeded to carry out his statutory duty by imposing the only sentence available for this crime, using the minimum number of words required:

The prisoner, Stephen Leslie Bradley, is sentenced to penal servitude for life.

Again there was an enormous uproar in the court. The *Herald* reported that 'screaming women surged forward and were controlled only by the outstretched arms of Sheriff's Officers and police'.[2] Justice Clancy and his associate hurriedly left the Bench by the judge's door, while Bradley was slowly led down the bleak, steep, stone stairs beneath the dock amid further abuse hurled at him from the back of the courtroom. Friends and relatives crowded around Bazil and Freda, and members of the public came to shake their hands. Eventually, the Sheriff's Officers cleared the courtroom and large groups of people assembled outside in the courtyard and on Oxford Street to discuss the outcome of the trial. The *Herald* reported that:

> *The scene outside resembled a carnival with about 400 people, many of them carrying and wheeling small children and babies, had gathered. Television floodlights and photographers' flash bulbs revealed people with sandwiches and vacuum flasks, youths with transistor radios, young couples, and a small boy who had climbed a pillar. People rushed forward as Mr Knight tried to leave. They mobbed his car amid calls of 'good on yer, Bill'.*[3]

As Bazil and Freda Thorne left the court, they were besieged by reporters and well-wishers in the courtyard and outside on Oxford Street, however they studiously kept silent and refused to comment on the verdict, other than to thank the police for all the work they had done. Stephen Bradley was whisked out a back entrance to a laneway behind the court where a prison van took him to the State Penitentiary at Long Bay. As the van exited to the street, crowds jeered and hurled abuse at him. Fred Vizzard felt utterly deflated and emotionally stung by the outcome of the trial, thinking that he must have done an inadequate job to warrant the result that was unexpected only to him. He knew he faced a hostile reaction from the crowd outside, so he lingered inside the court, not quite knowing what to do or where to go. Vin Wallace, junior counsel for the Crown, sympathetically offered him a lift home in his car, which was parked within the grounds of the courthouse, so that his former opponent would not have to undergo the ordeal of a media ruckus outside the gates, and Vizzard gratefully accepted. Immediately after the trial, Fred Vizzard left Sydney on a month's leave to recover from the ordeal and refrained from leaving his contact details with anyone.

***

Shortly after the sentence was pronounced, journalist Tom Prior went to the apartment on the other side of Taylor Square where Magda Bradley was waiting. She took the news stoically and enquired how Stephen had accepted it. Prior informed her that Stephen seemed to take it pretty well, but that he had made a bit of a speech saying that he hadn't been able to tell the full story. After inquiring about where her husband would be taken, Magda wanted to discuss with him how much she should charge for interviews, and which of the television stations would be likely to pay more. Prior offered to talk to his newspaper, as the proprietor, Sir Frank Packer, also owned a television station.[4] Prior and Magda then went briefly to a restaurant in Surry Hills, before Magda returned to the People's Palace, where, in a state of unbridled agitation and confusion, she took a sleeping pill, went to bed and promptly fell asleep.

When Magda awoke from a deep, drug-induced slumber the next morning, she heard the verdict on the radio. Her immediate concern was for the children and how they would cope with the news that their father and stepfather was not coming home for a very long time – if ever. She wept for their loss, and was overcome by waves of fear at the gaping hole that appeared all around her, barring every step in any direction. It was clear that she would have to return to England, where she could at least walk the streets without having vile comments hurled at her by strangers.

By the afternoon, Magda had recovered her composure sufficiently to make the journey to Long Bay, where she had again been given special permission by the Minister to visit. As a convicted prisoner, Stephen had been moved to a different part of the gaol, where the atmosphere was more menacing. This was the first visit where a warder was not only present, but within earshot the whole time. If there had been an emotional gap between husband and wife on the previous occasion, there was a chasm now. They hardly knew what to say to each other, and there were long periods of silence. She was determined to be of as much support to him as she could, but he seemed remote and distracted. She mentioned her plan to return to London with the children, and he begged her to stay until his appeal had been heard, which Vizzard had assured him would be in a month or so. Of course, she agreed to delay her departure. Stephen said that he was confident of success on the appeal, as the evidence against him at the trial had been flimsy, and he reiterated his view that the verdict had been based on mere prejudice. At the end of the visit, he asked her to tell all three children how much he loved them.

They were permitted to embrace in the knowledge that it was probably for the last time.

A newspaper report several days later quoted Magda as saying: 'I do not know when I will see him again. He told me he would appeal against his conviction.'

***

Magda made an application to the Attorney-General's Department to remain in Sydney at government expense until after the appeal, on the basis that if a retrial was ordered by the Appeal Court, she would have to be available to give evidence again. After considering the cost of the alternatives, the government agreed to Magda and the children remaining in Sydney at public expense. As the time for the appeal approached, Magda told a journalist, 'I have begun to feel the effect of months of strain and worry.'

On Friday, 19 May 1961, exactly six months to the day after he had been returned to Sydney under escort from Colombo and nearly two months since his trial, Stephen Bradley appealed his conviction to the Court of Criminal Appeal, comprising Chief Justice Dr HV Evatt, Mr Justice Herron and Mr Justice Collins. As was the custom in those days, Bill Knight QC again represented the Crown, this time juniored by Mr CD Cullen.[5] Bradley, who remained at the prison during the appeal hearing, was again represented by Fred Vizzard QC, instructed again by Mr Pat Smith. Vizzard complained that Mr Justice Clancy had delivered an unbalanced summing up to the jury by giving too much weight to the Crown case and too little to the defence. Vizzard also submitted that the identification evidence had been tainted by the publication of Bradley's photograph in the Sydney *Daily Mirror* on 11 October, well prior to the identification by Mrs Lord and that the judge had failed to properly put to the jury the defence case on this, and on many other issues. Vizzard concluded by submitting:

The more serious the charge, the more necessary it is that the defence should be carefully put, because I think it has been said that even the vilest criminals are entitled to have a clear, careful trial.

The Chief Justice observed during argument that perhaps an overwhelming factor in the case was that Bradley's wife had gone on a trip to Surfers Paradise the day the boy was kidnapped, and he suggested that her trip was 'a strange interlude at a time when tragedy was overtaking the boy with tremendous speed'. At one point during argument, Vizzard justifiably felt that the members of the Bench had already made up their minds against him, prompting him to say:

It appears to me that Your Honours are looking at the Crown case and assuming it must be valid.

To which Mr Justice Collins testily snapped:

I don't see what reason you have for making such a statement.

The hearing had not been completed by the end of the first day, so it was adjourned until Monday 22 May for Bill Knight QC to make his submissions. On resumption of the hearing, Mr Knight submitted that legal authorities showed that the trial judge was not required to give a full exposition of the whole case for the Crown or for the defence, but could pick out salient features on both sides. He submitted that the Crown case was not merely strong and convincing, but overwhelming. It did not depend on one category of evidence, but rather could be divided into three compartments: confessional, circumstantial and identification. He argued that Justice Clancy had adopted 'a mode in his summing up which was very much in Bradley's favour'.

Following those submissions, the Court of Criminal Appeal handed down its decision in which all three judges rejected the appeal out of hand, declaring that the defence had been properly explained by Mr Justice Clancy and that there had been no miscarriage of justice. The Chief Justice complimented the work of the Crown Prosecutors and the police, and remarked:

> *The crime was so brutal and cruel as to be beyond human experience and belief … [Bradley] had every lie ready to deceive the unwary.*

Mr Justice Herron commented:

> *Mr Justice Clancy is a man of experience and wisdom and I think it must be said he very fairly put the facts of the case to the jury … I doubt very much if I have ever met with a case in which a confession made in the accused's own handwriting is more convincing for its truth … So strong was the Crown case that I feel it fair to say that a jury which failed to convict on this evidence would have failed in their duty as citizens.*

Bazil and Freda did not attend the appeal hearing, but, on being informed of the result, were greatly relieved. The prospect of a retrial – however unlikely – had hung over them for the weeks since the verdict.

Magda Bradley likewise did not attend the appeal hearing. When a journalist approached her at the People's Palace to tell her that the appeal had been dismissed, she opened the door a few inches to hear the news, and when told the result she appeared stunned, saying, 'Oh, no. Are you sure? It couldn't be true. I don't know what I'll do now.' She told the journalist that the strain of the trial and appeal had been 'almost unbearable'. Conjecture in the papers continued to tarnish Magda with the brush of complicity in, or prior knowledge of, the kidnapping. It was clear that while she remained in Australia she would be subjected to unrelenting public antipathy that would make it impossible to lead a normal life.

***

Magda made one final visit to Stephen at Long Bay shortly after his failed appeal. He told her he had already made application for legal aid funding to support his last avenue of appeal – to the High Court of Australia. He maintained his belief that he would ultimately be vindicated, but acknowledged that it would take some time for this appeal to be heard. When Magda told him that she intended returning soon to London with the children, he readily agreed that in the circumstances it was all for the best. They parted on cordial terms, but it was clear to both of them that their former intimacy had been irretrievably shattered.

***

In early June 1961, about a fortnight after the appeal, Stephen Bradley was transferred from Long Bay Gaol to Goulburn maximum-security gaol. In November 1961, the New South Wales Government refused an application by Bradley for legal aid to appeal to the High Court of Australia on the grounds that the appeal had no reasonable prospects of success, and Bradley did not pursue the appeal further.

***

While the jury's verdict, the sentence and the appeal ended the judicial process for Stephen Bradley, it was not the end of Magda Bradley's ordeals with the law. Just seven days after the verdict, she was served with a number of commitment warrants in relation to the twelve parking offences she had committed prior to her departure from Australia. She was compelled to hand over the sum of £47.10.0 from her meagre funds or face the prospect of being gaoled for three months.

After the trial, Magda was repeatedly besieged by reporters and was subjected to numerous suggestions that she must have been involved in her husband's plans, or at least had prior knowledge of them. In the public eye, she was almost as hated as her husband, and sometimes more so, because, as a woman, she was expected to have had more sympathy for Graeme's ordeal and the agony his parents had undergone. As a result, as soon as the appeal was over Magda was desperate to return to the relative safety and comfort of London. However, her departure was delayed by actions that threatened her custody of the two older children, Paul and Helen. Nobody seemed keen to seek custody of poor Ross, now six, who once again had been boarding at St. Gabriel's School for deaf children. Paul, now fourteen, had decided for himself that he did not want to return to England, but rather wished to live with his father in Leura. Magda did not challenge Paul's choice, as he was now of an age when he could make an informed decision for himself. Of more concern to her was her custody of Helen, now nearly eight years old.

As soon as Magda and the children had landed in Australia in mid-March 1961, Dr Frank Laszlo had gone back to his lawyers in Melbourne. Following Bradley's unsuccessful appeal, in June 1961 he commenced an action in the Equity Division of the Supreme Court of New South Wales seeking custody of his granddaughter, Helen.

The first hearing was a very brief one on 30 June before Justice Jacobs, in which Magda was represented by the Public Solicitor. Magda, Helen and Ross were due to travel back to England at government expense, leaving two days later on 2 July on the Sitmar Line ship TV *Castel Felice* bound for Southampton. Barrister Mr Derek Cassidy, who appeared for Dr Laszlo, was granted an adjournment of the custody hearing for four weeks until 28 July, which legally prevented Helen from leaving Australia until the next court appearance. Whether it was because she was worn down by the repeated criticisms in the papers, or because she was emotionally exhausted from the whole ordeal and desperate to get back to London, Magda reluctantly agreed to temporarily relinquish custody of Helen to Dr Laszlo and his wife, Ilse, until the hearing on 28 July, thereby conceding to them a huge tactical advantage. This freed Magda and Ross to leave on the *Castel Felice* as planned on 2 July.

Helen flew to Melbourne with her grandparents on the evening after the interim custody hearing. They all used the false name 'Lenner' on the plane's passenger list in a failed attempt to avoid newspaper photographers. Journalists reported that at Sydney airport Helen boarded the plane clutching a doll and a pink handbag. She and her grandparents shielded their faces from the press photographers, while Dr Laszlo refused to make any comment, reminding the media throng that the matter was still before the courts. In Melbourne they sheltered behind closed doors from a fresh group of photographers, while an Ansett-ANA official collected their luggage and brought it to them, whereupon they disappeared into a waiting taxi.

On the day before Magda was due to embark on the *Castel Felice*, she told a journalist: 'I'm not even sure that I'll catch the boat. I'm too heart-broken about the children to talk. I have no plans for the future. I don't know what I'm going to do.'

The following afternoon, Magda and Ross boarded the *Castel Felice* at Wharf 7 at Woolloomooloo. She declined to tell journalists whether she would continue the legal battle for the custody of Helen. To a journalist from the *Telegraph* she said she had not visited Bradley since he was transferred to Goulburn Gaol, but she had received several letters from him. She said that she had secured a job in London as a writer of television documentaries and that she would also help with the publication of a book she had written about her life.[6]

Once ensconced in her cabin on the ship, she gave an interview to a journalist from the *Sydney Morning Herald*. He reported:

Seated on a bunk smoking a cigarette, Mrs Bradley said she was leaving Australia because both she and her husband felt she would have a better chance to start life again in England.

'I am broken-hearted at having to leave,' she said. 'I don't know when I will be coming back. I'm going to London where I have a job arranged for me – writing commercial music for television. That's my profession. Stephen, whom I last saw a few weeks ago, wants me to go.' Magda Bradley said she believed that something would happen to prove her husband's innocence.[7]

Another journalist reported quite differently:

When at last she opened her cabin door to reporters she said 'I sincerely believe in my husband's innocence.' She said she would stay in London for about a year and work. Then she would return to Australia and wait for her husband – 'no matter how long it takes'.[8]

The ship sailed at 5.30pm on 2 July. Having left Australia behind, Magda lost her determination to fight for Helen to join her. On 4 August 1961, Justice Jacobs made a consent order officially granting custody of Helen to Frank Laszlo and his wife until the child turned sixteen.

When Magda arrived with her younger son in London, she was heartbroken, emotionally devastated and completely impoverished.

After leaving Australia, Magda never saw Stephen again. In 1965, she divorced him. While there continued to be occasional conjecture in the newspapers that she must have had some involvement in the kidnapping, she was never charged and she always denied any knowledge of her husband's vile plan.

***

The initial period of Stephen Bradley's incarceration in the prison system was fraught with hostility and the constant threat of violence from other prisoners. News reports soon after his conviction mentioned that warders had heard through the prison grapevine that Bradley was a marked man, and that several 'lifers' and a number of men serving long sentences had vowed to get him at the first opportunity. As a result, the prison authorities kept Bradley in strict protective custody and allowed him little contact with other prisoners. In November 1961, the *Sun* newspaper reported:

> *Friends of prisoners say letters from the gaol suggest that Bradley has completely changed from the self-assured, slightly arrogant man, as he was when he first arrived at Goulburn. They say he has become withdrawn, and his pallid features reflect the wall of silence erected around him by other prisoners. Warders speak to him only when necessary – at the five daily musters when his number (46) is called, and he must salute and answer 'sir'. Bradley is reported to be working in the prison tailor shop, 'doing it hard'.*

Eventually, however, Bradley's genial and engaging personality resulted in him becoming quite popular with both warders and fellow prisoners, although he had a reputation for telling tall stories when the truth would have readily sufficed. In Goulburn Gaol he was able to continue his work in the medical field by working as a prison hospital orderly.

Stephen Bradley's life sentence turned out to be much shorter than anyone had expected. On 6 October 1968, eight years after his arrest, he was enjoying a game of tennis with other prisoners at Goulburn Gaol when he suddenly dropped to the ground motionless. He was immediately taken to the prison hospital; where life was pronounced extinct. He was forty-two years old. A post-mortem examination disclosed that he had died of a heart attack. He continued to the end of his life to maintain his innocence of the kidnapping and murder of Graeme Thorne, and he never disclosed any further details of how the boy had come to die. Nor did he ever express any regrets or sorrow for Graeme's death or the hardships that the Thorne family had endured.

***

Police made recommendations for the government reward to be shared between: Douglas Palmer, Cecil and Dorothea Denmeade, Dorothy Lord, Hector and Eric Coughlin, David and Philip Wall and Theo Joseph (Christies Motors). It appears that no recognition was given to the information provided by the Telfords or Mr Browne. Detective Sergeant Ray Kelly's astounding intuition was never given public recognition.

***

Shortly after the trial, Bazil and Freda wrote to the Commissioner of Police expressing their appreciation for the efforts of the police during the investigation and their gratitude for the care they had been shown:

With the closing of the case against the accused, Bradley, our thoughts go back over the past nine months to those who worked relentlessly and with neither normal rest or thought of reward, to bring our son back to us and when this was known to be impossible to pursue untiringly until justice was done …

We feel we must at this time mention two of your officers in particular, Detective Sergeant Dave Paul and Detective Constable Lloyd Noonan. As you are aware, either one or the other of these officers was in constant attendance at our flat at Bondi during the first six weeks from 7th July, 1960. Normally Mr Noonan would remain for six days continuously and then be relieved by Mr Paul on the seventh day. During our long and terrible ordeal, no small part was played by the aforementioned officers, and we have to mention Mr Noonan especially, in counselling us on our many hopes and wishes whilst doing all to sustain our morale. It was also mainly because of these officers that our daughter Belinda was kept from realising what was occurring at the time.[9]

If Bazil and Freda Thorne thought that the verdict would give them some closure and equanimity, they were sorely disappointed. While they were gratified at the verdict, and felt that justice had been convincingly done, the yawning chasm of grief for the loss of their beautiful son opened wider and deeper. Whereas they had previously been distracted by eagerly awaiting the next step – the arrest, the extradition, the Inquest, and then the trial – now they had nothing to divert them from the gaping hole in their lives and the agony of years ahead without their son. It was only their other child, Belinda, who still needed her parents' love and attention, who brought them back from the brink of utter despair. Everything in their lives that had previously given them joy was now tinged with sorrow. Even their memories of events that had occurred before Graeme's death were overshadowed by an overlay of grief. For Belinda, the spirit of her deceased brother hung heavily over their home. As a child, she was unable to overcome feelings that she was not entitled to any happiness in her life when her parents were suffering so much, and even a sense of guilt for being alive when her beloved elder brother had been 'lost'. Graeme's murder cast an unrelenting pall over the lives of his parents and sister forever.

Soon after the trial, Bazil and Freda Thorne moved from their home at Bondi and eventually settled in Beresford Road, Rose Bay. As could be expected, they never got over the death of their son. Bazil passed away in 1978 aged 56 – his family insisting that he had died of a broken heart. Freda lived a long life, passing away in 2012 at the age of 86. Cheryl, still institutionalised, died in her fifties. Belinda, thankfully, has established an immediate family of her own.

***

One of the great ironies of this case is that by depriving Bazil and Freda Thorne of their son, Stephen Bradley ended up depriving his own daughter, Helen, of her father and the only mother she had ever known. All three of Stephen and Magda's children faced the complex task of dealing with the loss of the family life they had known and the public opprobrium of their parents. Bradley's crime cast a pall of unjustified shame by association over the lives of his child and stepchildren. Despite having no responsibility for his actions – legally or morally – his daughter

and stepsons continued to grapple with a sense of familial dis-
honour, rather than seeing themselves as secondary victims, as
they truly were.

In an interview with journalist Tom Prior in 1986, twenty-
five years after the trial, Helen Bradley told him 'I can't
remember my father clearly at all. I suppose I should. I was old
enough to remember him, and Magda. My grandparents were
very protective and discouraged questions about the past. It
was their private sorrow. We didn't talk about the past at all,
but it was always there and caused a lot of unhappiness.'[10]

Several years after the trial, Magda quietly returned to
Australia. She passed away in 2002.

**

Soon after the kidnapping and death of Graeme Thorne,
arrangements were introduced to all State lotteries to allow for
the privacy of winners' details.

**

In September 1960, one of the many people who had attempted
to extort money from the Thornes, and one of the few to be
caught and prosecuted, pleaded guilty in the Sydney Quarter
Sessions.[11] Forty-four-year-old Newcastle photographer Alfred
Vercoe appeared for sentence charged with attempting to obtain
£25,000 from Bazil Thorne by falsely pretending that he was
in a position to assist in the return of Graeme Thorne. In a
written statement, Bazil Thorne testified that on 4 August
1960 after speaking to a man on the phone who claimed to

be holding Graeme, he went to Newtown Railway Station and spoke to a man whom he identified as Mr Vercoe. The man told him that Graeme was safe and would be returned on payment of £25,000, claiming not to have actually participated in the kidnapping, but to have been in the same street when the boy was taken away. Bazil decided that the man was not telling the truth, and so he neither offered him nor gave him any money. Mr Vercoe admitted in court that he had said the things as alleged by Bazil Thorne, but denied that he had had any intention of obtaining money when he met with Bazil. He told the court, 'I wanted to make myself big in confronting Mr Thorne.'[12] As a result of raising this exoneratory explanation, Vercoe's plea of guilty was rejected and he went to trial in May 1962 before Judge Clegg and a jury. In his dock statement, Vercoe agreed that Bazil Thorne's evidence was correct, but again asserted that he had not intended extorting any money, saying:

> I wanted to be seen with Thorne and let everybody know that I had been with him. Why I did this I am simply at a loss to explain.

Vercoe was convicted by the jury on 25 May 1962. When sentencing him, Judge Clegg told Vercoe that he had been callous and inhuman to prey on the mind of a man who did not know if his son was alive or dead. Referring to a recommendation for mercy from the jury, the judge said:

> I regard your crime is almost deserving of the same penalty as awarded the actual kidnapper. The law provides a maximum

sentence of five years for this type of offence. Until I heard the jury's recommendation, I had intended to impose that sentence on you.[13]

Vercoe was sentenced to imprisonment for two years.

***

In December 1961, the New South Wales Parliament passed an amendment to the *Crimes Act* which introduced the new crime of kidnapping (detention for ransom or any other advantage). To the author's knowledge, there has not been another kidnapping for ransom of a child in Australia.

16

HYPOTHESES AND SYNTHESES

The evidence linking Stephen Bradley to the kidnapping and death of Graeme Thorne can only be described as overwhelming. The combination of direct evidence (the identifications and confessions), circumstantial evidence (the car, accent, previous connection to the location of the body, statements consistent with expected future wealth) and the expert scientific evidence (plant material, mortar, hair, tassels, rug, twine, string) amounted to a case that would be the envy of any prosecutor in a homicide trial. The extent of the police investigation was unparalleled at the time, and rarely matched to this day.

Stephen Bradley's assertion to the police in his oral and written confessions that Graeme Thorne sat meekly in the front passenger seat of his car while he drove through the city, over the Harbour Bridge and down to the Spit Bridge was quite

275

unbelievable, as was the idea that he left Graeme unattended in the car while he made the ransom call to his parents. It was equally incredible that the boy remained calmly in the vehicle while Bradley drove into his own garage, and that it was only when they were inside the garage that Bradley forced him into the boot.

It is inconceivable that Bradley left Graeme in a conscious state in the boot of the car while the removalists went about their work just metres away, or that he left him there from approximately 10am (when they arrived at Clontarf) until it was dark (at about 5.30pm in July) – a total of over seven hours – before he went back to the boot to find that he was dead. It should be noted that when the body was found there was no twine wrapped around Graeme's wrists – only around his ankles. If he had been confined to the boot in a conscious state, he would surely have used his hands to remove the gag in order to breathe more freely and to call out for help. The time of Graeme's death, based on the forensic pathologist's examination of his stomach contents, was at least two or three hours after Graeme had ingested his breakfast. The mode of death – a combination of blunt force trauma to the head and asphyxiation – is consistent with him being locked in the boot of the car while *un*conscious, after a severe blow to the head and at a time when his breathing was restricted by the gag and the close confines of the Customline's boot. By the time they arrived at Clontarf, it is likely that Graeme was already suffering from oxygen deprivation. In hitting him on the head with a metal tool, Bradley had no idea how hard he should strike in order to render him unconscious for an extended period of time. This was not something he had planned in advance.

Stephen Bradley's attempts to explain the death as a tragic accident that occurred through no fault of his own were seriously flawed and inherently unbelievable at the time, and with the benefit of hindsight they are equally unconvincing now.

It is quite plausible, however, that Bradley had no intention to kill Graeme Thorne. He would have realised how the boy's death would make it far more difficult to obtain payment of the ransom. It can be accepted that Bradley did not realise that, with the scarf tightly wrapped around Graeme's mouth and the boot lid closed, there was very little fresh air entering the confined space, so that even without a blow to the head he was at risk of dying from asphyxiation. The question arises: assuming that Bradley did not intend Graeme Thorne's death, was he properly convicted of murder?

Because Stephen Bradley adopted the defence at his trial that he had had no involvement whatsoever in the kidnapping, there was little consideration given to the question of his liability for murder in the event that Graeme's death had been unintended. In fact, neither counsel referred to this issue in their closing address, leaving it to Justice Clancy to explain this question of law to the jury. If Bradley had taken the same approach at his trial as he did during his police confession – that Graeme's death had been accidental – this issue would have loomed much larger.

Murder occurs where the accused has caused the death of another person with the intention either to kill or to do 'grievous bodily harm'. Grievous bodily harm means very serious bodily injury. To deliberately render someone unconscious by striking them on the head undoubtedly amounts to grievous bodily harm. Based on the scenario described in this book, involving the use of chloroform to render Graeme unconscious, and later a deliberate blow to his head to maintain that state of unconsciousness, Stephen Bradley was undoubtedly properly convicted of murder. Even if Bradley's oral police confession had been true (which clearly it was not), and Graeme somehow violently struck himself on the head while enclosed in the boot, Bradley would still have been legally liable for murder, because there was another category of murder in which the accused has acted with 'reckless indifference to human life'. Reckless indifference did not require any particular intent on the part of the accused to cause harm to the victim, but merely a 'don't care' attitude to whether the victim lives or dies.[1] It was inevitable that the jury would have found that merely by imprisoning Graeme in the boot of the car with the scarf wrapped around his mouth, Stephen Bradley was recklessly indifferent to the risk of the boy dying from a lack of oxygen.

Bradley's tactic when he was interviewed by the police – of trying to minimise his responsibility for Graeme's death – was therefore doomed from the start. Even if he had admitted his involvement in the kidnapping at the trial, his lame account to the police of how the boy had died would not have spared him from a conviction for murder. In fact, whatever approach Bradley could have taken at his trial, he was inevitably facing a conviction for murder.

***

The author's hypothesis about what happened in Centennial Park is based upon a synthesis of all of the evidence. The Senior Crown Prosecutor who conducted the trial clearly came to the view that Centennial Park was the location where the initial violence occurred. However, it would appear that the police were rather sceptical about this scenario. In a 1991 letter to journalist and author Malcolm Brown the retired Detective Sergeant Brian Doyle wrote:

> *I refer to Knight's mention of Centennial Park. As I told you at my place, there was never any evidence or even a suggestion of anything happening in Centennial Park. That was a shock suggestion by Knight himself at the trial, and for the very first time. It was pure speculation. There had not been any previous mention of it. Some of us for weeks later wondered where he had got the idea from, and what effect it may have had on the jury. In all our discussions with him he never mentioned it.*[2]

On the other hand, Detective Inspector Albert ('Bert') Windsor, the acting chief of the CIB who was extensively involved in the investigation, told journalist Bill Archibald:

> *There seems some doubt where and when the murder was committed. I suggest that the most likely spot was Centennial Park. I believe Bradley drove to a secluded spot in the park and then hit the boy on the head with a heavy instrument. I believe he then bundled the boy into the boot of the car.*[3]

The author's Centennial Park scenario is based on the assumption that Stephen Bradley would never have taken the risk of conveying his kidnap victim in the front seat of his car across the Sydney Harbour Bridge, where he had to briefly stop to pay the toll to a collector. By that stage, if Graeme had been unrestrained, he would certainly have been panicking that this man had taken him far away from his school. This version is also based upon a complete rejection of Bradley's account that he left the boy calmly sitting in the car while he went to the telephone box near the Spit Bridge and made the first ransom demand. The author has concluded, as Bill Knight QC clearly also did, that at some stage between Bondi and the Sydney Harbour Bridge Bradley converted a voluntary lift into a forced abduction. By the time he arrived at the Harbour Bridge, he must have been satisfied that Graeme was safely secured in a manner that did not allow any possibility for the boy to communicate with the toll collector. The most obvious location for rendering the boy immobile and unable to communicate was in the ample, green spaces of Centennial Park, which was sufficiently close to Bondi so that Graeme would not yet have panicked.

The author's hypothesis about the use of chloroform is predicated on the ready availability of that substance in 1960. Its use as an anaesthetic had been widely known since its discovery in the 1840s and there were numerous references to the criminal uses of it in literature and film. Chloroform was the way in which Bradley could most rapidly and easily render Graeme Thorne unconscious, with the least likelihood of being observed or of contaminating his car with obvious clues of a violent altercation. He could well have believed that he would not cause any long-term harm to his victim by using chloroform, despite the dangers associated with it. The state of Graeme's body when it was found many weeks after his death meant that it was impossible at that time to detect any trace of the substance. The author has prosecuted a more recent case of kidnapping of an adult for ransom – also a rare crime in Australia – in which the convicted perpetrator was in possession of a bottle of chloroform at the time.[4]

***

In assessing the police investigation with the benefit of hindsight and more than 50 years of progress in forensic science, it is important to remember that many of the techniques that were used by the police to weave the web of evidence against Stephen Bradley had never been used before. I doubt that there had been a case before this one where so many different strands of forensic science had come together to implicate an offender. However, despite the impressive array of scientific techniques that were used, there were other aspects of the police investigation that can, in my view, be legitimately criticised.

In retrospect, it seems obvious that the perpetrator of the kidnapping and murder was an inherently careless and lazy person. On the day of the kidnapping, the police already knew that the kidnapper had shown himself to the Thornes three weeks earlier. This was an incredibly brazen and unwise step. When Graeme's school bag and its contents and his cap were found, it was clear that no attempt had been made to properly dispose of these items or to conceal the fact that they had belonged to Graeme Thorne. When the body was found one suburb away, the killer had left a number of items of personal property with it. Putting all of this evidence together, the police ought to have deduced that the killer was an inherently careless and lazy person. For this reason, it now seems like an egregious error for the police to have assumed that the kidnapper would not have used his own car when carrying out the kidnapping. If they had not made this assumption, it is likely that Stephen Bradley would have become a suspect much earlier. It should also have been a priority for the police to focus their search for the car and the kidnapper much closer to where Graeme's property and his body had been discarded. Instead of questioning many thousands of owners of 1955 Ford Customlines on a statewide basis, if they had begun by questioning owners within a five-mile radius of the Wakehurst Parkway and Grandview Grove, again they would have located Stephen Bradley much sooner.

It is hard to criticise the police for the shortcomings of the running sheet system of recording information in a massive investigation like this one, because this was the first major case in which it had been used. Today, there are many techniques to try to avoid shortcomings of the kind that arose when the police received, but ignored, the valuable information from the Telfords and Mr Browne – information that was duly filed away in the running sheet archives, where it remained until after Bradley had been identified by other means as the principal suspect. There have been other major criminal investigations since in which highly valuable information has similarly been ignored and filed away. Police are constantly seeking to adopt measures to deal with this pervasive problem, especially in investigations involving large teams of detectives. The advent of computers has only exacerbated this issue.

***

Magda Bradley was subjected to an enormous amount of public odium at the time of the trial. The combination of her convenient trip to Queensland on the morning of the kidnapping and the covert travel arrangements to book their passages on the *Himalaya* convinced many police,[5] journalists and members of the public that Magda had known all along about her husband's plan. Crown Prosecutor Bill Knight QC clearly put to her in cross-examination that she had had advance knowledge of the kidnapping and had deliberately placed herself far from the action by flying to Queensland on the morning of the crime, thereby leaving the house at Clontarf free for her husband to use as a staging post. Knight also insinuated that it was not a mere coincidence that Magda had purchased berths on the *Himalaya* for herself and Paul the day after the police had first interviewed Stephen at his workplace. Magda's explanation in evidence – that she was planning to depart Australia, leaving behind her beloved husband, her handicapped son and the stepdaughter she adored – defies belief. It is much more credible that Stephen and Magda made separate bookings to disguise their planned departure – but from whom: from the police or from Paul and Ross's father, Gregor Weinberg? At the trial, it was never explored with Magda what she knew about Stephen's many early morning departures from their house to conduct surveillance on the Thornes in the weeks before the kidnapping.

The tumultuous row that the neighbours heard coming from the Bradley household on the night of 6 July was undoubtedly about the sudden change of plan that meant that Magda and the two older children would fly to Queensland the following morning instead of driving in the car with Stephen.

But who had come up with this? Was it Stephen attempting to ensure that he had a free rein in the house the next day, or was it Magda – as she asserted at the trial – insisting on flying because she had tired of the packing and wanted to start her holiday immediately? Alternatively, was Bill Knight QC right that Magda had learnt of her husband's plans for the next day and wanted nothing to do with it, and so decided to insulate herself by going as far away as possible with the children?

The author is of the view that Magda had no prior knowledge of Stephen's plan to kidnap Graeme Thorne. If he had told her, she would surely have appreciated the extraordinary risks that the plan entailed for their whole family and would have refused to allow him to pursue such a venture. However, she must have read or heard of the kidnapping when she was in Queensland, and would also have learnt at a very early stage that the kidnapper had a foreign accent. Did the early publicity cause Magda to harbour suspicions that her husband had been involved? Did she suddenly understand why he had been taking her around to look at expensive homes that they could not afford? The discovery of Graeme's body and his belongings so close to their home must also have deepened her suspicions. There is a good basis for concluding that at some stage after the kidnapping Magda secretly feared that her husband had been responsible for the kidnapping and death of Graeme Thorne, and at the same time desperately hoped that her suspicions were wrong.

The author has prosecuted and defended many cases in which spouses, partners and other family members turned a blind eye to overwhelming evidence of an accused's involvement in a serious crime, because the idea was just too horrible to contemplate. By the time Stephen informed Magda that he had been interviewed by the police at Nutt & Muddle, she must have had a fair idea of his involvement. Magda's cooperation in the surreptitious and sudden departure from Australia suggests that by that stage she knew or suspected the real reason they needed to leave. Her continued support of him suggests that she grappled with those suspicions and tried to dismiss them, based upon her knowledge of the man she had married and lived with for some years. If one reads between the lines, Magda's unpublished manuscript, written in London in 1961 before the trial, describes this internal struggle.

***

Stephen Bradley's greed for the ransom money was so intense that it created a form of psychological tunnel-vision that prevented him from seeing what other people would have viewed as patently obvious: that his venture was fraught with a high risk of failure or misadventure and that the chances of eventual detection were high. It was as though blinkers had been placed around his eyes, like those on a racing horse that force it to look only straight ahead so as to prevent it being distracted by anything on either side. Bradley's psychological blinkers prevented him from seeing how likely it was that his plan would come unstuck, and how great was the risk that he would be caught. His sense of entitlement to the money was so strong that he gave not a moment's concern to the long-term psychological harm an abduction would inevitably cause to Graeme or the torment that would be suffered by Bazil and Freda. He also failed to appreciate the depth of feeling that would likely be engendered in the community towards a monster who could commit such a heinous crime that sought to take financial advantage of the greatest bond of love – between parent and child. His utter commitment to achieving his goal led to a brazenness and overconfidence in his own capabilities and judgement, so that he remained unaware that many of his actions were needlessly foolhardy and incautious.

A common feature of those who commit murder for greed is the quality of narcissism. Narcissism is far more than a mere focus on self or an overly selfish attitude. The classic narcissistic murderer has so little capacity to empathise with other people that he, or less commonly she, can kill without any sense of personal responsibility. Narcissists have an implacable belief in their own superiority and the priority of their own needs over those of others. They consider that they can perceive connections that other people miss and that their capacity for planning makes them immune to detection. In fact, their delusions are so profound that they fail to see that their chosen path will almost inevitably lead to detection, denouncement and doom. Stephen Bradley falls firmly into this category.

I can do no better to convey the qualities of the narcissist than to quote the words of a modern-day Sydney forensic psychiatrist, Dr Michael Diamond, in a completely unrelated matter:

Narcissism refers to a very insecure, very fragile sense of worthiness of a place in the world that causes the individual to feel very precariously placed and very much in need of incessant reassurances. The way it is manifested with [the offender] was in his behaviour towards other people. A large part of his effort habitually goes into ingratiating himself to people in doing things in a way that is likely to elicit support and affirmation that he is a worthy person; to be really quite obsessively focused on that need to overcome any sense of vulnerability and insecurity.

But the underside of that behaviour is his inability to take criticism, his inability to be advised. It takes the form of opinionated or grandiose views of his ways of dealing with the world around him, and it is well evidenced by his treatment when he clearly was not coping with life events. There were very serious parts of that where an overriding part of his nature is to be concerned about his own self needs and a deficiency to properly consider the needs of others.

That might sound reasonably trivial, and I might assess that as being selfish, but he is far beyond that. This is an inability to balance up one's own needs against the needs of others. Perhaps that goes to the heart of this particular condition.

The narcissistic state is not simply one of being overly selfish or overly opinionated or overly concerned at how others see you. It is really the extreme effect that it has on the way people make decisions and behaviour. It is far beyond the scope of normal behaviour. The other part of his behaviour is the histrionic and dramatic way he expressed his concern to me because he was prone to be a little larger than life, a little more colourful and seductive in a way to try and get people to see his way.[6]

These words describe Stephen Bradley as though they were written about him. If Magda's 1960 manuscript is to be accepted, Bradley had a childhood in which he was deprived of love and attention. Such a poor start in life can result in the adult constantly looking for external, self-affirming support and verification. The fear is that if the scaffolding around self is removed, the edifice will collapse into nothingness. The fear is so great that the person is oblivious to the needs and rights of others – even the right to life itself. The kidnapping and murder of Graeme Thorne were crimes of the ego, frantically trying to protect itself from disintegration into oblivion. Stephen Bradley's lack of thought for the welfare of Graeme or his family demonstrates these same qualities. Even after being apprehended and while on his way back to Australia, his only concern was what would happen to himself. Even when he admitted his involvement in the kidnapping to the police, he completely distanced himself from how the boy came to die, as though the eight-year-old child was somehow to blame for his own, and Bradley's, misfortune. At no time did he acknowledge the enduring agony he had caused to Freda and Bazil. Nor was there any sense of having brought any misfortune upon his own family. His idea that Helen should be returned from Aden to a convent in Sydney to await his return and release illustrates not only his lack of reality about his own prospects, but also his preoccupation with his own needs above those of his daughter.

The author has come to the conclusion that an irrepressible and profound need to possess and impress (which often go hand-in-hand) drove Stephen Bradley to commit the kidnapping and murder of Graeme Thorne. Bradley's unrelenting needs derived from the lack of a solid core of the personality; from a frantic desperation to build a scaffold around that personality to prop it up, lest it collapse into nothingness; from a sense of panic and unrelieved anxiety that without the physical and monetary acquisitions and frequent self-accolades, the very essence of the individual would crumble; and from a fundamental laziness that impelled him to seek a quick and easy path to the riches that he so desperately craved.

The lack of an inner core, in my view, derives from the very earliest years of life. Whether it is caused by poor parenting or by an underlying, innate incapacity within the young child to attach to his or her primary carer, I do not know. At its base, I believe that it is caused by a deep fear of being unloved, unlovable and abandoned to death. Murder for greed is the unrequited cry of the infant, demanding to be loved and cared for, echoing endlessly unheard through the decades of adulthood. Murder for greed is essentially a crime born of an abject fear of nothingness.

END NOTES

Chapter 1

1 The equivalent of about $4 million today. The magnitude of the prize can be understood by the fact that a modest Sydney home could then be purchased for about £8000.

2 The equivalent of about $350,000 today.

3 It was not until October 1960 that the French police received their first serious lead in the investigation, and only in February 1961, ten months after the kidnapping, that the world was informed of the arrest of the three kidnappers. They had already spent virtually the entire ransom. The following year they were sentenced to imprisonment for twenty years.

4 In fact, it later appeared that some others had taken tentative steps towards carrying out a similar crime against the Thorne family.

5 The Goggomobil was a micro-car, originally produced in Germany from 1955 to 1969. An Australian sports version, known as a Goggomobil Dart was produced between 1957 and 1961.

6 Hire purchase was a means of buying an item on credit with

payments by instalments. It has largely been superseded by leasing arrangements.

Chapter 2

1 I have used pseudonyms to protect Magda's two natural children, who were incidental, secondary victims, and do not wish to have their identities disclosed. This has necessitated using the same pseudo-surname for their father and for their mother before she married Bradley.

Chapter 3

1 For the basis of this version, see the Preface.
2 In those days it was not as commonplace as it is today for people to use the park for daily exercise during the working week.
3 At that time, chloroform was readily available as a solvent cleaner.
4 Now the suburb of Beauty Point. The modern-day Spit Bridge had been opened in 1958.

Chapter 5

1 For the basis of this version, see the Preface.

Chapter 6

1 The kidnapping of Charles Augustus Lindbergh, the son of the famous aviator, Charles Lindbergh, in March 1932.

Chapter 7

1 5 and 10 degrees Celsius.
2 *Sydney Morning Herald*, 3 April 1961.
3 Within a short time of this investigation the 'running sheet' had become standard practice. About thirty years later, the running sheet became computerised.

4 An exercise on a comparable scale to locate a vehicle – not subject to such flaws – was conducted by NSW police investigating the 1997 disappearance of Kerry Whelan. A number of even more extensive searches – this time for a missing child, and subject to serious flaws – were conducted by police investigating the disappearance of baby Tegan Lane, who vanished days after her birth in 1996.

Chapter 8

1 The author, who was the same age as Graeme Thorne, had a newspaper photograph of him which he pasted onto a cupboard in his bedroom.

2 Submission to the Attorney-General by the Under Secretary of the Department, 24 October 1960 (State Records NSW).

3 At this time, the police had still not disclosed to the public that they were looking for a blue Ford Customline.

4 See *Australian Dictionary of Biography*, http://adb.anu.edu.au/biography/kelly-raymond-william-10678.

5 In the case of the disappearance of baby Tegan Lane, the investigation only began in earnest more than seven years after her disappearance in 1996. The searches for her were seriously flawed in that the police sent questionnaires to every primary school throughout Australia asking for information about any girl called Tegan or Lane whose birth had been registered on the day of Tegan's birth, or on the two days on either side of it. This failed to take into account that a person who may have informally adopted her – as her mother Keli Lane claimed – could have changed Tegan's name or registered her birth as having occurred on another day. At the trial, the Crown admitted that the searches could never definitively prove that Tegan was dead. They merely showed the extent to which the police had gone in their attempts to find her.

END NOTES

Chapter 9

1 *My Story*, unpublished manuscript by Magda Bradley, 1961 (courtesy of the Justice & Police Museum, Sydney Living Museums, NSW). This manuscript was written about four months after their departure.

2 op. cit., Part 5, pages 2–3.

3 op. cit., p10.

4 op. cit., p11.

5 op. cit., pp11–12.

6 op. cit., p12.

7 *Sun Herald*, 25 September 1960, page 3.

Chapter 10

1 It is unlikely that modern-day forensic pathologists could be any more precise than this.

Chapter 11

1 The *Himalaya* remained in service with P&O until 1974.

2 *Sydney Morning Herald*, 21 October 1960.

3 *Sydney Morning Herald*, 26 October 1960.

4 *Sydney Morning Herald*, 9 November 1960.

5 The SS *Strathmore* was much older than the SS *Himalaya*, having been constructed in 1935. In 1961 she was converted into a single-class ship, and her final voyage as a P&O liner was made in 1963, when she was sold to a Greek shipping line. She was demolished in 1969.

6 The author has been involved in only one extradition – of one of the murderers of heart surgeon Dr Victor Chang, who was extradited from Malaysia.

7 Now the Central Local Court.

8 *Sydney Morning Herald*, 18 October 1960.

9 Corea was later released and gave evidence for the prosecution at the trial of the assassins in 1961.

10 *Sydney Morning Herald*, 23 October 1960.

Chapter 12

1 *Sydney Morning Herald*, 19 November 1960.

2 *Police Monthly*, May 2014; see also: http://www.police.nsw.gov. au/__data/assets/pdf_file/0008/292490/The_incredible_career_ of_Det_Sgt_Jack_Bateman.pdf.

3 *Sydney Morning Herald*, 20 November 1960.

4 *Sun-Herald*, 20 November 1960, page 2.

5 op. cit., pages 2, 4.

6 op. cit., page 4.

7 It was not the practice at that time for police to record interviews, as the technology was not yet generally available to police. All police interviews are taken from the trial transcript: R v. Stephen Bradley, Supreme Court, 1961.

8 The author was an articled clerk to Mr Richard Holt of Gilbert M Johnstone and Co in 1972–73. At the time this was the practical training required for those intending to practise law.

9 Bill Archibald, *The Bradley Case*, Horwitz Publications Pty Ltd, 1961, page 77.

10 Today, the previous identification and the earlier publication of the photograph in the paper would render inadmissible any evidence of a subsequent identification.

Chapter 13

1 Today in New South Wales there are more than twenty-five.

2 Manuscript by Chester Porter QC, written for the opening of new Chambers for the Public Defenders, 2012.

3 Today almost any confession to the police is inadmissible unless it has been electronically recorded, so challenges to police interviews are almost unknown.

4 In the event of jurors failing to reach unanimity, they would eventually be discharged and the trial brought to an end. The matter would then be referred to the Attorney-General for a decision whether a retrial would take place. In the event of two hung juries, the matter would almost invariably not be tried a third time. Today the law allows for majority verdicts of 11 to 1.

5 Although there were a handful of female barristers in New South Wales at this time, they almost exclusively practised in family law and did not appear in criminal trials.

6 The Clerk of the Peace was an office that had existed in New South Wales since 1817. Its role was to act as the solicitor for the Crown in criminal cases and Inquests, and also to provide administrative support services for the operation of the criminal courts. In 1986 it was replaced by the Solicitor for Public Prosecutions and by separate court registrars.

7 *My Story*, manuscript by Magda Bradley, 1961, part 2, page 2 (courtesy of the Justice & Police Museum, Sydney Living Museums, NSW).

8 op. cit., part 2, page 3.

9 op. cit., part 6, pages 8–9.

10 Robert Reginald Downing AC QC (1904–1994) was an Australian lawyer, textile worker, union organiser and politician. He was a member of the New South Wales Legislative Council for the Australian Labor Party for 31 years from 1940 to 1972 and in that time served as Attorney-General and Minister for Justice, as well as Vice-President of the Executive Council. The Downing Centre court complex in Liverpool Street, Sydney, is named after him.

11 *Daily Mirror*, 13 March 1961, page 6.

12 Vladimir Nabokov's novel about a man's obsessive love for his twelve-year-old step-daughter was first published in Paris

in 1955 and later in New York in 1958. *Lolita* was banned by Australia's Literature Censorship Board in 1958. The ban was not lifted until 1965.

Chapter 14

1 Now Court 5 at Darlinghurst Courthouse.

2 In fact, women had been legally permitted to serve on juries in New South Wales since 1947, but the commencement of this reform was delayed due to 'accommodation difficulties' – a euphemism for separate dormitories and toilet facilities, and the appointment of female Sheriff's officers. Until 1968 women were required to apply to the Chief Constable of their police district to be included on the jury roll.

3 Bill Knight was the fifth Senior Crown Prosecutor for New South Wales. There have only been fourteen since the first was appointed in 1920.

4 Vin Wallace was later to become a QC and Senior Crown Prosecutor.

5 Bill Job also later became a QC and Senior Crown Prosecutor, and occupied this position when the author was appointed a Crown Prosecutor in 1983.

6 A trial of similar complexity today would last at least three months, and up to six.

7 *Canberra Times*, 21 March 1961.

8 The whole evidence from both prosecution and defence consisted of fewer than 350 pages of transcript. Today, a case of this complexity would likely extend over 3000 pages of transcript.

9 The unsworn statement from the dock was abolished in New South Wales in 1994.

10 Bill Archibald, *The Bradley Case*, Horwitz Publications Pty Ltd, 1961, page 96.

11 *Canberra Times*, 28 March 1961.

12　Knight QC practised at a time when it was considered acceptable for a Crown Prosecutor to adopt a hostile and antagonistic
attitude in cross-examining defence witnesses. According to
Chester Porter QC, Knight had a reputation for being 'aggressive, bullying and overwhelming' in his cross-examination of
accused persons. Today a judge would prohibit gratuitous hostility towards any witness by either counsel.

13　Bill Archibald, *The Bradley Case*, page 103.

14　By the time Bradley returned from Queensland in the Ford, the
kidnapping was well and truly over. I am sure that Knight meant
to say, 'your Ford had been used in the kidnapping'.

15　Bill Archibald, *The Bradley Case*, page 111.

16　Proceedings for contempt of court had been commenced against
the *Daily Mirror* and its executive editor arising out of the publication of this photograph.

17　The order of addresses is now reversed, so that the defence
always gets the last address.

18　*Canberra Times*, 29 March 1961.

19　Tom Prior, *The Sinners' Club*, Penguin Books, 1993, pp 19–21.

Chapter 15

1　This account of what occurred in the jury room comes from a
post-trial interview with a juror by journalist Bill Archibald. See
Bill Archibald, *The Bradley Case*, Horwitz Publications Pty Ltd,
1961, page 117.

2　*Sydney Morning Herald*, 31 March 1961.

3　ibid.

4　Tom Prior, *The Sinners' Club*, Penguin Books, 1993, pp 19–21.
In fact, Sir Frank Packer refused to pay any money to Magda
Bradley.

5　Today it is highly unusual for the trial Crown Prosecutor to
also appear at the appeal. It is considered desirable for another

Crown Prosecutor, with a fresh approach to the case, to represent the Crown. In this way, the trial prosecutor is not put in a position of having to justify his or her own actions. It is more common on the defence side for the same barrister to appear at the appeal.

6 The *Telegraph*, 3 July 1961.

7 *Sydney Morning Herald*, 3 July 1961.

8 *Canberra Times*, 3 July 1961.

9 Bill Archibald, *The Bradley Case*, page 129.

10 *The Sinners Club: Confessions of a Walk-up Man*, Tom Prior, Penguin Books Australia, 1993. Tom Prior was an Australian newsman during the 1960s to 1990s. He worked for 28 years with Melbourne's *Sun News-Pictorial*, specialising in crime and sport.

11 Now the District Court.

12 The *Age*, 1 September 1960.

13 *Canberra Times*, 26 May 1962.

Chapter 16

1 Reckless indifference murder now requires the prosecution to prove that the accused appreciated the likelihood of death, but at that time the words were given their ordinary English meaning.

2 Letter dated 29 July 1991. Presumably it was written after Doyle had read the manuscript of *Justice and Nightmares – Successes and Failures of Forensic Science in Australia and New Zealand* by Malcolm Brown, Paul Wilson and Judith Whelan, New South Wales University Press, 1992.

3 Bill Archibald, *The Bradley Case*, Horwitz Publications Pty Ltd, 1961, page 128.

4 *R v Bruce Burrell*, Supreme Court of New South Wales, 2005 & 2006.

END NOTES

5 See Doyle's letter to Malcolm Brown dated 14 July 1991.

6 For another excellent description of narcissism, this time from the realm of fiction, see the main character, Rodion Razkolnikov, in *Crime and Punishment* by the Russian author Fyodor Dostoevsky.

BIBLIOGRAPHY

Official records

Transcript of the Supreme Court trial of *R v Stephen Leslie Bradley*, courtesy of State Records New South Wales.

Court of Criminal Appeal decision in the case of *R v Stephen Leslie Bradley*, courtesy of the Justice & Police Museum, Sydney Living Museums.

Police Brief and File of the Clerk of the Peace in the case of *R v Stephen Leslie Bradley*, courtesy of State Records New South Wales, including statements by witnesses to police, summaries and notes by the Clerk of the Peace Officer and the Crown Prosecutor.

Newspapers and journals

Numerous contemporary newspapers, including: *Daily Telegraph, Daily Mirror, Sun, Sydney Morning Herald, Sun-Herald, Sunday Telegraph, Canberra Times.*

'The Jack Bateman story', *Daily Mirror*, 8–9 March 1966.

'Scientific Aspects of the Graeme Thorne Kidnapping and Murder', by Detective Sergeant AF Clarke (New South Wales Police), Australian Police Journal, July 1963 Volume 16, Number 3, pages

BIBLIOGRAPHY

181–237; reprinted in Australian Police Journal 50th Anniversary Edition, September 1996 (Volume 50, Number 3A, pages 68–95):

Books and manuscripts

Bill Archibald, *The Bradley Case*, Horwitz Publications Pty Ltd, 1961.

Magda Bradley, unpublished manuscript *My Story*, 1961, courtesy of the Justice & Police Museum, Sydney Living Museums.

Tom Prior, *The Sinners' Club*, Penguin Books, 1993.

Larry Writer, *The Australian Book of True Crime*, Pier 9, 2008.

Credits and permissions

Transcripts of the committal and trial of Stephen Bradley are reproduced with permission of the Chief Justice of New South Wales.

Newspaper extracts from the *Sydney Morning Herald* (21, 18, 23 October 1960; 9, 19, 20 November 1960; 31 March 1961; 3 April, 1961; 3 July 1961), the *Sun* (November 1961), the *Sun-Herald* (25 September 1960), the *Daily Mirror* (13 March, 1961), the *Canberra Times* (21 March 1961, 3 July 1961, 26 May 1962) are reproduced with permission, with thanks to Copyright Agency Limited in association with Fairfax Syndications and News Limited.

Copyright material by Magda Bradley is reproduced with permission, with thanks to the estate.

Copyright material by Detective Sergeant Brian Doyle is reproduced with permission, with thanks to Stephen Doyle.

Copyright material by Dr Michael Diamond is reproduced with permission.

Copyright material by Bill Archibald is reproduced with permission, with thanks to Susan Horwitz.

Images from the Justice & Police Museum Collection, Sydney Living Museums, are reproduced with permission.

Images from Fairfax Syndications are reproduced with permission.

The image of Frederick Vizzard QC is reproduced with permission, with thanks to the estate.

ABOUT THE AUTHOR

Mark Tedeschi AM QC is the Senior Crown Prosecutor for New South Wales. He has practised in the criminal courts for 38 years, both for the prosecution and the defence. He is a Visiting Fellow at the University of Wollongong, a Member of the Board of Directors at the National Art School, and a Trustee of Sydney Grammar School. He is also an accomplished photographer, whose works are held in many galleries and private collections. Mark lives and works in Sydney.

For more information, see his website:
www.MarkTedeschi.com.